IN PURSUIT OF EQUAL LIBERTY

IN PURSUIT

★ ★ ★ OF ★ ★ ★

EQUAL LIBERTY

George Bryan and
the Revolution in Pennsylvania

Joseph S. Foster

The Pennsylvania State University Press

University Park, Pennsylvania

Library of Congress Cataloging-in-Publication Data

Foster, Joseph S.
   In Pursuit of Equal Liberty : George Bryan and the revolution in Pennsylvania / Joseph S. Foster.
      p.   cm.
   Includes bibliographical references and index.
   ISBN 0-271-01074-6
   1. Bryan, George, 1731–1791. 2. Politicians—Pennsylvania—Biography. 3. Pennsylvania—Constitutional history. 4. Pennsylvania—Politics and government—1775–1783.
5. Pennsylvania—Politics and government—To 1775.   I. Title.
F153.B88F67   1994
974.8'03'092—dc20   93-6902
                                                                        CIP

Published by The Pennsylvania State University Press,
Barbara Building, Suite C, University Park, PA 16802-1003

It is the policy of The Pennsylvania State University Press to use acid-free paper for the
first printing of all clothbound books. Publications on uncoated stock satisfy the mini-
mum requirements of American National Standard for Information Sciences—Perma-
nence of Paper for Printed Library Materials, ANSI Z39.48–1984.

Frontispiece: Painting of George Bryan by an unknown artist (Society Collection, Historical Society of Pennsylvania).

For Debby
and our children
Rachael, Hannah, and Jonathan

Contents

Preface

Few events, if any, in the history of Pennsylvania can rival for both significance and drama the American Revolution and its aftermath. Within the space of one year, the colony's ruling oligarchy, a relatively stable political entity, was overthrown dramatically by revolutionary partisans—or "Whigs," who used the rebellion against England as a means to extend to the local level the full force of their radical ideology. Previously obscure men emerged to fill the positions of power in the wake of the sudden collapse of traditional authority, as few individuals who were part of the colony's ruling structure survived the political upheavals of 1776. For a brief period, the ideological force that erupted that year represented the united goals and aspirations of the Whigs; but almost as quickly as the Whigs seized power, they fell out among themselves and split into opposing factions. For fourteen years the two factions fought for the right to define the terms upon which political stability would be restored. Pennsylvania's revolutionary movement reached its conclusion with the 1790 state constitution, which represented a synthesis of the ideals and realities that emerged from the internal conflict between the competing Whig parties, as well as from the revolution itself. Moreover, during the first several years of that partisan contest between the opposing Whig factions for political and ideological supremacy, Pennsylvania was thrust into the middle of an exhausting war. As is usually the case in violent conflicts, the bitter memories of the war's hardest days tinged future relationships and politics.

One of those obscure men elevated to prominence by the upheaval of 1776 was George Bryan, whose role within the revolutionary movement was clearly visible. He expounded the political beliefs of those men and women who demanded the violent termination of Pennsylvania's subservience to

England and the overthrow of the colony's ruling elite. Assuming a prominent role within the factional conflict that occurred immediately after independence, Bryan promoted the partisan ideals expressed in the 1776 state
constitution and the policies of his party throughout the revolution and
postwar period. He remained active in politics until his death in 1791.

Yet, despite his significance in American and Pennsylvania history, Bryan
has remained an elusive figure. Through an unfortunate loss of many of his
personal papers and letters, Bryan has escaped the grasp of the historian,
and in the process he has been relegated to the background of the American
Revolution. Many years ago, when I first embarked on this project, a
prominent Pennsylvania historian observed to me that retracing Bryan's
steps was similar to entering rooms that Bryan had just left, leaving behind
him few clues to the events that had transpired there. This biography will
try to resolve some of the mysteries surrounding one of Pennsylvania's most
prominent revolutionaries and the causes he espoused.

In that event, I hope that I have been fair to George Bryan, portraying
him as close to the mark as possible. Granted, Bryan would have probably
preferred to tell his own story—a circumstance, however, that would not
have been any more objective than if that task were left to his bitterest
enemies. But by sidestepping to some degree the more partisan descriptions, what emerges from the extant record is the picture of a sensitive and
complex individual who attempted to resolve to the best of his capabilities,
and under the guidance of his own worldview forged by the experiences
of his life, the crises of rebellion and political upheaval as they unfolded
before him.

I need to be equally fair, however, on a different level, by acknowledging
my appreciation and gratitude to those historians and archivists who advised and assisted me in writing this biography. I particularly wish to thank
Howard A. Ohline, P.M.G. Harris, Alan F. Davis, Michael Zuckerman,
and the staffs of the Library Company of Philadelphia and the Historical
Society of Pennsylvania. On a more personal note, I owe an enormous debt
to Craig W. Horle, whose invaluable assistance and tireless efforts helped to
flesh out both the writer and the historian within me. Lastly, but always
first, I also wish to thank my wife for her patience and encouragement.

All primary printed and manuscript quotations have been modernized in
capitalization and punctuation. Spelling, however, has been retained as in
the original. All superscripts have been lowered and expanded where necessary. All ampersands and abbreviations have been spelled out. The thorn in
all cases has been rendered as "th."

Introduction

On 23 May 1778, in the crowded confines of a makeshift meeting room of the Supreme Executive Council in Lancaster, Pennsylvania, George Bryan at age forty-seven sat among his fellow councillors and announced the death of council president Thomas Wharton. According to the state constitution Bryan, as council vice president, ascended to the position of president of the commonwealth of Pennsylvania, assuming the full powers and authorities of that office. It was a remarkable moment. An Irish-born Philadelphia merchant who during the colonial period had been simply a local religious and political leader, George Bryan had emerged out of the upheavals of 1776 to become one of the principal political figures of the state.

Initially, revolution had carried with it the potency and excitement of an aphrodisiac, but by the time of Bryan's assumption of power a sense of despair had seized many of the participants. The American Revolution was passing through its darkest hours in Pennsylvania. The Indians were poised to strike the settlements along the frontiers, the British army lay hold of the city of Philadelphia, toryism reached unprecedented heights, the economy teetered on the brink of collapse, and support for the revolutionary state government faltered among the state's citizenry. Bryan's task, from which he never wavered, was to shepherd Pennsylvania safely through its time of crisis.

Beginning in 1776 and for the next several years as councillor, acting president of the state, and legislative assemblyman, Bryan threw his enormous energies behind the success of the revolution in Pennsylvania and the stabilization of the state government. After the war he continued in his capacity as one of the state's leading politicians, heading a political party that unsuccessfully opposed ratification of the 1787 federal constitution and the enactment of a new state constitution.

His life spanned nearly forty years of Pennsylvania history, embracing the colonial, revolutionary, and postwar periods, an era that witnessed the transformation of the colony into a state, and into one of the leading centers of discussion over liberty and republicanism. During the turbulent days of war and the uncertain days of peace, Bryan played an integral role in the critical decisions and debates and, in his capacity as leader of his political party, attempted to influence public policy wherever he could.

His story is truly the story of the American Revolution. Active in the resistance movement, he emerged, as did many men, out of the ranks of revolutionary politics to become one of the leading provincial and national figures during the war for independence and the postwar period. On the other hand, *if,* in the counterfactual world of make-believe, the revolution had been somehow avoided at the last moment and the two sides had reconciled their differences amicably, what then would have been George Bryan's history? Most probably he would have remained a local politician who would have lived out his life holding various elected or appointed offices under the proprietary government. Although Bryan's thoughts on that afternoon in Lancaster will never be known, one might well ponder whether he himself speculated, however fleetingly, on that identical question; in any event, he must have realized that his life would never be the same.

Historians of Pennsylvania's revolutionary period have always recognized the importance of Bryan as a political leader during the war and the significance of his party, the Constitutionalists, and of the Antifederalist forces, but the paucity of Bryan's extant papers has made it difficult to gauge the depth of his political beliefs and activities. Consequently, Bryan has remained a relatively obscure political figure. In fact, many of the Constitutionalist leaders have suffered the same fate for similar reasons. Bryan's papers, located at the Historical Society of Pennsylvania, contain important letters and addresses on politics and on his personal life, but generally the letters, private papers, and notes on court cases are limited. Other sources, however, help fill the void: the Atlee Papers, Peter Force Collection, and George Bryan diary at the Library of Congress; the Reed Papers at the New York Historical Society; the church minutes at the Presbyterian Historical Society; and the official letters and documents, as well as council and assembly minutes, of the state of Pennsylvania. Despite these collections and the published articles that have been identified as his, there remain serious gaps.

Little or nothing is known of the behind-the-scenes political transactions in which he engaged during the war, or of the political intrigues and conferences he conducted while on circuit as a supreme court justice visiting the county seats. Consequently, more questions remain than answers; nor can comfort be taken from the rumor that Bryan allegedly wrote an autobiography, which, if true, has never been found.[1] Nonetheless, sufficient information exists to permit a deeper and more thorough examination of the politics and ideologies that motivated George Bryan than has hitherto been accomplished.

Some aspects of Bryan's personality emerge from the evidence. He was controversial and at times reckless, often allowing his temper to cloud his better judgment and earning for himself the censorious description by Frederick Muhlenberg of "archpartisan" and "brawler."[2] Another critic charged Bryan with "consummate arrogance and self-importance."[3] Even Bryan once admitted sheepishly to his wife that he was "more discreet" when recently dining with members of Congress at the City Tavern than he had been "on a day in March Last." He was, he continued, "on . . . guard."[4] In cooler moments, however, Bryan was calm and deliberate and, according to John Ewing, possessed an "unaffected humility and easiness of access upon all occasions," with a "readiness to forgive" the injuries of a "misjudging world."[5] Another friend observed that his "judgment was cor-‐ rect, his modesty extreme, his benevolence unbounded, and his piety unaffected and exemplary." Possessing a "mildness of temper" that "never changed," Bryan had a "firmness of resolution" that was "invincible." This last description, of course, was perhaps a polite way of saying that Bryan was inflexible.[6] Apparently as he grew older he became milder and less antagonistic. By then, however, he was the leader of his party and bitter feelings toward him were well entrenched. Bryan himself never quite overcame his prejudice against the Quakers, or his antipathy for James Wilson.

A salient feature of Bryan's personality was his remarkable memory. Contemporaries were astounded at his ability to recall the minutest of details with amazing accuracy. "A memory surprisingly tenacious," commented Ewing, "his mind was the storehouse of extensive information on a great variety of subjects."[7] Although impressed, Alexander Graydon jested that Bryan recalled the most tedious of facts as well as the most important. His natural intellectual powers and retentive skills, however, explain in part how Bryan was able to become a leader of his party and of the state in the late 1770s. A more melancholy aspect of Bryan's life was his chronic bad health in his last twenty years. A satire written about Bryan by members of the opposition mentioned the disfigured right side of his face, perhaps the result of a stroke.[8] Yet while Bryan, according to a friend, exhibited "for many years" the "visible marks of weakness and decay," his mind remained strong—"unruffled and unbroken."[9]

Some features of Bryan's character, however, are less easily understood, let alone explained. Alexander Graydon in his reminiscences observed that Bryan liked "to identify himself with the *people,* in opposition to those, who were termed the *well-born,* a designation conceived in the genuine spirit of democracy." Furthermore, recalled Graydon, Bryan was a "staunch patriot" who, like his Irish brethren, was "in the antipodes at all points, to whatever was English."[10] Although Graydon's feelings toward Bryan were on the whole uncomplimentary, he never doubted Bryan's sincerity. His remarks about Bryan's black-and-white dichotomy of society into two antipathetic groups, the "people" and the "well-born," were accurate; Bryan certainly viewed the world that way. Ironically, however, Bryan was the product of a wealthy middle-class family, with many advantages that most of the "people" did not possess. Admittedly, by 1776 Bryan no longer enjoyed the prosperity he once did, and by the time of his death he was living in near poverty. But there may be more to his stark characterization of society than a simple explanation of wealth lost and poverty gained. In many respects, Bryan's reasoning was often more emotional than logical, his analyses more instinctual than reasoned. The Irish versus the English, the people versus the well-born, both suggest a confrontational, tunnel-vision mentality.[11] Alternatively, however, there was a grain of truth to those divisions for a man like Bryan; Irish Presbyterians were antagonistic toward England, and many of the leaders of the party opposed to Bryan and the Constitutionalists were of a higher economic status. Nonetheless, on a personal level Bryan's experiences as a highly successful merchant and as a leader in his church provide little incentive for a bias against the wealthy or the English, any more than against any other economic or ethnic group.

Yet the inconsistencies of his personality run deeper than specific issues. Bryan was by nature at varying times reasonable and inflexible, friendly and resentful, accommodating and confrontational. Usually fixed in his opinions, he may have been the type of individual who thrived on emotionally gratifying certainties but had difficulty adjusting those needs in a complex world filled with subtlety, confusion, and differences. At times he proved to be very capable at reconciling outstanding differences, especially among those with whom he was associated, as in his church or his political party. On other occasions, however, he simply refused to recognize an opponent's point of view as worthy of any merit. In the event, he was a man of strong emotions, which proved to be both his weakness and his strength. His tremendous energy helped to carry the state through the war, stabilize its government, and establish a political party that embodied the philosophy of Bryan and his peers. His emotional reactions to more complex issues, however, obscured his vision and caused him to lose touch with the democratic society he helped to create. What follows, then, is the story of a remarkable man, tough-minded, passionate, intelligent, and often unyielding, whose strengths guided his state through revolution and radicalism but whose weaknesses undermined his political career and destroyed his party.

1

"To Be Known and Regarded"

SAILING UNDER THE POWER of a strong spring breeze, the ship *Crawford* in 1752 tacked its way up the forest-edged Delaware River, passing the small port settlements of Wilmington and Chester. Standing along its bow, the twenty-year-old George Bryan observed for the first time the outline of Philadelphia, with its bustle of activity along the riverbanks. Like the masts of tall ships, the steeples of Anglican, Dutch Calvinist, and Presbyterian churches stood above the clumps of warehouses, shops, and homes huddled among one another and confined by winding cobblestone streets. Gazing upon the provincial courthouse standing beyond the High Street wharf, Bryan was drawn to the imposing statehouse tower that dominated the city's skyline. One day George Bryan would dominate Philadelphia from the same structure that occupied his attention, but that event lay twenty-five years in the future. Perhaps he was absorbed by the cacophony of urban noises as he made his way through the crowds of Irish, English, and German merchants, of traders, artisans, farmers, laborers, and slaves. He may have been struck, in particular, by the numbers of plainly garbed Quakers. Seeking directions to the corner of Water and Market streets, commonly called Bourne's Corner, Bryan could not have known the turbulent political career that lay ahead of him; he was consumed instead with the thoughts of his new enterprise and of becoming a successful merchant.

Bryan was ambitious, having traveled three thousand miles from home in order to launch his career in the New World. He would prove to be diligent, clever, and aggressive, qualities that were required in the often risky and unforgiving world of international trade. He was determined to succeed, both as a merchant and as a community figure; the two goals were intertwined. Besides the attainment of a comfortable standard of living, Bryan sought the social status that traditionally accompanied the life-style of a profitable trader. While hoping to become "known and regarded" among Philadelphia merchants and businessmen, and possibly among the political elite of the governor's council, Bryan also desired the respect of the people whom he knew, if not personally, then through his ethnic-religious inheritance—the Irish Presbyterians.

These years were critical for Bryan. While some of his early dreams would be shattered in later life, others would come to fruition. Bryan was to become a prominent leader of his fellow Irish, acting as a spokesman for their interests in the political arena. Although his mercantile career ended unhappily for him, his ambition for success set the context that defined his life. Arriving at his destiny and lowering the trunk that contained his belongings on the steps before the door, Bryan, with letters from family and friends tucked inside his waistcoat, stood before the firm of Wallace and Bryan, Merchants. Passing through the entrance of the store, Bryan took his first steps in a long, and often controversial, life in Pennsylvania.

II

On 11 August 1731 Sarah Dennis Bryan, wife of the successful Dublin merchant Samuel Bryan, gave birth to their first son, George. Sarah Bryan had already borne three daughters, Eliza, Anne, and Nancy, and would have three more sons, Arthur, Samuel, and William.[1] She and her husband were devout Presbyterians who intended to provide their sons with sound educations and careers in the mercantile world. George Bryan's early life in Dublin remains shrouded in obscurity; in 1751, however, his father arranged for him to become a partner with the Philadelphia merchant James Wallace. A Presbyterian of either Scotch or Irish descent, Wallace was known to Samuel Bryan through business connections, particularly a brother-in-law who lived in Philadelphia.[2] At the same time that George Bryan's mercantile career was being arranged, his father Samuel, relative William Bryan (who was either George Bryan's brother, cousin, or uncle), and James Wallace were pooling their resources to finance the construction of a fifty-ton ship, the *Friendship*, at Marcus Hook, Pennsylvania.[3]

As merchants, Samuel Bryan and his sons were participating in one of

the most dynamic enterprises of the eighteenth century. Trading throughout the Atlantic community, international merchants with their extensive
correspondence and movement into distant ports were engaging in exciting
as well as profitable exchanges with different cultures and countries. They
were in the forefront of an emerging world economy—organizing financial strategies, developing extensive concentrations of capital, and creating
complicated but essential lines of credit that brought together the needs of
northwestern Europe, North America, the West Indies, and certain markets
of southern Europe. Involved at all levels of the social and political economies of the international market, the merchants united the interests of the
farmers and the artisans throughout the Atlantic trading world by exchanging the produce and products of various communities to meet the demands
of other burgeoning markets. A merchant could earn great wealth, with
concomitant status; but the trade was competitive and risky, always holding
the possibility of failure and bankruptcy.[4]

Samuel Bryan not only assisted his eldest son, but also secured the interests of his firm when he relocated George to Philadelphia. Such a practice
was not uncommon, as merchants often placed a son or a relative in over-
seas operations.[5] Vital to the success of any importer and exporter was a
trustworthy partner with whom he could trade goods and vital information
about foreign and domestic markets. By locating his son in Philadelphia,
Samuel Bryan anchored the family's business to the growing Pennsylvania
market. Nor was this effort the first such venture for George Bryan. According to a 1748 Philadelphia ship registry, one of the three owners of the
June, a forty-ton brigantine, was a George Bryan of Saint Kitts, British West
Indies.[6] Although he would have been only seventeen years old at the time,
Bryan may have been sent by his father to gain valuable personal experience, as well as to provide firsthand knowledge of the profitable West Indies trade.

In the spring of 1752 George Bryan, still only twenty, arrived in Philadelphia as the junior partner in the firm of Wallace and Bryan. Unlike the
thousands of Irish Presbyterians streaming into Pennsylvania during the
eighteenth century hoping to free themselves from poverty, Bryan had im-
migrated simply to further an already established career. He was part of that
small proportion of Irish emigrants who were merchants, professionals, or
artisans, and who could afford to relocate to Philadelphia in some degree
of comfort.[7] Bryan had probably returned to Ireland from the West Indies
before embarking for Philadelphia.

Leaving family and friends must have been difficult for Bryan, although
he might have been ambivalent about residing in Dublin. Perhaps he intended to return to Ireland after staying a short time in Philadelphia, for

his father certainly expected to see him again. But Bryan never returned home and, according to the extant evidence, never gave a hint of homesickness. He may well have enjoyed his continued liberation from parental authority, having begun three years earlier in the West Indies, or perhaps he simply became absorbed in the excitement of a growing colonial metropolis. In any event, Bryan settled comfortably and permanently into his new environs.

His father feared that his son's independence could result in indolence. Writing to him in September 1752, Samuel Bryan focused specific attention on his son's amusement of "boating on the river" and on his association with a fellow Irish Presbyterian John Bleakley. While Bleakley was "honest," he was not the man, warned Samuel Bryan, "I should choose for my companion," for there was never anything "in his young days that could polish his person and manners." Samuel reminded his son of the "long letters" he had given him outlining appropriate behavior, and he now further recommended "dancing, fencing, the use of the small sword, taking a glass of wine or punch" with "men of manners, sense, etc.," as the means to become "known and regarded." He also advised his son to keep the best company, "men in business, men in conversation and good manners" and not to become the "rustic or tar, but the genteel pretty agreeable fellow as well as the complete sensible merchant." His father urged Bryan to forgo boating and any other such nonsense. "I am doing everything in my power to advance you in the world and establish you as my son," continued the elder Bryan. "Do not defeat it."[8] Bryan may have ignored his father's advice about choosing friends, but he fully shared the expectation of becoming "known and regarded."

The firm of Wallace and Bryan, located on the corner of Water and Market streets, operated for more than two and a half years. Its first advertisement promoted the sale of potential servants recently arrived from Ireland. Far more common, however, were notices listing a variety of dry goods, manufactured products from England, Irish beef, and sundry wines and ales. Acting on the request of Bryan's father for products to be shipped to Ireland, the firm exported cranberries, pickles, peaches, hickory sticks, and other items, including fish. At one point, however, his father cautioned Bryan not to send any more sturgeon, as it was "very bad," and "not worth a penny." The senior Bryan added with exasperation that the fish had not been "saved in the Dantzick way"—apparently the method Samuel Bryan approved for shipping them. Samuel also advised his son to be routinely informed of the price of flax seed in Pennsylvania, one of the most important trade items between Ireland and Philadelphia.[9]

Wallace and Bryan expanded their profits by owning several ships. Although the cost of maintaining a ship and crew and associated expenses was often substantial, the two partners believed that shipping produce and goods to ready markets for a quick profit was preferable to dependence on the time schedule of another merchant's vessel. They also earned revenue by shipping the goods of other merchants.[10] The *Jenney*, a thirty-five-ton brigantine, and the *Lucas*, a fifty-ton snow, commanded by the Philadelphia Irish Presbyterians Alexander and Nathaniel Magee, respectively, regularly sailed for the firm to both the West Indies and the British Isles. The partners sold produce to Jamaica, Barbados, and Saint Kitts, while purchasing in return rum and molasses. From Ireland and England they bought Irish linen, dry goods, and manufactured products, while selling on the Irish market flax seed and other goods. They did not restrict themselves to their own ships, however, for they often shipped and imported goods in other vessels.[11]

Wallace must have felt comfortable with the talents of his young partner, because in September 1752 he traveled to England, leaving Bryan in control of the firm.[12] In May 1753 Bryan also left the city. Possibly on business, or to inspect potential land purchases as investments, or merely for pleasure, Bryan toured New Jersey and western Pennsylvania, his fragmentary diary describing visits to Amboy, Brunswick, and Mount Holly, New Jersey, and a journey "westward for Carlisle," Pennsylvania.[13]

Despite the prosperity of the firm, Bryan and Wallace on 10 October 1754 announced its pending dissolution and requested all of their customers with outstanding debts to pay their balances. The dissolution, in fact, was probably anticipated by the two partners from the beginning since the average length of most mercantile partnerships in colonial Pennsylvania varied from two to seven years. Few businesses were permanent.[14] Bryan and Wallace most likely sold the *Jenney* and *Lucas* and divided the money from the sale between them. On 4 February 1755 the partnership was officially terminated; Wallace joined his brother in the short-lived firm of James and Thomas Wallace, while Bryan established his own merchant house on Front Street between Market and Arch streets.[15]

Bryan announced his debut as an independent merchant in an advertisement of 4 March 1755. He continued to advertise throughout the year, but less frequently afterward. Like many other Philadelphia merchants, he sold principally dry goods and clothing from England and Ireland—Irish linens, osnaburgs, Turkey quilts, and other cotton and wool products. He also imported for resale a variety of domestic goods, including shears, needles, tea-tongs, pins, and buttons as well as products from the West Indies.[16]

In 1756 Bryan teamed with the merchants Redmond Conyngham and John Nesbitt to construct the one hundred-ton ship *Hayfield*. To defray expenses, merchants frequently contracted among themselves to build and own ships while sharing an equal voice in the ship's management.[17] Although such cooperation sometimes led to difficulty, Bryan's arrangement with the firm of Conyngham and Nesbitt appeared to be successful. Upon completion, the *Hayfield* was sent to Newry, Ireland, to participate in the flax seed trade. It returned eleven months later from Newry, having probably made other calls as well within the British Isles. Leaving again for Newry in December 1757 to continue the trade in flax seed, the *Hayfield* also visited Dublin in March 1758 and Louisbourg, Nova Scotia (recently captured by the British), in the fall of 1758 before returning to Philadelphia. Sensing that a ready market existed in Louisbourg because of the presence of English forces, the three partners immediately reloaded the *Hayfield* in the remarkably quick span of seven days and ordered her captain, a man named Henderson, to sail back to that port. Upon the ship's return to Philadelphia in nine months, it was sent back to sea for Amsterdam in August 1759.[18]

Aside from his partnership in the *Hayfield,* Bryan joined Conyngham, Nesbitt, and Philadelphia merchant John McCullough in November 1759 in the purchase of the fifty-five-ton brigantine *Hannah,* which cleared for Dublin in December 1759. Bryan, in fact, dramatically expanded his involvement in shipping that year. He purchased on his own the *Patty,* a fifty-ton snow. He also joined a Captain Lake and New York merchant George Folliot, a business associate, in buying the ninety-five-ton ship *Speedwell* and acquired, with Folliot, the fifty-ton ship *John and William* and the fifty-ton snow *Charming Sally.* By 1760 Bryan, at the age of twenty-nine, could boast of maintaining at least six trading vessels.[19]

Although Bryan's prosperity in the 1750s owed much to his personal skills, he was also aided by external forces, especially the French and Indian War, which was primarily responsible for the increase of his financial success during the 1760s. Of the six vessels in which he owned an interest, four were French prizes purchased at auction. Bryan further strengthened his position by purchasing three more vessels between 1761 and 1762, the *Hibernia,* a sixty-ton brig; the *Greyhound,* a fifty-ton sloop; and a second *Greyhound,* a fifty-ton brig.[20] By 1763 Bryan's vessels were reaching all the major trading ports throughout the Atlantic community. While merchants usually owned or held interests in one or more vessels, Bryan's shipping interests were significant because he owned so many vessels at one time.[21] This development suggests that he was aggressively capitalizing on the profits available to merchants during the war.

Apparently, Bryan was not using these ships solely for his own cargo, for he could not have possessed enough products to fill the holds of six to nine vessels concurrently. Presumably, he used some of the ships for his own goods and either sold the other vessels for a profit after delivery of goods at different ports, or filled the ships with the goods of other merchants for a commission and then allowed the captain to find the best market he could, splitting the commissions with him. In any event, Bryan probably realized that ships were a good investment during a war; possession of several vessels protected him from a serious financial setback in case he lost property to French privateers. One thing is certain—Bryan was making money.

Bryan's financial success during the war was supported not only by his shipping interests but also by his ability to provide goods to war-created markets both at home and throughout the North American continent. In May 1756 Bryan supplied Pennsylvania's provincial militia with 757 shirts for a handsome gross profit of £391 14s. 4d.[22] In 1762 Bryan was advised by his New York friend and trading partner, the Irish-born Presbyterian William Gilliland, that an excellent market had been suddenly created in Quebec because of its capture by the British. After citing the source of his information, Gilliland named specific dry goods and domestic products, including twenty dozen military shirts and a variety of shipping gear such as canvas, rigging, and anchors with attached cables, that were in immediate demand. Gilliland had already shipped over £8,000 worth of goods to Canada before receiving this information but was unable to commit more. Knowing, however, that Bryan intended to send his sloop *Greyhound* to Quebec, he believed that the information would be of "no disservice" to him.[23]

There were, however, hazards in the war trade. Privateering posed a considerable threat to merchants, who could hope that their ship captains could outrun aggressors. Alternatively, they needed to make certain that the ships were adequately covered by insurance.[24] For example, in 1760 Bryan instructed the Philadelphia owner of the *Jenny-Sally*, which was returning from Leghorn (Livorno), Italy, via Lisbon, Portugal, to insure the cargo. Bryan's advice was more than a benevolent gesture—the cargo was consigned to him. He therefore added that if the owner needed the money to cover his insurance cost immediately, he should draw it from the London mercantile firm of Allen and Marlar. Disasters, however, were inevitable. In 1762 Bryan lost his investment in purchased merchandise with the seizure of the *Betsy and Nancy* off Antigua by French privateers.[25] Nonetheless, Bryan was fortunate in that such setbacks were never sufficient to offset the profits he reaped in the wartime commerce.

Bryan also faced other problems that were endemic to merchants whether during times of peace or belligerence. Debt collection, for example, was a perennial annoyance. North America was specie poor, and currency usually consisted of paper money issued by the various colonies and bills of exchange from the Atlantic trading community at large—creating a potpourri of currency exchanged in the marketplace. The principal technique in selling goods at the local market, however, involved the carrying of book debts for customers from three to twelve months.[26] While extended credit policies were necessary for a merchant hoping to attract customers, collecting debts was still troublesome. A year after Bryan and Wallace dissolved their firm, for example, Bryan continued to request their former customers to pay old liabilities.[27] Consumer debts were not the only concern for merchants like Bryan; the failure of a merchant with whom another merchant had credit also could have serious repercussions. One of Bryan's brothers, writing from Dublin, urged him to sell another merchant's vessel as soon as it arrived in Philadelphia. The merchant reluctantly agreed to liquidate the ship in order to repay the Bryans, as he was in debt to both George and his brother. The latter held George Bryan's bills of exchange, which were due for payment shortly, and therefore was anxious to receive the money from the sale of the vessel. He pleaded with his brother George not to lose "one instant of time," in sending the "remittances for the amount with damages" owed by the other merchant. Bryan's brother added that he would be "much distressed" if the payment was not expedited.[28]

Illegal trading activities were a regular feature in Philadelphia colonial and international commerce, and there is a suggestion that Bryan was not above the temptation. He apparently was willing to accept a shipment of shoes manufactured in Dublin for resale with the understanding that if the venture proved successful, more would be made available. There was one problem, however: the direct shipment of shoes from Ireland was prohibited by the Navigation Acts, a fact that was unquestionably known to Bryan.[29] In another instance that pointed to Bryan's participation in illegal trade, or at least his knowledge of it, Gilliland confidently informed him that Captain Albertson of the *Susannah* had left New York "without clearing" his departure with the Custom House. Also, while apprising Bryan later that year that Bryan's sloop *Greyhound* was unloading at New York, Gilliland added that Captain Albertson's cargo from the *Susannah* "was much in danger through the villainy of six rogues that threatened to inform," but that "their mouths were stopped at a small expense" and that "all is now well I hope."[30]

In the late 1760s Bryan was still acting as an importer-exporter and a retail merchant, although apparently by then he no longer owned his own vessels. He continued to trade heavily with the British Isles, with various points along the northern and southern coast of Europe, with the West

Indies, and with New England. By 1767 he had expanded his mercantile activities to include increased imports from the southern coast of North America, accepting cargoes from Baltimore and North and South Carolina. Cooperating with his brother William in Baltimore, Bryan concentrated on a variety of lumber exports—walnut, mahogany, and cedar, as well as white oak planks and boards for shipbuilding. The lumber was marked for both the Irish trade and the Philadelphia market. He also exported wheat and flour from Pennsylvania and Maryland to Ireland.[31]

Seeking additional revenues, Bryan acted as an agent and investor in two projects. He sought commissions in 1764 and 1767 for selling potential indentured servants arriving from Ireland, as well as for finding in 1766 an individual "skilled in the manufacture of paper" who was willing to relocate to Connecticut.[32] Bryan undertook a considerably larger proposition in 1765 during an investment mania among Philadelphia entrepreneurs for lands in Nova Scotia. Encouraged by Canadian local officials, several leading merchants and politicians of the Quaker party, including Benjamin Franklin, bought land rights in Acadia in June 1765. They hoped that settlers from the middle states would migrate to their land. In October of the same year, several leading Presbyterian merchants and other interested parties, known collectively as the Philadelphia Company, also bought property rights in Acadia. One of the investors was Bryan, who acted as the agent for clearing the passage of potential settlers. This speculative adventure proved to be relatively unsuccessful for both groups, and in May 1767 the Philadelphia Company granted powers of attorney to two of its members, instructing them to sell the land rights to the best possible advantage.[33]

Like many merchants attempting to augment their estates, Bryan diversified his investments by acquiring property. Most of the investments occurred in the early 1760s and apparently were intended either for speculation or for rental. The most significant purchase took place in 1761 when Bryan bought over four thousand acres in Sussex and Morris counties, New Jersey, from the London-based Pennsylvania Land Company for the substantial sum of £2,750.[34] Three years later, however, George Folliot became co-owner of the tract when he paid Bryan exactly half of the purchase price. Bryan then sold 201 acres of the Morris County acreage to George Keene and on 15 November 1768 sold the remainder of his share of the New Jersey properties to his widowed mother for £1,800.[35] The latter transaction probably involved unresolved book debts between the trading firms of Samuel Bryan and his sons, and therefore any assessment of the profitability of the total investment is difficult to ascertain. In another transaction, on 16 September 1761, Bryan bought a lot on Lombard Street in Philadelphia for £76, selling the property three years later for £120. By

1771 he also owned an eleven-acre farm in Roxborough and a one hundred-acre tract in Tinicum Township, Philadelphia County.[36]

Accompanying his success in business, Bryan also enjoyed a happy marriage. On 22 April 1757 he had wed Elizabeth Smith, the daughter of the prominent Philadelphia Presbyterian merchant Samuel Smith. The match was fortunate for Bryan because he married within his social status and increased his contacts among the city's Presbyterian merchants. More important, however, Bryan was genuinely in love. His letters to his wife were affectionate and caring; in one such missive, he described himself as her "devoted lover, partner & friend."[37] Between 1758 and 1774, Elizabeth Bryan delivered ten children, at least seven of whom survived to adulthood.[38] Although he owned several properties both in and outside of the city, Bryan apparently rented his lodgings, as there is no evidence to suggest he owned his own home. His family may have resided above his store, or lived nearby. In 1766 he moved his store from Front to Water Street below Market Street, and in 1767 he moved his business again, returning to Front Street off Walnut Street.[39] All of the locations were centered in the merchant district, situated around the wharfs and docks along the Delaware River.

Although he never ascended to the ranks of the very wealthy merchant elite, Bryan nonetheless flourished in his nineteen years as a Philadelphia merchant. Tax assessments are not necessarily sound measurements of an individual's worth because they often ignored other forms of wealth or underestimated the value of property, but they do provide a rough gauge of prosperity. In 1756 and again in 1765 Bryan's property was assessed at £50, placing him in the top fifth of those who resided in his ward at the time of the assessment.[40] The tax returns of 1767 and 1769 indicate, however, that Bryan's economic status had declined slightly, placing him in the upper third of those residents living in his ward.[41]

The tenuous nature of the mercantile world, however, was suddenly brought home to Bryan when his life was dramatically altered in September 1771. At that time Bryan was declared bankrupt, although little evidence exists to clarify the cause. One source indicates that the unanticipated "misfortunes of persons abroad" forced him to liquidate his assets, which included his one hundred-acre tract in Tinicum Township, in order to pay his debts.[42] By 1774, however, he had regained some measure of prosperity, albeit considerably less than that to which he had become accustomed. His tax assessment that year for the Dock Ward showed that he had one servant but that his rate was extremely low relative to that of the other residents, placing him in the lower half of those estates assessed. His mercantile career was over; his income after 1772 was dependent on his services as a city and county justice.[43]

III

Despite the turn of events in the early 1770s, Bryan should be viewed as a man who prospered for almost two decades as a Philadelphia merchant. Established in that career by his father, and possessing the aggressive and acquisitive qualities necessary for success, Bryan enriched himself in the expanding Philadelphia and international markets while capitalizing on the demands for goods created by eight years of warfare between 1756 and 1764. Fulfilling his father's advice to become "known and regarded," Bryan at age twenty-four started his own business and during the next sixteen years operated as a trader, shipowner and builder, investor, and land speculator. Although never a member of the colony's small circle of very wealthy merchants, he was comfortably situated in the upper sections of the amorphous but growing "middling" class.

Bryan's success as a merchant provided the context for his relationship with his peers. While Philadelphia merchants generally enjoyed enhanced social status within their community, they were most likely to possess a level of prosperity below that of the very wealthy and scarcely better than that of most successful artisans or traders. Furthermore, the Philadelphia mercantile community, as a recent economic historian argues, was not monolithic, but consisted of individual merchants who were often attracted to those institutions that had a stronger claim upon their loyalties, principally churches or ethnic associations.[44] This scenario clearly describes Bryan. By 1770 he had established himself as a successful businessman, as a leader in his church (as will be seen), and as a political spokesman for his community. The ability to attain such status, however, was entirely dependent on his success as a merchant. For example, his selection along with six others by the provincial assembly in 1762 to oversee the construction improvements along the Delaware River was in recognition of his successful career as a merchant and a community leader. The commission on which Bryan sat was authorized to build new piers, strengthen existing wharfs, and perform other works designed to improve navigation in the Delaware River.[45]

Given the scope of his success and the benefits he derived from it, both personally and politically, Bryan must have been traumatized by the crushing blow to his prestige and self-esteem of the bankruptcy. Besides a source of personal humiliation, the sudden collapse of his fortunes would have also caused a considerable strain on his large family. Furthermore, and perhaps not unconnected to his misfortunes, Bryan exhibited the first signs of failing health, which briefly incapacitated him in 1773.[46] What impact these developments had on Bryan's views and attitudes during the events leading to the revolution is difficult to ascertain. After the bankruptcy, Bryan chose to abandon the retail and merchant trade forever as his primary source of income, and pursued instead his expanding political and judicial career. In fact, his budding interests in politics and law must have previously distracted him from his business responsibilities. Although Bryan lacked formal legal training, he demonstrated by the 1770s a detailed knowledge of both the common law of England and the legal tradition of Pennsylvania, clearly the result of extensive reading. While he proved to be an apt student, his self-tutoring must have drained considerable time away from his ledger books. The bankruptcy was neither planned nor desired, but, ironically, enabled him to pursue interests that he had been developing since the mid-1760s and prepared the way for his dramatic entrance into Pennsylvania revolutionary politics.

2

"STRENGTHENING
THE PRESBYTERIAN INTEREST"

HIS LIFE SUBTLY WOVEN into the intricate layers of his ethnic community by ties of faith, family, and cultural heritage, Bryan became deeply
involved in the institution that gave his community its ultimate force and
meaning: the Presbyterian church. At the age of twenty-seven in 1758 he
was elected to the Congregational Committee, the lay governing body of
the First Presbyterian Church of Philadelphia. The following year he was
elected to the board of trustees for the Corporation for the Relief of Poor
and Distressed Presbyterian Ministers Etc.—an awkward title for the non-
profit organization that provided some financial security for their impoverished ministers. In these and other capacities, Bryan actively served the
church until his death in 1791.

Through these involvements, Bryan emerged within the Irish Presbyterian community as a well-known figure. Following the advice of his father
to establish himself in genteel company, to become known and regarded,
and not to permit the "carelessness of the world" to affect his obligation to
"God and religion," Bryan became a successful merchant and a participant
in church affairs.[1] In fact, his ascendancy into a position of leadership was
relatively easy. Successful in the respected occupation of merchant, Bryan
enjoyed an enhanced status among his peers. His generous contributions in
both time and money to the church further earned him the right to speak
on behalf of his fellow dissenters. He also enjoyed access to the leaders of

the church through his marriage to Elizabeth Smith, daughter of the successful merchant Samuel Smith, one of the founders of the Second Presbyterian Church of Philadelphia.

Bryan's entrance into church activity, however, occurred during a difficult period for the Presbyterians, as an "ugly, lean, jealous, ill-natured spirit," born of the Great Awakening, continued to haunt the church and divide its communicants and ministers between the New and Old Side factions. Upon his arrival, Bryan joined the Old Side First Church, presumably because he was more comfortable philosophically with its underpinnings than with the revivalist heritage of the New Side. Yet evidence is lacking to indicate that he was overly concerned with the theological debates that rocked the institution, or that he ever exhibited anything but a passing interest in the question of true salvation. Rather, his religious interests appeared to be more secular. In the event, he was confronted early in life with the necessity of transcending the great debate and striking a happy balance between the two sides. Bryan's marriage into the Smith family had brought him headfirst into church politics because that family belonged to the New Side Second Church, which owed its existence to the bitter schism of 1742. At the age of twenty-six, in one of his earliest acts of ecclesiastical diplomacy, Bryan sought to accommodate familial differences by taking the extraordinary step of maintaining pew rents in both churches and having most of his children baptized in the Second Church, while at the same time continuing his participation in the First Church.

II

Presbyterianism at the time of Bryan's participation was undergoing dramatic changes, still reeling at midcentury from the tremendous disruption of the Great Awakening. Briefly stated, the controversy had been fueled by the demand of the more emotional and revival-oriented Presbyterian faction known as the New Side that only those who could *testify* to having been "saved" by God could be members of the church. In contradistinction to this view, the subsequent Old Side faction argued against the likelihood that such a determination could ever truly be made by the saved and also questioned the ability of revivalist ministers to pass judgment on another individual's alleged salvation. The bitter schism among colonial Presbyterians that erupted over this issue beginning in 1742 ended at the 1758 Synod of Philadelphia. The issue was resolved through the Articles of Union, which would serve as the basis for compromise and governmental reorgani-

zation. Promoting the new harmony, both factions agreed that the controversial revival was the "blessed Work of God's [holy] Spirit in the conver-
sion of numbers." As a concession to the Old Side, however, the synod
added that persons who fell into convulsions and entertained visions of
Jesus were "under a dangerous delusion." Furthermore, the articles carefully decreed that the presbytery (the regional diocese for a given geographic area) alone could license, or ordain, ministerial candidates. For this
licensing to occur, the candidate must demonstrate both his "learning, and
experimental acquaintance with religion" and his acceptance of the Westminster confession of faith and the catechisms. The latter requirement was
usually, though not always, a routine matter, but the vaguely worded "experimental acquaintance" permitted a common foundation upon which
both the Old and New sides could agree. Finally, all past discussions, and
any recriminations over the recent schism, were declared off-limits in the
synod.[2]

The reunion of the two sides saved their unity but did not obliterate
their differences. In particular, they could never agree on the validity of
judging another man's claim of salvation. The New Side ardently believed
that the examination of a candidate's personal experience of God's salvation
was scriptural and necessary in order to bar hypocrites from entering the
fold. The Old Side agreed that a judicature might inquire if an individual
had experienced a work of grace but claimed that passing judgment on that
person's testimony was a pretense and a "meer human contrivance."[3] The
contest between the two groups was played out in the synod with its power
to create and redefine the presbyteries that would license ministerial candidates. Despite protestations by the minority Old Side that majority voting
was a "deaf, absurd thing," the New Side through its numerical superiority
attempted to isolate its theological opponents and insure that only candidates with New Side leanings could become ministers.[4]

In Philadelphia, the Old and New sides were divided between the First
and the Second Presbyterian churches, respectively. After the reunion, both
churches belonged to the Philadelphia Presbytery, which had a preponder-
ance of New Side ministers. The arrangement was not a happy one, and in
1762 the synod reluctantly agreed to separate the Old Side ministers into
a new Second Philadelphia Presbytery, while the remaining New Side ministers continued in the original presbytery (now called the First Philadelphia
Presbytery).[5] New Side ministers were outspokenly upset, however, about
the separation and determined that this act was one of the last compromises
the synod would allow the Old Side. Cutting off the supply of ministers
from the British Isles who had Old Side leanings, the synod ordered that it

must first approve all immigrating ministers. Old Side leader Francis Alison dubbed the synod's measure a "nonimportation act" and wondered how the vacant congregations would be filled.[6]

Revealing little or no interest in participating in the theological debate over salvation, Bryan was caught between the two antagonistic factions. His sole recorded reference to the Great Awakening and the subsequent schism was an offhand uncomplimentary remark about George Whitefield and his "tokens of regeneration."[7] More to the point, Bryan belonged to a post-Awakening generation that saw new opportunities in a revived Presbyterian faith. For Bryan, one important effect of the revival was the sweeping away of all assumptions about a unified church, thereby forcing the ministry to grapple with a splintered and divided laity. In order to survive in an increasingly competitive and pluralistic religious society, the church was compelled to strengthen itself through the increased activism of its communicants and to yield to men like Bryan a greater role within its hierarchy. From these positions Bryan and his peers would choose their own ministers, determine the church's finances, and subsequently participate with great energy in the ministerial intrigues of church politics.[8] But the visions created by these new opportunities were still dependent on the vicissitudes of New and Old Side antagonisms. For his part, Bryan attempted the difficult proposition of advancing the interests of the First Presbyterian Church while not overtly antagonizing the members of the New Side, and at the same time promoting the interests of the Presbyterian community. Whether Bryan's actions on behalf of his church were motivated by lofty idealism or personal ambition, both of which proved to be impractical, is debatable. Nonetheless, despite his best endeavors, he was eventually ensnared by the pettiness and suspicions of the two competing factions.

Bryan's initial association with the First Presbyterian Church occurred in June 1756, two years before the Articles of Union. His name was included among fifty-seven others in an official call to the Rev. Richard Godwin of Allerton, near Liverpool, England. The First Church had been unsuccessfully seeking to replace its aged pastor Robert Cross, who had been urging the congregation to act before his demise.[9] The congregation turned to the British Isles for a minister who was "polite, and sound in the faith, with a good learning, able to promote and defend the faith." They also wished that he would have a "peaceable healing temper"—a reflection of the fractured Presbyterian community in the wake of the schism.[10]

That the First Presbyterian Church should apply to England and Scotland for ministerial candidates was revealing. Since the schism, the Old Side had been reduced in size from twenty-seven ministers to twenty-three, averaging only one ordination per year while losing a total of eleven ministers through death or other circumstances. The New Side ministerial numbers, on the other hand, had swelled to seventy-three during the seventeen-year separation, enabling them to carry the evangelical message aggressively throughout New York, New Jersey, eastern Pennsylvania, and Virginia.[11] The Old Side might have found more willing congregations and popular support on the frontier, stocked with recent Scotch and Irish immigrants, but it lacked any ministers to send to those areas and consequently could only look on helplessly.

Most European ministers were reluctant to migrate to America under the best of conditions. The schism had only exacerbated matters.[12] Though the First Church claimed a large congregation, it was desperate for a pastor. Richard Godwin replied that he was a moderate Calvinist and somewhat accommodating to the Old Side First Church's specific needs. Nonetheless, he refused the call. By 1758 the committee for the congregation was asking its London correspondent for "anyone" who was available and could declare his belief in "the essential articles as his faith."[13]

Under these trying circumstances, George Bryan was unanimously elected a committeeman of the church in June 1758. In July, along with William Allen and several other committee members, Bryan visited the Rev. Andrew Bennet and officially extended to him the pastoral call. Bennet considered the offer but doubted whether he could accept the position because of his poor health and his personal reservations regarding the ordination ceremony as prescribed by the Old Side presbytery. Bryan, accompanied by John Mease, visited Bennet a second time; the two men gently expressed their concern over his reluctance. In the course of their conversation, however, Bennet made his refusal final.[14]

By September 1758 Bennet had left the city, but only after the committee had borrowed enough money from Bryan, Mease, and John McMichael to pay his expenses. The committee then inquired if the Rev. Joseph Cummings of the New Side New Brunswick Presbytery would be interested in the pastoral position. He was not. In the spring of 1759 the committee presented a call to a Rev. Monro, who appeared willing, but as he was already employed in the service of his majesty's government preaching to the Highlanders stationed in the city he was obligated to decline. Finally, a six-man committee including Bryan offered the call to the Rev. John Ewing, who, to their great relief, accepted.[15]

Ewing's appointment safely lodged the pastorate of the First Presbyterian Church in the Old Side hands of Francis Alison, the ailing Robert Cross, and Ewing. By 1762, with the organization of the Philadelphia Old Side into its own presbytery, the First Church began considering extending its

domain into the southern portion of the city. Anticipating a "great increase" in the city's population, church leaders then assumed the "probability" of a "considerable" increase in the number of Presbyterian families "in
a few years." They assumed therefore that a third place of worship would
need to be constructed.[16]

Bryan, who became an enthusiastic participant in the building of the
new church, was appointed with several others to consult with the prominent Shippen family about the availability of city lots below Market Street.
After several years of negotiations, the First Church successfully appealed
to the Penn family proprietors for a lot on the corner of Fourth and Pine
streets. As part of a six-man committee, Bryan visited William Allen; the
group expressed its thanks for his timely intervention with the Penn family
and began the process of transferring the property to the First Presbyterian
Church. The tedious but essential tasks of securing deeds and titles completed, the congregation then agreed to begin the construction of the new
house of worship immediately, with the costs to be paid by themselves. In
July 1765 a subscription was proposed, and Bryan, with William Rush, was
delegated the task of collecting the subscribed funds from congregation
families in the "upper part of the city."[17]

The establishment of the new church was as much a part of the Old
Side–New Side dispute as it was an anticipation of a growing Presbyterian
population. The capture of a new congregation for the Old Side's presbytery would provide that faction with a firmer foundation in its struggle to
survive within the New Side–dominated Presbyterian church in Philadelphia. Nonetheless, the 1758 reunion had been ostensibly intended to prevent open competition between the two sides, and the First Church correctly perceived that the failure to include the Second Church in the
creation of the new church was a breach of faith. The task of calling upon
the New Side Second Presbyterian Church to explain the actions of the
First Church leaders was left to Bryan, who either volunteered to do so or
was assigned the unenviable errand.

On 1 July 1765 Bryan presented his argument in writing to the Second
Presbyterian Church. He began defensively, commenting that the First
Presbyterian Church had "long laboured under a considerable difficulty to
accommodate the numbers of our society with pews in our church, our
house not being able to contain them all." To gratify the continued applica-
tions of new families for pews, he continued, the First Church had decided
to acquire property and begin construction of a new church. Bryan further
stated that the new structure not only satisfied those families seeking pews,
it also served as an "inducement to others of the Presbyterian persuasion,"
who were currently misspending their Sabbaths "in idleness and sauntering

thro' the streets to commons of the city." Bryan further cautioned that idle Presbyterians became prey to being "seduced by sectaries," who were taking advantage of the situation and were endeavoring "to undo & divide our congregations." The new meeting place, he insisted, would have the effect of "strengthening the Presbyterian interest" in Philadelphia "by a closer union," and thereby increase their numbers.[18]

Bryan understood that the New Side Second Presbyterian Church would be skeptical of his letter and of his congregation's professed sincerities. He therefore attempted to reassure the Second Church that "these & these only have been the motives which have carried us far in the prosecution of our present plan." Carefully wording his conclusion, Bryan suggested that it would have been "a breach of that charity and brotherly kindness which ought to subsist between our congregations" to have failed to communicate "our designs & intentions to you for your approbation and concurrence."[19]

Enclosed with the letter was a set of proposals that contained a complicated plan for rotating the ministers of the three churches until one minister could be settled among the new communicants. The ninth article of the proposals, however, suggested that once a minister was finally "fixed in the Third congregation," he was to alternate his preaching between the First and the Third churches *unless* all parties agreed to rotate their ministers among the three churches.[20] Given the differences between the First and Second churches, however, the likelihood of an agreement between them regarding the rotation of a minister was highly doubtful. The alternative, as outlined in the proposals, effectively excluded the Second Church from determining the preacher for the new congregation, while fulfilling the First Church's expectation that it would make that decision.

The reply of the Second Church indicated that Bryan's arguments had not been persuasive. Regretfully, the reply noted, a lot had been purchased, trustees appointed, and a plan of the new church settled without any prior consultation with the Second Church. If space had been the motivator, the reply continued, the Second Church had plenty of room, a whole gallery yet to be filled. The response also summarily dismissed Bryan's argument regarding the undue influence of sectaries. "We have not the least apprehension of danger from any *sectaries*," commented the Second Church, "nor do we see any probability of their doing much hurt to either of our congregations." The respondents further admonished Bryan to ignore the sectaries, adding that "public measures to oppose 'em seems to us least of all calculated to defeat their designs." Rather, the Second Church cautioned, Bryan should "*let these men alone; for party spirit never thrives so much as when it meets with opposition.*"[21]

The reply further observed bluntly that the proposals accompanying Bryan's letter were useless to any goal of unity, for the plan of rotating the ministers of all three churches seemed to invite "a refusal," and that the true intent of the proposal was to reduce the status of the Third Church to an "appendage to the first congregation." As a parting shot, the Second Church respondents added that even if they should agree to the necessity of a new church, they could not progress further in the matter until they consulted their presbytery, from which the First Church had seceded in 1762. For Bryan the response was particularly galling, for one of the signers was his father-in-law, Samuel Smith.[22]

Bryan's letter and the proposals (which he helped to draft) were evidence of his and the Old Side's dilemma. The problem was straightforward: to advance their interests without exacerbating the already strained relations with the Second Church. Bryan's desire in this instance to promote the welfare of the Presbyterian community rested on the assumption that what was good for one faction's perspective was also good for the whole community. Such assumptions were not inherently wrong, but given the attitudes of the two sides conflict would be the obvious and expected result. Bryan was not naive, and he undoubtedly realized that the Second Church would dissaprove of the unilateral actions taken by the First Church; the New Side's response confirmed that impression. His attempt, therefore, to smooth over the differences with his explanation of the First Church's actions and the proposed rotation plan, were, on the surface, disingenuous. Yet in fairness to Bryan and his colleagues, the letter and accompanying proposals were an honest outgrowth of their circumstances. Cooperation between the two churches over a third place of worship was, at best, unlikely, and both sides probably knew that. In the event, no further attempt was made to reconcile the two groups over the settlement of the new congregation, and despite the irritation caused by the affair, the matter seems to have been dropped by both sides.

The First Church continued its preparations, beginning construction of the new meeting place in 1766. Some members of the congregation questioned whether they could afford the new church and what its impact would be on the finances of the congregation. In response, Bryan estimated the number of families who would leave their church to assume membership in the new body and reported to his fellow committee members that the losses would be minor. Bryan and several others then decided to "use their prudence" in reconciling members who had concerns about the project's feasibility. Despite those doubts, the plans continued to go forward smoothly for the remainder of the year.[23]

Both Old and New sides were able to move beyond the issue of constructing the Third Church since neither was compelled to cooperate with the other in order to ensure the venture's success. That was not the case, however, when Bryan hoped that the Old and New Side factions would arrive at a mutual agreement regarding the College of New Jersey at Princeton. Although under severe criticism by both sides for its declining academic reputation and lack of strong leadership, the college was the only Presbyterian institution of higher education in America. Dissatisfied with New England's Harvard and Yale, Presbyterians were equally uneasy over their alliance with the Anglicans at the College of Philadelphia, raising doubts about its future as a seminary for dissenters. Francis Alison's New Ark Academy in Delaware was a competent school, albeit financially precarious, but it could not confer higher degrees. The only alternative for colonial Presbyterianism therefore was Princeton's College of New Jersey.[24]

Unfortunately, the Old and New Side dispute also affected the college, which had been founded in 1748 under the immediate auspices of leading New Side ministers and supporters, including William Tennent, Aaron Burr, and Jonathan Dickinson. The college's antecedents were the famous New Side Log College of Neshaminy, Bucks County, headed by William Tennent, Sr. Over the years, the presidents of the college were respectable, well-educated ministers with impeccable New Side credentials, but from 1757 to 1766 the presidents had an unfortunately high turnover rate: four in nine years, none of whom served for any appreciable length of time. After the death of Dr. Samuel Finley in 1766, the office remained vacant for two years under the temporary management of William Tennent. Nor was leadership at the top all that the college lacked. It was suffering also from a poor financial base, an inadequately funded staff that consisted of a series of temporary tutors, and a declining enrollment.[25]

Under these circumstances, members of the First Church believed the time was appropriate for achieving a measure of Old Side influence in the New Side college. Visiting the college's trustees in November 1766, a five-man committee, including Bryan, hoped to persuade the board to expand the college's staff by appointing "a president, a professor of divinity, and two professors of the sciences," with the appointments to be shared between Old and New Side educators. While the delegation suggested that a New Side minister should be appointed for the chair of divinity, they proposed that Francis Alison be appointed as professor of moral philosophy and John Ewing as professor of mathematics. The committee was further prepared to suggest two other Old Side ministers to those positions, Alexander McDowell and Matthew Wilson, if Alison and Ewing were too closely identified with the Old Side, as the committee anticipated they would be. The promise of considerable financial support from the Old Side accompanied the committee's aggressive proposals.[26]

The Old Side delegation wanted to present their proposals before the election of a new president by the trustees. They had kept their plans a closely guarded secret, fearing that premature disclosure would rally New Side opposition in time to squelch any Old Side presentation. The element of surprise might therefore provide the necessary momentum to obtain approval of the proposals before the New Side could react. The trustees, however, either learned or guessed the exact nature of the delegation's plans and quickly huddled together in one room and elected John Witherspoon as president while Bryan and his colleagues waited in an adjoining room. The delegation was greatly dejected upon learning of Witherspoon's summary election but nonetheless discussed with the trustees an impromptu plan for creating a permanent faculty as well as possible candidates for those positions. But the talks were fruitless. The trustees countered that without the promise of added financing they could not create the positions; the Old Side responded that without the promise of the appointments, they could not guarantee the financing. The talks came to an end, and the plan "to unite all the Presbyterians in the college of New Jersey" was shelved.[27]

Bryan and a new delegation met a second time with the college's trustees eleven months later. Witherspoon's refusal of Princeton's invitation to become its president prompted Bryan and his colleagues to recommend new proposals for a permanent faculty. The New Side, however, blamed the Old Side for Witherspoon's declination and accused Old Side member John Wallace of sending an "artful" letter to Witherspoon that was crafted in such a way as to ostensibly encourage him to accept the post while in fact discouraging acceptance. Wallace's letter described the Old Side's view that the college was "sinking" into oblivion. Yet Wallace never intended to dissuade Witherspoon from accepting the position. Rather, he and his Old Side brethren (probably including Bryan) believed that Witherspoon's accession was now necessary to restore the college's seriously impaired health and to bring the Presbyterian factions together.[28]

When the trustees met in October 1767, they were still without a president, and their meeting with the Old Side committee was, on the surface, friendlier than that held previously. The trustees agreed to the creation of three adequately funded faculty positions, with one chair, that of professor of mathematics and natural philosophy, scheduled for Old Side educator Dr. Hugh Williamson. The other two appointments were to go to New Side ministers John Blair and Jonathan Edwards, Jr. The college trustees then offered the presidency to the Rev. Samuel Blair of Boston. The success of the plan was dependent on the financial support promised by the

Old Side, although only one of the four suggested appointments was promised to the Old Side. Moreover, since the trustees decided that a year would be necessary to raise the required funding, none of the appointments except for that of John Blair was to be effective until that year had passed. Although their sincerity was questionable, the trustees in an apparent gesture of goodwill unanimously elected Bryan a member of their board. In December, however, the trustees learned that Witherspoon, in a stunning volte-face, had decided to accept the presidency. Dr. Blair of Boston hurriedly declined his invitation to the position, and the entire delicately crafted plan of a faculty quickly unraveled. Witherspoon's acceptance provided the trustees with the necessary excuse to quietly drop the faculty plan altogether.[29]

The negotiations at Princeton were clearly a failure. At their first meeting with the trustees, Bryan and the Old Side representatives had encountered "a cold reception"; the second meeting proved to be even less productive. The college made it quite clear that it had no intention of sharing the "management" with its brethren at Philadelphia.[30] Nor did the Old Side leaders fare any better in the synod, as they were consistently outvoted by numerically superior New Side ministers and elders. By 1773 Old Side leader Francis Alison bitterly described the synod as devolving into "private caballs out of doors, to secure a majority; and within doors, strife and contention and debates." He seriously doubted whether the union of 1758 was worth preserving.[31]

The inability of the two factions to find some level of agreement was frustrating at a time when leaders of the Presbyterian community like Bryan deemed unity essential, albeit on their own terms. The internal politics of Pennsylvania, the French and Indian War, and the imperial and ecclesiastical conflict between England and the colonies directly affected the immediate interests of Presbyterians during the sixties. The failure of meaningful compromise between the Old and New sides left their religion vulnerable. "Thus," lamented Francis Alison, "our enemies gain ground by our foolish animosities."[32]

The continued fracture between the two groups created dissensions among the Old Side members of the First Presbyterian Church as well. Such divisions chiefly occurred as a reaction to the increasing strain between the two sides and the extent to which they were willing to accommodate those differences. By 1768 Bryan's continued attempts to promote the welfare of the First Church and the society as a whole came under criticism by Old Side members who now viewed the New Side with open hostility. The pivotal conflict again revolved around the new church.

In March 1767 the Third Presbyterian Church was ready for occupancy and Bryan, along with John Wallace, prepared lists of families eligible for pews. Accordingly, the issue was raised of settling a minister at the Third Church; the First Church committee, considering the growing ministrations of the Scottish Church of the Seceders in the southern part of the city, felt that a minister was needed immediately at the Pine Street church. Therefore Bryan immediately requested that the Second Presbytery call a minister without delay.[33]

The calling of a minister to the Third Presbyterian Church proved to be unexpectedly disruptive. Initially, however, there was no sign of potential trouble, as several members, led by George Bryan and John Wallace, sought a minister for the Third Church congregation who would be acceptable to both the New and Old Side members. In March 1767 a great majority of the families, led by Bryan, favored the immediate call of the Rev. James Sproat of Connecticut, a pious, well-respected minister whose New Side ministry was innocuous to most communicants. The suggestion to call Sproat, therefore, seemed a reasonable decision, and for the greater part of 1767 it enjoyed the support of the majority of the congregation.

Although the decision to call Sproat was not final, there was little reason to believe that it would not be executed. The October 1767 visit by the Old Side committee to the Princeton trustees, however, apparently undermined the consensus. The continued failure of the Princeton negotiations stimulated a backlash among First Church members and resulted in a shift away from cooperative ventures and a movement toward a more pronounced antagonistic view of the New Side. In fact, the hostility within the First Church probably had been growing for some time. Francis Alison by 1766 was openly contemptuous of the "persecuting, narrow biggots" among the New Side ministers and displayed even less respect for the trustees of Princeton.[34]

Within the congregation, the political shift was led by William Alison, one of the members of the Princeton delegation, and by Dr. Hugh Williamson, whose name had been put forward as a potential professor and ultimately rejected by the trustees. In January 1768 Williamson along with William Rush told several families of the Third Church that if they would agree to call the Rev. Patrick Alison, a well-known Old Side minister, instead of James Sproat, then Williamson and Rush in return "would subscribe to a sum for three years and for some time longer" for the purpose of paying Alison's salary. In other words, the First Church members offered a minister *gratis*, provided the Third Church called the minister they proposed.[35]

In February 1768 Rush, Williamson, and James Craig conducted a survey of Third Church families and reported to the First Church committee that seventy-five families favored the call of Patrick Alison, while only eight or nine families preferred James Sproat. The committee, now dominated by Williamson and Rush, cautioned that it "never intended to infringe upon the rights of the congregation" in the "selection of a minister, and that they should vote on whom they want." Yet the committee in the same statement was quick to remind the Pine Street parishioners of their outstanding debts, and of the First Church's role in paying off those sums.[36]

The Market Street congregation rapidly divided between the Sproat and the Patrick Alison factions—the latter led by Rush and Williamson, who showed little inclination toward compromise. The committee appointed William Rush to speak with Bryan and with John Wallace, leaders of the Sproat faction, in an effort to convince them of the correctness of calling Patrick Alison. The contents of that conversation, unfortunately, were not reported, but in the event it would have made little difference. On 15 April 1768 the First Church officially called Patrick Alison for the ministry of the Third Church.[37] In a sharp and immediate retort, sixteen families led by Bryan sent a protest to the First Church committee outlining their grievances. Written by Bryan, the protest stated that the call to Patrick Alison was repugnant to the great majority of Third Church members, and that his election was "evasive" and had been influenced more by the promise of money from the old congregation than by a willingness of the Third Church to settle him as its spiritual guide. Bryan and his followers issued a second protest to John Ewing asking that the call be reconsidered. Ewing, however, deftly sidestepped the request by referring it to the lay committee under the leadership of Rush and Williamson, where the request was promptly tabled. As a final effort, fifty-one Third Church families led by Robert Knox, a former First Church member, sought redress from the 1768 synod against the Second Presbytery's call to Alison, but that too was ignored.[38]

The result of the Sproat–Patrick Alison controversy was unmistakable: for the first time in more than ten years, Bryan was out of step with his First Church coreligionists. To make matters worse, he and Wallace were ousted from the lay leadership of the church. Between 1768 and 1773 Bryan, once very active in his congregation, was conspicuously inactive. Although the debate over Patrick Alison proved to be so rancorous that Alison judiciously decided to decline the call, Bryan remained angry at his treatment and began attending Second Church services and meetings, where his name subsequently appeared on both a 1769 committee list and a 1772 pew rent increase petition. Furthermore, his seventh, eighth, and ninth children were baptized at the Second Church—ironically by the Rev. James Sproat, who had accepted the October 1768 call by the Second Church to serve as its pastor.[39]

Despite the dramatic upheaval engulfing the First Church in 1768, the departure of Bryan may have been less the result of fundamental differences of opinion than of the pent-up frustrations of years of bickering with the New Side. Certainly, Bryan must have resented the manner in which the Patrick Alison faction overtook and usurped his leadership position after years of service. In the event, and despite the previous dispute over the construction of the Third Church, Bryan was apparently able to shift his attendance to the Second Church comfortably. Four years later, Bryan returned to the First Church, entering the lists once again in yet another intrafaith squabble. Despite its rancor and continuing controversies, however, Philadelphia Presbyterian politics in the second half of the eighteenth century maintained a remarkable fluidity that kept the church from splintering into separatist movements or undertaking disownment of individual members.

III

In December 1759 Bryan's activities among Presbyterians had assumed a greater responsibility when he became a trustee of the newly created Corporation for Relief of Poor Ministers. The corporation was the brainchild of Old Side minister Francis Alison, who desired to create some financial security for the impoverished ministry. Observing that the chronic impecuniousness of the church "discouraged men of abilities" from serving "Christ and mankind in the ministry of the gospel," Alison feared that the dearth of ministers would threaten the ability of the church to keep pace with the demands of colonial Presbyterianism.[40] He unhappily concluded that many of the settlers were "readier to learn the vices of their Indian neighbors, than to teach them the more perfect ways of God."[41] Believing that the absence of a sufficient number of preachers would eventually "bring the gospel into contempt," and in an effort to attract ministers, Alison took upon himself the enormous task of organizing an insurance plan that would provide the widows of deceased ministers with a life pension.[42]

He began the project in 1755 and two years later applied to the proprietor for a patent of incorporation, which was granted in 1758. His next step was to create a sufficient foundation of capital for the fund. Accordingly, he reached out to the community for additional support, and on 17 December 1759 he added fourteen members to the original twelve-member board. Among the new members were George Bryan and his father-in-law, Samuel Smith.[43]

The immediate plan called for local communities to be pressed to contribute and for the bright and persuasively sincere Rev. Charles Beatty to be dispatched to England, Scotland, and Ireland for additional financial assistance. As a trustee, Bryan was assigned to committees that prepared a rough draft addressing Presbyterian communities in Pennsylvania and that oversaw on a daily basis the preparations for Beatty's trip. John Wallace provided sea stores and other necessities for the voyage, while Bryan provided letters of credit to northern Ireland. Beatty arrived in London on 15 April 1760 and remained in Great Britain for nearly two years, returning to Philadelphia by mid-1762.[44]

The horrible plight of their fellow Presbyterians at war with the Indians considerably moved the ministers and congregations "back home." Of the money Beatty collected, some was set aside for the minister's fund, while much more was designated for the relief of frontier victims. A committee was appointed to assist Bryan in examining Beatty's expenses and receipts and determining the manner in which the money was to be spent in accordance with the contributor's instructions. Bryan also served on a committee to return letters of thanks to the various donors and to compile an abstract of Beatty's journal that would be sent to the British Isles.[45]

Bryan was further assigned to manage the corporation's relationship with the synod regarding Beatty's money. For example, the Scottish Assembly directed that a portion of its donation was to be used for the distressed frontier inhabitants and the settling of a minister among them.[46] Such an order would normally be handled by the synod, which in May 1767 sent a committee to the corporation to inquire about the Scottish money. The synod specifically desired to know the total amount collected, whether it was available immediately, and the degree to which that body had power over its distribution.[47]

In a fairly stiff reply to the synod, Bryan cautioned that the corporation could not legally associate with nonmembers. Furthermore, although the conditions of the grant made by the Scots imposed upon the corporation a "joint" distribution of the money with the synod, the corporation was not responsible for the synod's ability to procure the money from the corporation. The synod was obligated, added Bryan, to send a representative to attend the corporation meetings if it intended to participate in the Scottish fund. Finally, concluded Bryan, the synod could expect £35 per year, to be jointly distributed with the corporation.[48]

This uneasy arrangement lasted the three years Bryan acted as chairman for settling their joint accounts; in 1771 a compromise was effected (during a period of Bryan's continued absence from the corporation) with the intention to "end all disputes." The corporation would automatically vote the synod £30 yearly, and the capital fund that created the allocation would remain undisturbed.[49] In all likelihood, Bryan's curt manner was in part a reflection of the ill will that existed between the two groups at the time. But of equal if not greater significance, Bryan was probably acting on behalf of the corporation, perhaps viewing himself as morally and legally responsible for its best interests. As such, he was unwilling to relinquish control over the distribution of the Scottish money.

In serving the corporation, Bryan participated in the usual business of an insurance company: examining the treasurer's books, determining policy on specific annuity cases or eligibility requirements, and constantly pleading with delinquent members to pay their premiums. Bryan also attempted to locate £500 entrusted in 1762 to Governor James Hamilton, who in turn had given it to an Indian commissioner for the ransoming of captives during the midcentury Indian wars. Though the corporation was able to secure the release of some prisoners on other occasions, the £500 was money ill spent. For the next twenty years Bryan and others, often threatening civil action, would demand an accounting of the funds. The money was never recovered, however, and was eventually realized as a loss.[50]

As a result of his political responsibilities during the revolution and postwar period, Bryan became less active with the corporation. In 1780, then a Pennsylvania Supreme Court justice, Bryan was elected president of the corporation following the death of Francis Alison. He held the title until his own death in 1791. Yet by the 1780s Bryan was absorbed in his judicial obligations and his political career, and the corporation was more concerned with the tedious business of running an insurance company and less preoccupied with war and the survival of the Presbyterian communities along the frontier. Bryan only attended eight of twenty-eight meetings held during his presidency.[51]

IV

Bryan's absence from the First Church was not permanent; by 1772 he again involved himself in First Church politics. The immediate crisis that he faced concerned the Third Church's claim of independence from its parent congregation. The First Church learned with "great surprise and concern" that its "brethren of the Pine Street Church have been so long blinded and misled by a very unaccountable misconstruction" of the rules and stipulations governing both churches. The Third Church had taken upon itself to call its own minister.[52] Despite the cautions of Francis Alison, a sizable faction within the Third Church had extended a call to the New Side Rev. George Duffield of the Donegal Presbytery, who accepted the call. The Third Church claimed that there was no binding agreement between the two congregations that restricted its right to extend a ministerial call on its own. The First Church responded that it had a "considerable share in the choice of ministers for Pine Street Church from its first formulation until the Late unconstitutionall proceedings."[53]

Bryan's opinion on the merits of the candidate Duffield remains unknown, but his objection mirrored that of the First Church, which denied the right of the Third Church to make the call at all. Attempting therefore to stop Pine Street's action, Bryan—again joined by his old ally John Wallace—provided the First Church in 1772 with a detailed summary of the legal and binding connections between the two congregations, including a history of their joint endeavors that served as precedent to the Third Church claim. Following the Bryan-Wallace presentation, a twenty-four-man committee was established to serve as the board of trustees for both churches. Bryan was elected as one of the twelve representatives from the First Church. The committee, dominated by First Church and several discontented Third Church members, decreed that the invitation to Duffield was invalid and ordered a new ministerial search.[54]

Bryan and his twenty-three colleagues on the committee also moved to solidify their position at law, promptly applying to the proprietor for a patent of incorporation that would sanction the committee as the legally incorporated board of trustees representing both churches. The patent was granted. The Second Presbytery of Philadelphia, led by John Ewing, then refused to prosecute the Third Church's call to Duffield, citing as the reason the extraordinary amount of dissension over his appointment.[55]

The Third Church, however, refused to yield, despite the formidable opposition of the First Church. Choosing to ignore the committee of twenty-four, the Third Church announced that the committee had "nothing to do with Pine Street congregation," and consequently that church would not "pay any regard whatever to it." Then the Third Church countered its Market Street brethren by appealing to the sympathetic New Side synod in 1772 against Ewing's refusal to call Duffield. The synod happily reversed the Old Side presbytery's decision and permitted Duffield's call to stand.[56]

In the following year the synod further decreed that George Duffield's subsequent complaint against the Second Presbytery was valid, and that he was to be removed to the First Presbytery of Philadelphia. In reaction and on behalf of an outraged First Church, Bryan delivered a furious letter to the synod accusing it of having "manifestly prejudged" the First Church's case, whereby the First Church would be foolish to pursue the matter further, for to do so would expose it to continued "ridicule," which was "unbecoming the gentleman and the christian." There was nothing left to do, exclaimed Bryan, except to withdraw the case from the synod—a circumstance that undoubtedly pleased that body.[57]

The First Church successfully argued in the court of common pleas and eventually in the Pennsylvania Supreme Court that it was the legal representative of the two churches. But the significant decisions were those of the synod in 1772 and again in 1773, which recognized the legal authority of the First Church in name but not in fact. The synod's indisputable right to uphold the call of a congregation to a minister was more important than the secular recognition of the First Church's property rights. The synod's decision allowed the Third Church to win the war, despite having lost the battle.[58]

The controversy peaked in September 1772. Armed with an injunction, the First Church ordered the doors of the Third Church locked, prohibiting the entrance of the recalcitrant congregation and its New Side minister. Duffield and the communicants entered the church through a back window and proceeded to engage in Sabbath service. A magistrate soon appeared, marched down the center of the aisle to the front of the pulpit, and ordered the congregation to disperse. He then began reading the Riot Act. His reading was short-lived, however, as Robert Knox, a physically imposing man, seized the magistrate and unceremoniously heaved him out the now unlocked doors. The following day Duffield was arrested, but the courts were reluctant to move against a minister and ordered the case dismissed.[59] Not until 1786 did the two churches forgo their differences and begin the necessary legal process for the Third Church's separate incorporation, which was completed in 1793. Presumably, Bryan supported the final outcome.

V

Bryan continued his involvement with the First Church until his death, serving three three-year terms between 1772 and 1784 on the board of trustees that oversaw both the First and the Third Presbyterian churches. Besides his continued association with the Corporation for Relief of Poor Ministers, he also maintained his connection with the Second Church, partly through his family and also through his friendship with James Sproat.[60] As evidence of Bryan's commitment to maintaining personal equilibrium between the First and Second churches, he continued his habit of paying pew rents to both. Because pew rent records for the two churches survive only for the 1780s and the early 1790s, it is impossible to confirm the date he began paying the double pew rents. More than likely, he had been doing so for some time. Seven of Bryan's children were baptized in the Second Presbyterian Church, and he and his wife were buried there.[61]

By 1776 and the outbreak of revolution, George Bryan had served as a member of the lay leadership of his church for eighteen years and was prominent in nearly all the major events that affected his Presbyterian community. He was a highly visible participant in the affairs of the First Church and was recognized as one of the community's religious and political leaders by the Second Church as well. Thus, for example, he represented the First Church in 1765 in negotiations with its New Side coreligionists over the establishment of the Third Church because at that time he was a provincial assemblyman and was related either by marriage, business, or friendship to many members of the Second Church. Moreover, within one year of his temporary withdrawal from the Market Street congregation in 1768 he was elected by the Second Church communicants to their governing lay committee. He further served as a trustee, along with some Third Church members, on the governing board that oversaw the management of the fractured Pine Street congregation. Whether in conflict or consensus, Bryan was an integral part and active member of his religious community.

Despite its many upheavals, the Presbyterian community constructed a new church in the southern part of the city to serve its increasing numbers, established the Corporation for the Relief of Poor and Distressed Ministers, finally initiated consideration of serious reform of its college at Princeton, and (no small achievement) remained intact. The lingering and often heated controversy between the New and Old sides, however, limited the progress the church could hope to attain. Whatever satisfaction Bryan may have felt, therefore, concerning Presbyterian achievements must have been tempered by the frustration and disillusionment of seventeen years of seemingly unrelenting factionalism in which he was a participant. A member of the post-Awakening generation eager for a united Presbyterian community to take a more active role in its external social and political environment, Bryan must have chafed at the inability of the Pennsylvania Presbyterians to find common ground.

In the event, an impression of his personality and the motivation behind some of his actions emerge from the years of his participation in his religious community prior to the revolution. One striking feature of Bryan's behavior was his secularism. Although deeply involved in the politics of the New and Old Side dispute, Bryan ironically displayed only a marginal interest in the theological underpinnings of the debate. For him, the opportunity to strengthen the "Presbyterian interest" in the community at large proved to be the overriding motivator. Yet Bryan was not simply an accommodationist, desiring to remain impartially above the fray, seeking compromise at all costs. He was also partisan, willing to engage in confrontation to obtain his goals as well as diplomacy. While he may have assumed that those goals were, *ipso facto*, best suited to the future well-being of the Presbyterian community, he often demonstrated a rigidity that was at times self-defeating.

As will be seen, Bryan was clearly not oblivious to the potential political significance of a cohesive, united Presbyterian community, both for the group and for himself. But his activism on behalf of the Presbyterian church as a whole indicates that he was not an ambitious careerist, willing to ally with any faction that would advance his political aspirations. In fact, if he personally harbored any serious political ambitions via a well-organized and disciplined Presbyterian presence in the colony, he certainly went about his task in a peculiar way. If his participation in the church was intended solely to promote his own career, Bryan would have been more successful had he abandoned the Old Side altogether. As a communicant of the New Side Second Church he would have been a member of the majority faction and therefore far better positioned for the struggles over the building and ministerial staffing of the Third Church and the reform of the college at Princeton. He would have enjoyed a leadership role in the Second Church and throughout the Presbyterian community and could have negotiated magnanimous compromises with the First Church from a position of strength. Moreover, since his wife was the daughter of one of the founders of the Second Church, Bryan had a plausible excuse for making such a transition. But he did not make that transition. Instead, whether from loyalty, stubbornness, perverseness, or a combination thereof, Bryan remained with the First Church, even returning to the fold several years after losing his leadership role.

Yet despite Bryan's attachment to the Old Side First Church, he was apparently admired, as events would prove, even by his Presbyterian opponents for the significant amount of time and energy that he devoted to the cause of Presbyterianism in Pennsylvania. That tireless activism, which would also be evident in his political endeavors on their behalf, won for Bryan by the 1760s the role of spokesman for the entire Presbyterian community.

With the onset of revolution, however, many of the conflicts that pervaded the Presbyterian church during the 1760s and early 1770s were swept away, as those issues rapidly faded in a new world of social dislocation, war, survival, and freedom. George Bryan also became absorbed in the revolution, thrust into leadership positions for which he had been honed by his Presbyterian experiences but which now ironically occupied so much of his time and resources that he was unable to continue to participate to any great extent in church affairs. Nonetheless, he remained an important voice for his religious brethren. Not surprisingly, however, the same characteristics that had marked his religious decisions would influence his political decisions. He would take controversial and often unpopular positions from which he would never waver, even when support for those positions crumbled around him. In effect, the same strengths and weaknesses that he had displayed in the realm of religion would surface in the realm of politics.

3

"OUR OWN HERO"
Bryan and the Emergence of Presbyterian Politics, 1755–1765

IN THE WORDS OF A PHILADELPHIA PRESBYTERIAN in 1766, George Bryan was "our own hero."[1] A talented and eager participant in the province's incessant political turmoil as early as 1755, Bryan emerged out of the shadows when Presbyterian political interests coalesced prior to the revolution, becoming one of the Presbyterians' principal leaders. As such, he reflected the values and needs of his ethno-religious community. Motivated by external events, the city Presbyterians between 1755 and 1766 slowly organized into a viable political faction whose power reached its apogee in the provincial elections of 1764; Bryan played a crucial role in those events. His political career therefore begins here.

II

In 1755 the younger Philadelphia dissenters, men like George Bryan and Charles Thomson, loosely identified with Benjamin Franklin and the Quaker party, while the ethnic community's elder spokesman, William Allen, solidly supported the proprietor. By 1764, however, circumstances had changed. The leaders of the Irish Presbyterian community—Bryan, Allen, and Samuel Purviance, Jr.—had united in a determined opposition to Quaker politics and Quaker society. Franklin was now in disfavor with the

Presbyterians, who had formed an alliance with the proprietary party.[2]
The emergence of Presbyterian politics during the era before the revolution crystallized in the early sixties, when the ethnic dynamics of political behavior became significantly more important than they had been in the past. There is, however, an essential caveat: the nascent Presbyterian political movement, centered in Philadelphia, enjoyed only brief success before it deteriorated as rapidly as it had come together. The ostensible basis for its existence began with the onset of the French and Indian War in 1755, but the underlying determinant lay with Pennsylvania's changing demographics beginning in 1725, when a large influx of Presbyterians from Ireland and Scotland were incorporated within the colony.[3] Their enhanced numbers, however, had little immediate impact on the influence of Presbyterian political impulses, in part because most Scotch and Irish Presbyterians settled along the back counties and frontiers, where they had little leverage in Philadelphia politics. That circumstance was ensured by Quaker politicians, who skewed the proportionment of assembly representatives in favor of the older eastern counties of Bucks, Chester, and Philadelphia, where they resided.[4]

Moreover, despite the reuniting of the Old and New sides in 1758, the continued divisive and vehement theological and clerical disputes undoubtedly hampered the ability of the Presbyterians to focus on other, outside political issues. Some Presbyterians realized the consequences of this behavior, observing that "some denominations openly insult us as acting without plan or design, quarreling with one another, and seldom uniting together, even to promote the most salutary purposes."[5] The fact that they could find common ground at all was in itself at times a notable achievement. Nonetheless, the events of the French and Indian War and the 1764 attempt to convert the proprietary colony into a royal colony served as sufficient stimuli to force concerted efforts among Presbyterians in Philadelphia and surrounding localities on behalf of all their brethren.

Without overstating the case, it may be said that the French and Indian War had a cataclysmic impact upon the colony's Presbyterians. The horrific stories of barbarities committed along the frontiers upon families, many of whom were Scotch and Irish Presbyterians, heightened and excited tensions and differences in a dramatic way. The war motivated Presbyterians to attempt to gain greater control over their communities and greater influence in the province. This effort in turn fostered the articulation of their special characteristics and prejudices, giving shape to their political expression.

Presbyterian political aspirations, however, intruded awkwardly upon a political system that had existed for over seventy-five years. Generally, colonial Pennsylvania politics centered on a prolonged antagonism between the assembly and the proprietor in a struggle for control of the colony.[6] In times of peace, this struggle was politically charged but never disruptive of the fabric of political society. Unfortunately, during the war, militia bills and desperately needed appropriations for defense either were not passed, were sabotaged, or were delayed for as long as six months to a year as each side sought to protect what it perceived as its constitutional right. Both factions argued over whom to tax, the appropriate system for collection of taxes, and control over the expenditure of the funds raised. In both 1756 and 1757 Lord Loudoun, commander of British forces in North America, was forced to intervene. With the implied threat of a thousand-man army, he ended the impasse over the quartering of troops and brought to fruition a £100,000 appropriation bill.[7]

Stalemate had long existed between the assembly and Thomas Penn, second son of William Penn's second marriage. Like his father, Thomas Penn remained in England (except for 1732–41), preferring to authorize appointed resident governors to represent his interests. To insure their faithfulness, Penn invariably required his governors to post a bond (usually £5,000) promising fidelity to his instructions.[8] Within the colony there existed a proprietary party—though the word *party* is an overstatement. More accurately, it was a faction led by men of sizable estates and considerable prestige within the province. But they generally lacked any unifying ideological purpose or political necessity other than an end to Quaker domination of the assembly. Although they provided legal and occasional moral support for the appointed governor, they were never an effective political opposition to the Quakers, and only once, in 1742, did they mount a campaign to unseat the Quaker party in the October elections. The Quakers, however, won handily, despite a particularly heavy-handed attempt on election day to overawe their supporters in Philadelphia.[9]

The Quakers owed their domination of the assembly to an efficient and exclusive political organization that admitted only Quakers or their close associates. For the first half of the eighteenth century, the Quaker assemblies adequately represented the needs of their constituents, providing honest government, levying minimal taxes, and supporting the rights of the legislature against the imposing demands of the proprietary landlord.[10]

In part, also, the continued success of the Quaker party lay in the colony's harmonious relations with its Indians. Furthermore, in its initial seventy-five years the colony, along with its immediate neighbors, had been spared the ravages of war between France and England. The French and Indian War, however, changed that reality with two significant military events—the defeats in western Pennsylvania of Colonel Washington and

General Braddock in 1754 and 1755, respectively. With the successful re-moval of colonial and British resistance, the Indians, believed to be under French influence, launched a frontier war in October 1755.[11]

Galvanized by these developments into a spirited force, Pennsylvanians in large numbers demanded quick and effective military measures from Philadelphia. Fighting their own war, the assembly and governor balked at action, thereby allowing Benjamin Franklin to step into the void. Deftly organizing the war movement into a political force, Franklin drove a wedge between the pacifist Quakers and the proprietor. By 1756 ten Quaker as-semblymen had resigned, six for reasons of principle and four because of increasingly strident pressure from reformers in their religious ranks, elimi-nating opposition to the legislature's enactment of military measures.[12] Those members were replaced by Anglicans friendly to Franklin, thus cre-ating a successful coalition between Franklin, his non-Quaker followers, and the remaining Quakers led by Isaac Norris II, who were comfortable with the passage of wartime legislation. The newly aligned faction pursued an active policy of defense, while continuing an equally active campaign against the proprietor. Despite the resignation of the ten Quakers, however, and the ascendency of Franklin among the Quaker politicians, the Quaker party for all practical purposes remained a viable and formidable organi-zation.[13]

III

While the vital factor in the origins of George Bryan's political career was the emergence of a Presbyterian political organization, his elevation into the political fray owed much to the relationship of the Presbyterians dur-ing the war with the two principal political factions in Pennsylvania, the Quaker and proprietary parties. Initially, Presbyterians like Bryan sup-ported Franklin because he was active in the prosecution of the war against the Indians. One of Franklin's earlier projects had been the organization of the 1747 Association, a volunteer militia, that protected the frontiers during King George's war. In 1755, while defense policy floundered, Franklin helped to rescue Braddock's expedition to Fort Duquesne by organizing the army's supply lines. He hired wagons and drivers to serve Braddock's forces for the duration of the army's presence in the west. Throughout the winter of 1755–56, Franklin visited and oversaw the construction of a line of forts along the northeastern frontier to the Susquehanna River.[14]

Franklin's aggressive prosecution of the war gained the approval of many Philadelphia Presbyterians, who in 1756 clamored for an energetic war program. "We beseech the Almighty to direct your honour," pleaded the Revs. Robert Cross and Gilbert Tennent of Philadelphia's First and Second Presbyterian churches to the colony's governor, "to repel the insolent incursions of our ambitious and cruel enemies, who have turned a once flourishing and happy province into a scene of blood and distress."[15] Motivated by the war, Bryan made his first known foray into Pennsylvania politics in November 1755. Together with Joseph Galloway and William Franklin, he authored an insulting satire on the elder Franklin's principal antagonist, Pennsylvania's governor Robert Hunter Morris. The satire, entitled *Tit for Tat, or the Score wip'd Off,* by Humphrey Scourge, Esq., was in response to a series of articles that had attacked the assembly under Franklin. The first article had appeared in September 1755 in the *Pennsylvania Journal,* which quoted London's *Gentleman Magazine* as saying that Morris's veto of assembly legislation that touched upon economic and defensive measures favorable to the House but not to the proprietary was personally approved by the king. A refutation appeared the following week, claiming that the people of England solidly supported the assembly. In October 1755 the *New York Mercury* published supplement no. 168, containing copies of letters favorable to the governor, and an article ridiculing the refutation as a "lame and ridiculous essay." If the Quaker party remained in power, according to the article, the province would either be "thrown into the enemy's hands," or rescued by the defensive measures enacted by the king and Parliament.[16]

Bryan and his co-authors in *Tit for Tat* responded in kind. Citing the supplement's "pretended letters from England," Humphrey Scourge revealed that he, too, had "letters"—from a captured Frenchman! The letters disclosed that Morris, an unemployed place seeker, originally contracted with the French to be governor of Pennsylvania in order to yield the colony to the invading armies. Morris was selected for the position because a "private enquiry" into his "character" had discovered "that he was a very proper person to make a tool of."[17] Scourge further revealed that the supplement contained "several Charges against the Assembly," which were specious, "dogmatical assertions" paraded as proof. The Quakers, Scourge reminded his readers, were a respectable people, "to whom England" was "more obliged than most people know." But, he continued, those individuals who believed that "conscience" had prevented the Quaker assembly from granting money for the war were "fond of saying the things which are not."[18]

Tit for Tat was particularly fascinating for the unlikely association of the three authors. Franklin and Galloway supported the Quaker party into the 1770s, but Bryan would become an ally of the proprietary party and an avid foe of the Quakers. The temporary union of interest of the three men in 1755 was predicated on their desire for an effective military response against the Indians, and on their belief that the governor was responsible for the colony's wartime inactivity. For Bryan and his fellow Presbyterians, the prejudices and tensions that would violently divide them from the Quakers had not yet emerged, and the distinction between Franklin's Quaker party and Quakerism would become significantly blurred for Presbyterians, who would in time equate the two as synonymous.

While Bryan, Galloway, and William Franklin were creating Humphrey Scourge, the assembly under Benjamin Franklin had passed a militia bill that organized volunteers into battalions and readied them for possible action. The bill was acceptable to Quakers because militia duty was voluntary, with neither obligations nor penalties imposed on pacifists. It appealed to Franklin because the officers of the militia were elected by the militia members, rather than appointed by the governor. The governor, however, viewed the act as totally deficient. Though the power to reject or commission the elected officers was reserved to him, his role as chief military commander of the province was effectively compromised. Morris also perceived that the bill's popularity elevated his enemy, Franklin, to unofficial leader of the colony's volunteers. Consequently, Morris in December 1755 contemplated vetoing the bill, ostensibly citing the questionable legality of its language. But he was forced to bow to public pressure and signed it into law. In February 1756 the city militia, as the proprietary party foresaw, elected Franklin to be its leader.[19]

Not surprisingly then, Bryan and his fellow satirists ridiculed Morris and those who opposed the militia law, suggesting that their opposition resulted from false claims of bravado rather than from legal niceties. It was "really piteous," mocked Scourge, "to see the present condition of those valorous knights, those sons of thunder, who, but a little while ago, made a 'loud and positive demand' for a militia law." But, he emphasized, "how the mighty are fallen!" There were, however, "certain eminent state-quacks employed in making a collection of simples, otherwise called, objections to militia laws; which wonderful medkament, if it has its designed effect, is to recover our heroes in the same proportion as it is swallowed by others."[20]

Though Morris signed the bill, he continued his opposition to Franklin's militia by staying the commissions of the city militia's elected officers. To an assembled group of officers, including Bryan, Morris argued that their election was irregular and that he was considering the attachment of the militia to the British regulars so that they might feel some "military discipline." Although Morris later claimed that he was misunderstood, and that he was only referring to the colony's frontier regular troops, the gathered officers took great "umbrage" at his remarks and promptly convened a meeting in front of his house. Then, in an "indecent and rude manner," they voted unanimously to ignore everything the governor had to say. Members of the Provincial Council, however, prevailed upon both governor Morris and the officers to accept a compromise. The officers agreed to resubmit a list of the voting electorate, thus satisfying qualms over the mode of election. The governor therefore issued their commissions.[21]

Morris, however, exacted a small measure of revenge. He refused to commission George Bryan, who had been elected lieutenant of the Chestnut and Walnut ward's militia. Bryan was explicitly rejected because of his participation in the production of "that vile paper, *Tit for Tat.*" Although the commissioned officers resented his displacement as well as that of another elected officer, also denied because of mutual ill feeling, they were generally pleased that the militia had been finally established. In an effort to demonstrate unity, the commissioned officers, with swords drawn, rode with Morris as far as Germantown on his journey to the frontier.[22]

Throughout 1756 the city's Presbyterians demonstrated staunch support for Benjamin Franklin's prowar stance while remaining politically nonaligned. Of the twenty-four elected officers in the city regiment, including Bryan, at least eight were Presbyterians.[23] Moreover, in June 1756 Quakers and dissenters united to defend the reputation of a Franklin political adherent, Daniel Roberdeau, elected to the assembly that month for Philadelphia County in place of one of the resigning Quakers. Roberdeau, an Anglican, had a chance encounter with the Rev. William Smith on the corner of Front and Market streets; in the ensuing conversation, according to Roberdeau, Smith identified himself as a supporter of the proprietary party against the Quaker party. This revelation swept through the city like a hurricane, for Smith not only betrayed his pretended impartiality but also helped to fuel the rumors that he was the author of an anonymous vitriolic anti-Quaker pamphlet, *A Brief State of the Province of Pennsylvania.*[24] Subsequent articles, believed to be by Smith, continued the vituperative assault against Franklin and his militia. The glib Smith denied Roberdeau's recollection of the conversation, and the two promptly filed depositions that were printed in the papers, recounting their sides of the story. Forty-seven individuals, including George Bryan, signed an affidavit attesting to Roberdeau's integrity—obviously, the signers believed that he was telling the truth and that, conversely, Smith was lying. The signatories also included such prominent figures as Gilbert Tennent and Israel and John Pemberton, as well as other noted Presbyterians and Quakers.[25]

Franklin, however, never completely secured the Presbyterians to his cause. For example, in an attempt to insult Franklin's militia a Captain

Vanderspiegel organized an independent militia company to be at the disposal of Governor Morris. Subsequently, Gilbert Tennent, the prominent Presbyterian pastor of the Second Church, at the request of Vanderspiegel and in the interest of impartiality delivered a prowar sermon to Vanderspiegel's militia in February 1756.[26]

Nor were the Presbyterians happy when Nathaniel Grubb, a Quaker party assemblyman from Berks County, allegedly commented in June 1756, when informed that several backcountry frontiersmen had been murdered by the Indians, "that they were only some Scotch-Irish killed, who could well enough be spared." Grubb publicly denied the report. But isolated incidents soon yielded to a general feeling of tension and anxiety between Quakers and Presbyterians. By late fall 1756 rumors circulated that the Quakers were speaking "mightily ill of all Presbyterians."[27]

The changing relationship between Quakers and Presbyterians was partly inevitable and partly determined by the fate of Franklin's political move-ment. Franklin had successfully removed the Quaker party's pacifists from office in 1756 and had created, at least in theory, a more representative party. He could not avoid, however, two persistent, underlying themes in Pennsylvania's colonial history that threatened any long-term political harmony—the Quaker peace testimony and the perennial struggle for power between the proprietor and the assembly. Franklin's primary goal had been to exclude Quakerism, not necessarily Quakers, from his party; from his perspective he had succeeded. Yet Franklin's "half and half" Quakers could not completely shed their religion's central tenets, especially in time of war, and inevitably Quaker pacifism would resurface. Presbyterians, whose theological beliefs did not preclude support for a just war, understood the Quaker dichotomy and therefore added their voices to the common belief that provincial policy was often determined at the Philadelphia or Burlington Yearly Meeting.[28]

To the concern over renewed pacifism, Presbyterians could soon add the resumption by Franklin's Quaker party of the struggle waged by previous Quaker assemblies against the proprietor. Consequently, Presbyterians lost faith in Franklin's patchwork party. The assembly-proprietary rivalry had little meaning to Presbyterians in time of war; quarrels over supply and revenue bills, or proprietary instructions, were regarded by them as distractions from the real issue—defeating the Indians. The insinuation advanced by some Quakers that the war had resulted from proprietary land frauds and from the coaxing, even manipulation for propaganda purposes, of the Indian chief Teedyuscung at peace negotiations, confirmed Presbyterian fears that the Quakers lacked the will to fight the war and were indifferent to the lives of the frontier families.[29] Aggravating the relationship were the peacemaking efforts of some Quakers led by Israel Pemberton. They presented gifts to the Indians with whom they conducted protracted negotiations in the vain hope of ending the war. But as the hostilities continued and the number of frontier victims increased, enraged Presbyterians saw the Quaker pacifists as deliberately supporting the murderers. "In all our troubles," wrote one critic, "the Quakers, at least a Quaker faction, have secretly supported the Indians, held treaties and correspondence with them in our wars, and bestowed on them arms and ammunition, and tomahawks, even when they were murdering our frontier inhabitants."[30]

Not all Presbyterians were alienated from Franklin's party. Charles Thomson, for example, continued harmonious relations with both Franklin and the Presbyterian politicians. Francis Alison, a personal friend of Franklin's, was chagrined to find that Presbyterian opposition to the Quaker party meant cooperation with William Smith, leader of the Anglicans who supported the proprietor. Alison despised Smith and suspected him of plotting to establish the Church of England as the colony's official religion, to be followed by religious tests that would exclude nonconformists from public office. "The mice and frogs may fight," observed Alison, referring to the Quakers and Presbyterians, "till the kite devours both."[31]

Nonetheless, between 1757 and 1764 Presbyterians were disassociating themselves from Franklin's Quaker party and moving closer to the proprietary faction. The governor's sphere was a logical choice for the Presbyterians, not only because of the avowed support for strong military measures against the Indians but also for the pivotal role played in proprietary affairs by the city's most prestigious Presbyterian, William Allen. Having supplanted Andrew Hamilton in the 1740s as the leading spokesman of the proprietary faction in provincial politics, Allen remained adamantly opposed to the Quaker party. In the late 1750s he helped to sponsor a petition to the Board of Trade demanding the removal of Quakers from the assembly during time of war.[32] A critical difference existed, however, between Allen and the younger Presbyterians. Allen was a proprietary man and a Presbyterian, while the younger leaders were Presbyterians temporarily aligned with the proprietor. After all, remarked George Bryan in an offhand manner that belied the significance of the statement, he and his colleagues craved "only for a removal" of Penn's "perpetual right of government." The young leaders knew that they represented an ethnoreligious community that sought political recognition on its own merits. John Armstrong, Presbyterian leader and provincial troop captain from Cumberland County, reminded the proprietor of their growing importance, pointing out to him that the Presbyterians were increasing in population, wealth, and status. He stressed their continued "loyalty and military spirit" and observed that they had constituted "the far greater number both of the officers and soldiers raised by this government." Moreover, he reiterated "the difficulties and loss of blood they have sustained on the frontiers during the Indian war," and therefore advised Thomas Penn that the Presbyterians "should not be overlooked."[33]

As some Presbyterians attempted to form a politically conscious community, George Bryan represented those who were most antipathetic toward the Quakers. He had defected early from the Quaker party, at least by 1758, and nursed a growing hostility to what he perceived as the party's unshakable stranglehold on the assembly. Bryan doubted Quaker sincerity in both prosecuting the war and fighting for the rights of the assembly against the proprietor. Rather, he believed their true purpose was the aggrandizement of their power. "It is for power and influence our folks contend," Bryan commented in reference to the Quakers, "to preserve which they will leave no stone unturned." Quaker assemblymen, argued Bryan, "made a bustle of defending theirs and the peoples privileges against the proprietaries, merely to keep up a dust, that their unfitness for government in time of war, might be less attended to." Quakers, he concluded, "leave nothing unattempted to secure to themselves the direction of government."[34]

Bryan also accused the Quakers of manipulating the Indians into claiming that the war had been caused by proprietary land fraud. "This affords a fine handle for clamour," he wrote in his diary, that "puts the consideration of their unfitness for publick offices out of people's heads." With bitter invective and a touch of hyperbole, Bryan added: "It would be endless to mention all the artifices used to divide those who are not of their society; lying, misrepresentation and false reports are hourly practiced."[35] He was impressed by a cartoon that appeared in Philadelphia in 1764 portraying an Irish settler being ridden by a Quaker, who was preventing him from defending his home and family from an Indian attack. Another cartoon that caught his eye depicted a Quaker leading a German settler by the nose. Bryan lamented that his "fellow subjects on the border are in great measure abandon'd to a relentless enemy, and many when they lye down, have great cause to dread they shall not rise in safety."[36]

Bryan desired direct military confrontation with the Indians. "There is nothing here to bring the Indian enemy to reason," he observed, unless they were a "good deal sobered by a spirited attack on their villages"; otherwise, "we can expect no lasting peace." As for recently captured Indians, they were to be put to death as an example: "It would look more like a war, and have lasting good consequences, from the spirit of revenge which Indians cultivate as a virtue—this would defend us better than fifty battalions of regulars." Indians in general, Bryan concluded, were useful in a "commercial way." But owing to their habit of killing the animals on which their subsistence depended in order to sell the skins, as well as their personal way of life (including drinking), Bryan anticipated that most of the province's Indians would be extinct within fifty years.[37] Unlike some contemporaries, Bryan never envisioned the Indian as the "noble savage," nor did he ever appreciate the role of the European in that process of extinction he so casually predicted.[38]

The combustible mix of tensions caused by the war and by the assembly-proprietary feud and the growing discontent of the Presbyterians finally exploded in 1764, a watershed year in Presbyterian relations with the Quakers. The news of peace between England and France was quickly countered by Pontiac's Rebellion. As the Indians under Chief Pontiac continued their brutal offensive against the back counties, the colonial government was again unable to respond quickly or effectively, crippled as it was by arguments over proprietary instructions and assembly liberties. In the winter of 1763–64, back county "rangers" from Paxton Township, Lancaster County, descended on Lancaster and murdered several peaceful Indians who were Christian converts, ironically lodged in the town for their own safety. The rangers returned a second time and massacred the survivors of the first attack, who had been moved to the town jail for their own protection. Pennsylvanians were stunned. But the incident, like all momentous events in Pennsylvania, was quickly absorbed into provincial politics. Franklin and the Quaker party accused the governor and the proprietor of secretly acquiescing in the massacre, while the proprietor viewed the Paxton rangers as the inevitable outgrowth of assembly mismanagement.[39]

In February 1764, having disposed of the Indians in Lancaster, the "Paxton boys" (as the rangers were called)—many of whom were Scotch and Irish Presbyterians—turned their murderous attention to about 140 Northampton County Indian refugees housed in Philadelphia, whom they had threatened earlier, and to Israel Pemberton, whom they regarded as an Indian-loving traitor. About 250 of the vigilantes marched from Lancaster County toward the capital city. While the marchers were met at Germantown and temporarily pacified by a delegation of provincial officials including Benjamin Franklin, considerable alarm spread through the city. The militia was mobilized, volunteers armed themselves, and cannons were mounted in strategic locations, as rumors were rife of an impending attack by the Paxton marchers. Pemberton himself fled the city to the dismay of some Quakers and relatives. The rush to arms, however, of some 200 Quaker youths shocked and angered many citizens, fanning the flames of denominational hostility within the city.[40]

The Paxton march occasioned a sudden outpouring of angry and accusatory pamphlets, exposing a Quaker-Presbyterian antagonism that had been smoldering for nine years. While the Quakers themselves apparently maintained a discreet silence,[41] their apologists defended their war record and expressed outrage over the Indian massacre at Lancaster and the subsequent "revolt" of the Paxton boys against the government. Presbyterians were denounced for their rancor toward the Quakers: "Tis grievous to see what Heat and bitterness subsists in the breasts of many Presbyterians in this town, as well as in the country against the people called Quakers," concluded one Quaker supporter. Another Quaker apologist, reflecting on the ethno-religious makeup of the marchers, wondered if any Presbyterians, past or present, were ever loyal to their king, for in both "ancient and modern history, *Presbyterianism* and *Rebellion* were twin-sisters, sprung from faction, and their affection for each other, has been ever so strong."[42]

That George Bryan was not a participant in the pamphlet war is hard to imagine, especially as Presbyterians vented their anger against the Quakers in equal measure. Yet his role as a public apologist for his brethren in 1764 remains a secret of the past. Nonetheless, Presbyterians accused the Quakers of placing greed over public virtue, of befriending the Indian rather than the Scotch-Irish settler in time of war, and of indifference in prosecuting the war effort. In *The Cloven-Foot Discovered,* the author observed that while the Quakers talked "of the happiness and justice of their administration," the "glaring evidences" pointed to "their unjustifiable usurpation, their thirst of power, their want of the principles of justice and the common feelings of human nature for the distressed." He concluded that the Presbyterians had little choice but to blame the Quakers "as the cause of many of our sufferings."[43]

The flagrant rebellion of the Paxton boys against authority, however, placed Bryan and many of his peers in an awkward position. Bryan, although unsympathetic to the Indians, was appalled by the Lancaster massacre and alarmed by the "danger of mobs." He reminded dissenters of the "necessity of supporting order," and he described the Paxton marchers as the "mean and lower sort of people." Philadelphia's leading dissenters, while sympathetic to the frontiersmen, were careful not to condone the marchers' inversion of the society's social and political order. While John Penn and his advisers, camped at the house of Benjamin Franklin, momentarily joined hands with Franklin's party in order to resolve the crisis, Presbyterian leaders were unsure of their own role. Many of them remained silent in Philadelphia, while in Paxton Township the Presbyterian minister John Elder, who had organized the rangers into a militia unit against the Indians, had been unable to dissuade them from their drastic action. Meanwhile, Anglicans like Edward Shippen referred to the rangers as "rioters" and stressed the city's determination to support the "government" and to defend the colony's "liberties and laws."[44]

Ultimately, however, Presbyterian leaders like Bryan, bitter over the obloquy heaped on the Paxton boys by the Quakers and others, fell back on the argument that the Quaker assemblymen had sown the seeds for the violence. The frontiersmen, according to this line of reasoning, had been abandoned by the government and consequently forced to fend for themselves during the emergency. "Necessity has no law," observed Bryan in his diary. Thus, desperate people would employ desperate measures, and, he insisted, "for any government to drive people into such proceedings is neither polite or safe." The populace, he made clear, was "indeed dreadfully incensed and an armed mob may turn its strength the wrong as well as the right way." John Ewing angrily complained that the marchers had been unjustly accused of attempting to overthrow the government. Rather they had journeyed to Germantown "to inquire why Indians, known to be enemies, were supported, even in luxury, . . . at the public expense, while they [the frontiersmen] were left in the utmost distress."[45]

Bryan was outraged that some Quakers insisted that the "insurgents should have been reduced by force." That was typical, believed Bryan, of the perpetually hypocritical Quaker political clique. "You have no idea of the arrogance of a Quaker," Bryan recorded in his diary incredulously, "who refuses to take up arms himself," but "should assume such language." Bryan feared, however, that the Quaker party, with its "foolish fondness of the Indians," would remain in power despite all that had happened. The Quakers were "more unhinged in their government than ever before, but," he concluded, "their known craft will set all right again."[46]

The decisive stroke that terminated any further possibility of harmony between the dissenters and the Quakers, however, was Franklin's ploy to break the legislative-executive impasse by petitioning the king-in-council to remove the proprietor and bring the colony under royal government. The Scotch and Irish Presbyterians, victims of royal rule in the Old World, completely opposed Franklin's strategy. "I can truly say," asserted William Allen in a letter to Thomas Penn, "that the Presbyterians" were "united to a man" in their opposition to a royal stewardship and their support for the proprietary government and the Charter of Liberties.[47]

In the spring of 1764, amid the turmoils of the Paxton pamphlet war, Franklin decided to present officially to the electorate the Quaker party's case for transferring Pennsylvania's government from the proprietor to the king. In his tract *Cool Thoughts on the Present Situation of our Public Affairs*, written on 12 April 1764, Franklin contended that the province, once the "land of peace and order," was heading "fast into anarchy and confusion," and that unless the crown saw the "necessity of taking the government into its own hands," there would soon be "no government at all." Almost three weeks earlier, on 24 March 1764, the assembly under Franklin had charged that the proprietor, although owning all the best lands, refused to pay any real estate taxes in support of the war. Furthermore, the proprietor had unscrupulously attempted to "extort privileges from the people" in time of war while not "permitting them to raise money for their defence, unless proprietary arbitrary will and pleasure" were secured first. The assembly demanded that the proprietor relinquish his authority to the king, because any hope of good government under the Penns had ended.[48]

Bryan viewed the Quaker party's drive for royal government as the height of hypocrisy, for its true purpose remained, as always, power through deception. The petition claimed to champion the liberties of the people, argued Bryan, while masking its real intention—the augmentation of Quaker power. Bryan calculated that the Quakers were "playing a very deep game," for they themselves were leery of such a fateful step. It would be "impossible to know how far the present policy of the ministry would lead them in new-modelling the government of a province whose inhabitants appear factious and troublesome in their eyes and in the world," observed Bryan. Not only would Quakers jeopardize their political status under royal authority, but Presbyterians were threatened as well. "Dissenters from the Church of England would do well to consider," concluded Bryan, "how far their privileges would be likely to be impaired."[49]

Bryan's characterization of the Quaker party as "unhinged" was correct, for the petition for royal government not only caused tremendous opposition but fractured the party that proposed it as well. The plan for royal government electrified an already agitated citizenry and created a visible and controversial issue for the October 1764 assembly elections. Isaac Norris II, the aged and venerated Quaker politician and speaker of the assembly for fourteen years, opposed Franklin's plan. Norris favored abandoning the entire project, and rather than sign the petition to the king, as the office of speaker would have required, he resigned the chair, although explaining that his absence was due to ill health. The Quaker party received another setback when Israel Pemberton also declared against the petition. Fearing the potential loss of religious and political liberties under an ambitious Whitehall, Pemberton successfully urged the Quaker Yearly Meeting to oppose the royal petition. Nonetheless, the Quaker party tried to create a strong popular base for its campaign for royal government by circulating petitions among the citizenry in support of the requested transfer of power. To its dismay, only 3,500 signatures in favor of the proposed transfer were obtained, while a subsequent counterpetition secured an astonishing

15,000 names, an obvious and significant indicator of discontent with the plan for royal government.[50]

The Presbyterians were an essential component in the opposition to Franklin's plans and in the subsequent attempt in the October elections to oust Quaker party assemblymen in favor of proprietary candidates. While the hostility and prejudice that surfaced during the Paxton affair served as the impetus for the effective organization of the Presbyterian electorate, the proposed introduction of royal government into the colony raised the specter of an official church and possible test acts designed to exclude dissenters from the social, economic, and political benefits of the province. A century of such experience in northern Ireland intensified their apprehensions.

Successful opposition to the Quaker party and its petition, however, required political unity among the several ethno-religious communities of Pennsylvania. The Presbyterians found ready allies among many of the colony's Anglicans, led by William Smith, a veteran foe of the Quaker party. Although some Anglicans wished to remain neutral, perhaps seeing an enhanced role for the Anglican church under the crown, others were less reticent.[51] For example, the Rev. Jacob Duche, pastor of Saint Peter's Church in Philadelphia, once considered a "mere Franklinist," cast his lot with Smith and the Presbyterians. The common interest between the two religious societies had been the College of Philadelphia, of which Smith was provost and Francis Alison its leading professor. That relationship was tenuous at best, as each side vied for hegemony over the college. Their unity in 1764 aimed at preventing the Quakers from accruing any further political advantage through a change in government. The Anglicans were perhaps one-fifth as numerous as the Presbyterians in Pennsylvania and were fairly equally divided on the issue of royal government and the October elections, but the alliance of the Anglicans' most visible leaders with the Presbyterians gave the latter's cause respectability and vitality.[52]

The pivotal group, however, was the Germans. Traditionally the German churches and religious sects had aligned themselves with the Quaker party, and proprietary efforts to detach them from the Quakers had been fruitless. But the Germans situated along the frontiers and within the back counties were forced to reassess their political allegiance under the exigencies of the Indian war; and, as for many Presbyterians, the assembly-proprietary debate was, in wartime, at best irrelevant and at worst dangerous. Anxious for stiffer wartime measures, German Lutheran and Calvinist communities were being slowly galvanized into supporting an alliance with the proprietary faction. The plan for royal government proved to be the final straw, prompting those Germans into breaking completely with the Quakers.

Again like the Presbyterians, they feared the revocation of the Charter of Liberties that guaranteed religious freedom from a state church. This toleration was especially crucial to the Germans, for they were well aware of their alien status in an English-speaking world.[53]

The transformation of the ethno-religious communities into an effective political organization against the Quakers, however, depended on the skills of a handful of leaders. The Revs. William Smith, Jacob Duche, and William Barton were active within the Anglican community, while the Rev. Henry Melchior Muhlenberg was influential with the colony's German population. William Allen, on the floor of the assembly and in direct contact with Thomas Penn, orchestrated the proprietary cause.[54]

What then of the Presbyterians? George Bryan assumed a prominent role in the organization of the Presbyterians of Philadelphia. He participated in the establishment of a twenty-seven-man political committee to oversee the assembly election in their district. The committee consisted of the ministers of both the First and Second Presbyterian Church along with other prominent city Presbyterians. Bryan was a member, as were his father-in-law and brother-in-law, Samuel and Thomas Smith. The committee was also, as a secondary function, to correspond with Presbyterians throughout the province and "to give and receive advices, and to consult what things may have a tendency to promote our union and welfare, either as a body, or, as we are connected together in particular congregations." Moreover, the committee requested that each county committee, consisting of the leading Presbyterians of that community, appoint one member to act as its secretary.[55]

In the Philadelphia committee, Samuel Purviance, Jr., was appointed secretary and was instrumental in creating a network of correspondence and cooperation among the opposition leaders throughout the colony. In Lancaster, for example, Purviance and the proprietary forces were compelled to adjust their campaign strategy against the Quakers. In prior elections, political factions had agreed on a slate of known and respected candidates in an attempt to create a measure of harmony, but feelings over the 1764 elections were too "warm." The Quaker party assembled a strong Quaker-Mennonite coalition and consequently refused any cooperation with their opponents. By the same token, the "New Side" (as the anti-Quaker forces were called) rejected any candidate who either was a Quaker or had supported the proposed transfer of government. Negotiations, doomed from the start, failed completely, and the New Side endeavored to defeat the Quaker party at the polls outright. Purviance advised that at least two Germans be added to the proposed slate in order to split the German vote. Purviance was confident that supporters in Bucks and Chester counties would also elect candidates who were opposed to the petition.[56]

In Philadelphia, the anti-Quaker forces, or the "New Ticket," decided on a slate of candidates who would appeal to the greatest number of voters. They immediately proposed Isaac Norris II and Joseph Richardson in an attempt to attract those Quakers who opposed the petition. The Quaker party, although chagrined at their opposition to the petition, either would not or could not abandon these two popular and highly visible party leaders. They were therefore incorporated as well into the Quaker party ticket.[57]

Not included on the Quaker party slate was John Dickinson, who had delighted proprietary party leaders with a forceful and eloquent defense of the old charter in the assembly in the spring of 1764. Joseph Galloway had not been as pleased, however, and the two joined in a spirited debate climaxing in fisticuffs near the assembly doors.[58] Dickinson subsequently ran on the New Ticket. The antipetition party also put forward two Germans, Frederick Antes and Henry Keppele, to represent their community. As one New Ticket writer explained, those two men were promoted because the Germans "have thought themselves too long denied the equal privilege of having some of their own people among their representatives." Amos Strettle, Henry Pawling, and Henry Harrison were nominated by the New Ticket for the remaining Philadelphia County seats.[59]

George Bryan and Thomas Willing were selected by the opposition for the formidable task of ousting the two most prominent Quaker party leaders, Benjamin Franklin and Joseph Galloway, from the city's two seats. Willing was a former mayor of the city and a highly successful merchant. Bryan, while also a successful merchant and recognized for his services as one of the pier and river commissioners, was chosen primarily for his standing in the Presbyterian community. He had proven himself to be a vocal opponent of the Quaker party and a trusted member of the religious and political leadership of the Presbyterians. He was, as Quaker party member Hugh Roberts ruefully remarked, the Presbyterian community's "champion."[60] The two men were strategic choices. Willing represented Philadelphia's wealthy and genteel society and was the leading importer of German immigrants.[61] Bryan appealed to the growing number of Calvinists, whether of Scotch, Irish, or German heritage. Both candidates were also ideologically sound: they not only opposed the change of government but were vigorous supporters of an energetic war effort.

Bryan's reputation as a fervent Presbyterian politician, however, worried some New Ticket men. One apologist for the anti-Quaker coalition, sensitive to the possible fears of the electorate that the ticket was a cabal of Presbyterians plotting to seize the government, pointed out that Bryan was the only Presbyterian on the Philadelphia New Ticket. Presbyterians, he continued, were sufficiently moderate that although "they are well entitled to their proportionate share of representatives, they have constantly declared that it is indifferent to them of which persuasions the new members are, provided the present betrayers of our rights are turned out."[62]

The October 1764 election was one of the most exciting and hotly contested in the history of the province. Nearly thirty-nine hundred voters participated in the Philadelphia County elections alone—probably its highest turnout before the revolution. William Franklin excused himself from his duties as royal governor of New Jersey and traveled to Philadelphia to campaign for his father. Benjamin Shoemaker and William Logan dropped any remaining pretence to impartiality, despite their membership in Governor John Penn's Provincial Council, and openly solicited votes for the Old Ticket. From 9:00 A.M. until midnight voters streamed into the polling place, creating long lines outside the courthouse doors. Finally, at 3:00 A.M. on 2 October, New Ticket party men called for the closing of the polls. The Quakers refused. They knew that several hundred lame and elderly supporters were to arrive shortly. New Ticket men quickly dispatched a rider to Germantown to summon as many Germans as were still available. The Germans complied and descended upon the courthouse in great numbers. At 3:00 P.M. on 2 October, an astonishing thirty hours after their opening, the polls were officially closed.[63]

In a stunning upset, albeit by the slimmest of margins, Bryan and Willing defeated the favored incumbents Franklin and Galloway, as a total of eight of the ten New Ticket candidates narrowly won in the city and county of Philadelphia. Presbyterian leaders were elated, while Franklin was more amazed than embittered and accurately analyzed the defection of the German vote as the reason for his loss. Galloway simply sulked.[64]

At the age of thirty-five, George Bryan began his official public career in the colonial assembly. But Bryan's election must be placed in its proper context. Contemporaries viewed the defeats of Franklin and Galloway as more significant than the victories of Bryan and Willing. Bryan's popularity was confined to his Presbyterian community, while his victory was the result of an unwieldy temporary alliance between Irish, Scotch, and German Calvinists, Lutherans, Anglicans, and disaffected Quakers who opposed the royal petition.

In any event, the New Ticket celebration proved to be short-lived. After the remaining counties filed their returns, the Quaker party still maintained a commanding majority. The New Ticket reelected William Allen in Cumberland County, two members from York, and one from Lancaster and gained a partisan from Northampton County. But Chester and Bucks counties returned strong Quaker party delegations, and all other Old

Ticket men were reelected. Moreover, despite Franklin and Galloway's loss their influence remained, the party routinely caucusing with these two leaders on the nights before sessions.[65]

Within five days of the legislature's meeting, the assembly minority, which included Bryan, pressed the issue of the proposed transfer. Isaac Norris II, the speaker, remained cool to his Quaker party's petition and recommended that the assembly reinstruct its agent, Richard Jackson, not to present the petition without an express order from the House. Despite the opposition of Norris, however, motions to recall the petition were easily defeated by the majority Quaker party. One motion, a Quaker compromise intended to soften the impact of the petition by guaranteeing civil and religious liberties, was rejected by the minority, making it clear that, in their view, the petition under any circumstances was repugnant.[66]

Bryan and the minority were equally helpless when the Quakers moved to send Benjamin Franklin to London to act as co-agent with Richard Jackson, a move intended to ensure a vigorous lobby for the petition before the ministry. Bryan and the minority opposed Franklin's appointment, at one point proposing to adjourn the House for two weeks to give them time to devise a new and more successful strategy to sabotage Franklin's mission. But that motion as well as all of their opposition was futile, and the minority's only satisfaction was an official protest published in the *Philadelphia Journal* shortly before Franklin's departure.[67]

Bryan was one of the signers of the protest, probably written by John Dickinson, that outlined the reasons for the opposition by the minority to Franklin's appointment. According to the protesters, Franklin was the "Chief author" of the petition, which, in turn, had been responsible for the "uneasiness and distractions" among the people. The protesters stressed that Franklin's known enmity toward Thomas Penn precluded any likelihood of a just accommodation with the proprietors. Citing Franklin's defeat in the recent election, the protesters emphasized the overwhelming unpopularity of the proposed transfer. In conclusion, they launched a personal attack on Franklin and complained of the public expense of the appointment. The heart of the argument, however, lay in the protesters objection to the petition: "any further prosecution of the measures for a change of our government at this time, will lay the foundations of unceasing feuds, and all the miseries of confusion, among the people we represent."[68]

It was a calmer assembly that reconvened on 7 January 1765, and Bryan, with Joseph Richardson, was appointed to present the new speaker, Joseph Fox, to Governor John Penn. In the previous October, Norris had again resigned the chair rather than participate in his party's pursuit of the petition. Franklin's wing of the Quaker party promoted George Ashbridge to replace Norris, but most Quakers were hesitant, preferring Fox. The latter, like Norris, was unenthusiastic but less vocal about the petition. Fox won handily. The political turmoil of 1764 had certainly dampened the rural Quakers' spirit for royal government, and Fox's victory indicated that the Quakers were beginning to proceed more cautiously. The New Ticket minority including Bryan sided with the Quakers who supported Fox, momentarily isolating those members favoring the petition. The appointment of Bryan and Richardson to wait upon the governor possibly indicated that the two men played a significant role in the struggle over the speakership.[69]

In the assembly's routine business, Bryan, as a junior member of the House, was generally assigned to less important tasks. When he was appointed to important committees, they were usually dominated by veteran assemblymen. Nonetheless, Bryan was honored with selections on two of the four standing committees of the House—grievances and accounts. An examination of committee appointments for the 1764 assembly indicates that they were usually dominated by Philadelphians, in part for practical reasons. They resided in the city or nearby and were available for work that often stretched beyond session dates. Such assignments to standing committees, however, were also politically motivated. The Quaker party hated William Allen, and John Dickinson was quickly reaching similar status. Although both were from Philadelphia, they were appointed only to the least significant standing committee—to revise and correct the minutes before they were printed; they were joined on that committee by Isaac Norris II and Joseph Fox, the leaders in the House of the Quaker party. Appointments to the Correspondence Committee, perhaps the most important standing committee, were reserved only for the Quaker party. Bryan and fellow minority appointees to the other two standing committees were outnumbered by Quaker party members.[70]

Bryan was appointed to ad hoc committees to bring in bills regarding the construction of a poorhouse and the regulation of election inspectors and bread prices, and to hear various grievances ranging from debt relief to road tax relief.[71] Bryan also sat on a five-man committee that created legislation overseeing the importation of Germans by Philadelphia merchants into Pennsylvania. Interestingly, and probably because of the German role in the election, Speaker Fox appointed four Philadelphia New Ticket members to this committee, which also included the Quaker party's Joseph Richardson. Caught between its German allies and the merchants, the committee, not surprisingly, wrote a bill that satisfied the Germans over the angry protests of the importing merchants. Bryan and Richardson oversaw the bill's passage through the assembly and into law.[72]

Bryan assumed, however, a far more important role in the Stamp Act crisis. He and several other members were appointed to an open committee to consider a circular letter sent by Rhode Island expressing concern over the Sugar Act and a rumored Stamp Act. In June 1765 Joseph Fox received a circular letter from Massachusetts requesting delegates for a proposed Stamp Act Congress to be held in New York City. The Quaker party, unsure of the role it should play, and yet in agreement with the grievances, preferred to remain aloof from treasonable projects and from the Presbyterians, who were vehemently opposed to the Stamp Act. On 10 September 1765 a tumultuous and bitterly divided House appointed four delegates including Dickinson and Bryan, both of whom were outspoken against the Stamp Act, to meet with other colonies over the crisis.[73] Of the eight members selected to prepare instructions for the delegates to New York, six were of the minority party—four of whom were Presbyterians, including Bryan.[74]

By 1765 the political atmosphere in Philadelphia had changed dramatically from the preceding year, completely altering Bryan's political career. The controversy over the Stamp Act quickly overshadowed the question of the petition. Moreover, by the spring of 1765 the proprietary faction was increasingly confident that the petition would end in failure. That assumption, along with the conclusion of Pontiac's Rebellion early in 1764, obviated any further need for the anti-Quaker alliance that had voted Bryan into office. Determined to regain its lost status, the Quaker party mounted an intensive campaign in October 1765.

In comparison with the election of 1764, that of 1765 was placid and even more decisive for the Quaker party, which reasserted its traditional hold on the electorate. Of the ten members of the minority party, only four were returned, three of whom were from the safe counties of Cumberland and Northampton. Only Thomas Willing retained his city seat. (Henry Pawling, who ran on the 1764 New Ticket, switched to the Quaker party. He was reelected.) Bryan attended the New York Stamp Act Congress during the election, and in an unusual development both he and James Pemberton, who had been specifically chosen by the Quaker party to oppose Bryan, received 902 votes each. The new assembly decided after "some debate" to hold a special election. On 23 October the Quaker party redoubled its efforts and secured the election of Pemberton by 171 votes over Bryan, despite extensive efforts on Bryan's behalf by the Presbyterians. His loss was attributed to the Germans, who, while supporting him, did not turn out as they had in the previous election.[75]

The following year, the New Ticket proposed to run Bryan against Pemberton a second time. But Bryan agreed to step aside in order to propose John Dickinson as the candidate. Bryan, Samuel Purviance, Jr., and

Table 1.

Committee members	Church	Occupation	Church officer
Allen, John	First	Merchant	y
Alison, William	First	Merchant	x
Bayard, John	Second	Merchant	x
Bryan, George	First	Merchant	x
Chevalier, P., Sr.	First	Merchant	x
Henry, William	First	Merchant	
Hodge, Andrew	Second	Merchant	x
Huston, Alexander	First	Merchant	x
Humphreys, William	First	Merchant	x
McCullough, Hugh	Second	Merchant	x
MacPherson, J.	(?)	(?)	
Mease, John	First	Merchant	x
Montgomery, Thomas	(?)	Shopkeeper	
Pettit, Charles	First	Merchant	z
Purviance, S., Sr.	First	Artisan	
Purviance, S., Jr.	First	Merchant	x
Redman, John	Second	Doctor	x
Rush, William	First	Artisan	x
Smith, Isaac	(?)	(?)	
Smith, Samuel	Second	Merchant	x
Smith, Thomas	Second	Merchant	x
Snowden, Isaac	Second	Tanner	x
Snowden, Jedediah	Second	Cabinetmaker	x
Wallace, John	First	Merchant	x
Wikoff, John	(?)	Merchant	
Williamson, Hugh	First	Doctor	y

Source: The committee list is located in "Circular Letter" in Joseph Galloway, *Historical and Political Reflections on the Rise and Progress of the American Rebellion* (London, 1780), 49–53. Also, Minutes of the First, Second Presbyterian Church, PHS; Philadelphia Will Books, 1747 to 1800; Robert F. Oaks, "Philadelphia Merchants and the American Revolution, 1765–1776" (Ph.D. dissertation, University of Southern California, 1970), 216–36; and Philadelphia tax lists for 1767 and 1772.

Notes
x = first served as a church officer prior to 1764
y = first served as a church officer after 1765
z = first served as a church officer after 1776

other New Ticket party men hoped that Dickinson would appeal to a greater number of voters, for Bryan was too closely identified with the Presbyterians. But by 1766 the New Ticket coalition had even less reason to exist than in 1765, and Dickinson was easily defeated.[76]

IV

The emergence of Bryan's political career occurred during the late 1750s and early 1760s and was directly related to his visible role within the Presbyterian community, to his outspoken opposition to the petition for royal government, and to his vigorous promotion of military measures within the colony. He helped combine the interests of all Presbyterians in 1764 through his participation on their election committee. That committee revealed the basic organizational structure of Presbyterian leadership in that year and demonstrated the fusion of political and religious roles by men who had served in their church's lay leadership and were responsible for the articulation of the Presbyterian community's political goals. Table 1 shows the equal representation of both the First and Second churches and the domination of the committee by merchants and professionals.

On the surface, the Presbyterians in Philadelphia appeared to have been unable to form an effective alliance with the back counties because of the latter's underrepresentation, and because the continued relationship between some western leaders and eastern Quaker politicians combined to prevent the creation of a permanent anti-Quaker faction. In reality, Philadelphia dissenters ultimately failed in their attempt to create a broad-based anti-Quaker party because, irrespective of the disruptions of the early sixties, the Quaker party continued to represent the will of the local communities, as it had for decades. Conversely, the Presbyterians, who were themselves racked with internal dissension, did not have a specific agenda that could form the basis for coalition, except for an energetic war program and opposition to a royal takeover. With the decline of those issues, the purpose of an alliance came to an end.[77]

For George Bryan, the demise of the brief moment of Presbyterian political organization resulted in the temporary termination of his career in elected office. Despised by the Quakers, Bryan could only fulfill his ambitions via the proprietary faction—which he did, through his appointment as a justice to the county court. But provincial politics would soon be overshadowed by the imperial crisis of 1766 to 1776, bringing Bryan once again to the fore, this time in opposition to England.

4

"WHAT TIMES ARE WE
FALLEN INTO?"

BETWEEN 1765 AND 1775 GEORGE BRYAN'S LIFE underwent dramatic changes. Whereas during the years from 1752 to 1764 Bryan experienced growth, prosperity, and success, the ten years prior to the revolution were marked by personal and public setbacks. As previously discussed, Bryan's prestige within his church was marred by the Sproat-Alison controversy and the separatist movement by the members of the Third Church. In 1771 Bryan went bankrupt; two years later he suffered a serious setback to his health, which appears to have incapacitated him for more than a year. Moreover, three of his ten children died in their infancy in the early 1770s.

Politically, the success Bryan enjoyed in 1764 would not be repeated in the remaining prerevolutionary years. The political coalition that was established in response to events of the early 1760s could not be sustained throughout the decade. Nor would the Presbyterians maintain the high level of organization that existed in 1764 and that had resulted in the apogee of Bryan's colonial political career. Bryan would, however, receive a judicial appointment as a consequence of his political activities, which proved to be a fortuitous placement because it not only provided him with an income after his bankruptcy, but also kept his flickering political career alive by maintaining him in the public eye.

Overshadowing Bryan's personal and public life was the growing imperial crisis. Although he did not become a highly visible leader of the resistance movement, he certainly opposed the Stamp Act, the episcopacy, and proposed colonial legislation emanating from England. While his personal commitments prevented him from assuming a more active role in the emerging opposition, he anxiously anticipated the results of the American resistance. For example, in 1775 he reported to his friend the Rev. John Ewing, who was visiting London, on the defeat of the British regulars at Boston: "Will not the rout of Lexington bring you home?" he asked. Yet at the same time he could not help but speculate about the tremendous changes occurring around him, asking rhetorically, "What times are we fallen into?"[1] Ironically, that sentiment could be applied to his personal experiences in the years leading up to the revolution as much as to his apprehension about the future.

II

The short-lived New Ticket political experiment collapsed shortly after the 1764 Indian war ended and the petition campaign for a royal government lost momentum. In the wake of these events Pennsylvania politics, like the flow of unimpeded water, took on a new course as circumstances dictated. The political alliance of the Anglicans and the Presbyterians split apart. While retaining cordial relations with the proprietary through William Smith, the Anglican community initiated its own campaign with London for an American episcopate, provoking immediate and uncompromising opposition from the Presbyterians. The rancor over the project rendered impossible any future political cooperation between the Episcopalians and the Presbyterians.[2]

Equally important was the changing relationship between the Quaker party and the proprietary. The ending of demands for immediate military appropriations and revenue acts returned to the Quaker party a measure of internal stability, while the proprietor's knowledge that the petitions for royal government were permanently tabled by Whitehall officials provided each side with a sense of security for its political status within the province. These conditions were necessary for the surprising parallel interests the two sides assumed in facing the problems of the late sixties and early seventies.[3]

The relationship between the assembly and the proprietary improved, but it was never completely comfortable. Governor Penn continued to resent the assembly's dictation to him "in matters which relate to the executive." Similarly, the assembly complained of the governor's calculated attempts to disturb the "harmony which ought to subsist between the branches of a legislative body." Nonetheless, their disputes were no longer over the validity of each other's existence; rather, they were over the administration of policy. As Galloway observed, the "future safety of the people and the honour of government are most intimately concerned."[4] Increasingly, the executive and legislature had more reason to agree than to disagree.

Both sides were alarmed over the steady assault on the legitimacy of provincial authority in the turbulent western counties during the imperial crisis. They strove to restrain the white frontier population from upsetting the fragile Indian peace, and they were shocked over the invasions of the Wyoming Valley by armed Connecticut settlers and of southwestern Pennsylvania by Virginia militiamen. Other problems they faced included floundering negotiations with Maryland and Virginia over the western border and an economic recession among many Philadelphia merchants during the late 1760s.[5] Furthermore, as the imperial crisis grew both the assembly and the proprietary under John Penn embraced a pro-American stance, but the two sides were increasingly out of step with the resistance movement. In the confused politics prior to the revolution, the proprietor and the assembly, and their few remaining adherents, became equally horrified spectators of Pennsylvania's march toward independence.[6]

Under these circumstances, the proprietary faction was less inclined to continue its support of the antagonistic policies of the Presbyterians. As early as 1767 William Allen remarked that the proprietary faction's new election strategy was to "sit still" and not oppose the Quaker party, as a demonstration of proprietary goodwill toward it. By the early seventies, the Quakers and the governor were enjoying an unusually good-tempered relationship. Therefore, as it turned out, another reason for the inability of the Presbyterian party of the early 1760s to have realistically sustained itself was the increasing distance the proprietary faction placed between itself and the Presbyterians over the ensuing years.[7]

While the decline of the Presbyterian political movement attested to the end of Bryan's ambitions for serving in the assembly, it did not mean the end of his public career. Governor Penn appointed Bryan a justice of the city and county of Philadelphia courts of common pleas and Quarter sessions in 1764 as a reward for his support and that of the Presbyterian community. The appointment proved to be invaluable for Bryan, both as a source of income during a period of personal financial difficulty and as a source of enhancement for his position as a community leader by giving him political visibility among his peers from 1764 to 1776. In 1776 he would be called upon immediately by Pennsylvania's revolutionary government to continue his judicial services.

Bryan's appointment to the bench in 1764 was solely the result of partisan politics. The newly appointed governor, John Penn, remarked with dismay that the executive branch regularly filled judicial and civic posts with men who were violent in their opposition toward the proprietary. The power of patronage, lamented Penn, was never employed to its full advantage. He hoped to reverse that practice despite the cautionary line of his advisers, who reminded him that partisan appointments in communities where the Quaker party was strong would only bring the authority of the proprietary into greater contempt. These men recognized that the ability of the justices to enforce the law was dependent upon the community in which they resided. Consequently, governors had been forced to fill important judicial and county offices in southeastern Pennsylvania with politicians and supporters of the Quaker party.[8]

The campaign for royal government, however, provided the necessary impetus for a change in proprietary strategy. As early as 1761 John Penn removed several pro-Quaker justices, and in 1764, despite the advice of William Allen, he refused to make an appointment to the supreme court because of the nominee's Quaker party allegiance. The election of Bryan and Willing to the assembly from the city of Philadelphia allowed Penn to continue his program of removing Quakers from the bench. Buoyed by the New Ticket party's upset victory in the city, Penn decided to reissue the judicial commissions for the city and county of Philadelphia.[9]

Commissions were distributed to proprietary supporters such as Thomas Willing, while several pro-Quaker justices like Henry Pawling were dropped. Hoping to strengthen the allegiance of his new allies, Penn granted commissions to members of the Presbyterian and German communities who had supported the New Ticket. "As a reward to this sect," wrote an angry Quaker supporter referring to the Presbyterians, "Mr. Geo. Bryan and Mr. Alexander Huston, two fiery bigots, are appointed justices, for this city and county." Joseph Galloway commented in disgust that worthy men were turned out of their commissions because they supported the assembly petitions for royal government while Presbyterians were "to fill their places," and he specifically cited Bryan as one of the Presbyterians. Despite the disapproval of the Quaker party, Bryan and the newly appointed justices assumed their commissions on 19 November 1764. Bryan's commission was renewed by Governor Penn on 23 May 1770 and again on 22 April 1772.[10] Apparently, Bryan's recommissioning as a justice had less to do with partisan politics than with his diligent devotion to his work on the bench.

Most judicial appointments in eighteenth-century Pennsylvania went to men who were prominent within their respective communities, not necessarily to those trained in the law. Of the thirty-eight appointments by Penn for Philadelphia in 1764, no more than five or six were actually lawyers.

Judicial appointments were issued at the pleasure of the governor, who commissioned judges whenever he perceived the need. He was not legally bound (nor did he ever choose) to solicit the advice and consent of the assembly. The governor could remove judges on his own initiative, or he could dismiss them upon the request of the legislature. Penn extended his executive power over the judiciary by including members of his Provincial Council in the commissions for all the counties. In Philadelphia, for example, sixteen of the commissions in 1764 went to members of the executive council, while twenty-two went to gentlemen of the city and county. Although thirty-eight men were appointed, not all of them actually served on the bench. Normally, in fact, only a handful of the appointments would choose to become working judges.[11]

By 1764 the Philadelphia County court system was divided among common pleas, orphans, quarter sessions, and the mayor's court—the last so called because citizens were summoned by the mayor of the city to act as jurors in minor criminal cases. The line dividing the functions of the various courts, however, was not always clear. For example, judicial commissions did not distinguish court assignments, so that judges sat in one particular court, or in all four courts, depending on their personal preference. Furthermore, the legislature throughout the century expanded the responsibilities of the various courts, often overlapping their jurisdiction.[12]

The orphans court appointed guardians, divided estates, determined inheritances, assessed probate inventories, recorded property titles, and performed other functions associated with the transfer of property. Common pleas decided civil cases such as personal lawsuits or actions of debt, and granted writs of replevin.[13] It was authorized to take deeds and had jurisdiction over suits for recovery of legacies. Quarter sessions, as established by the 1722 assembly, was empowered to take recognizances and obligations, and to hear criminal cases not tried in courts of oyer and terminer. But its powers were expanded to include setting prices on bread, liquors, and other commodities or services. It also supervised the construction of roads, the appointment of some local officers, the management of the poorhouse, and the collection of poor relief. Justices were able to perform their legal responsibilities in private sessions as well. When the courts were not convened, judges were permitted to take recognizances, bonds, and affidavits, and to issue certain writs.[14]

Unlike the courts established at the end of the century, colonial courts also possessed executive and legislative authority, as illustrated in the 1770 presentment by the grand jury and the justices of quarter sessions to the commissioners and assessors of Philadelphia. The court ordered the assessors to repair the Pennypack Bridge on the Philadelphia-Newtown road and to finance the project from revenues already collected. The assessors were further ordered to report to the court upon completion of the repairs.[15]

George Bryan's only pre-1764 legal experience consisted of several debt suits against delinquent customers, and grand jury duty in 1761;[16] as soon as he was commissioned, however, he began regularly attending court sessions. In terms of his attendance, Bryan was one of the more consistent judges of the orphans court sessions from the time of his appointment until the closing of the colonial courts in 1776, although he had two unexplained periods of absences, probably due to ill health and domestic pressures: 2 July to 12 November 1772, and 22 September 1773 to 28 December 1774. In that last period he attended only three of twenty-six orphans court sessions. Bryan also attended approximately one-third of the quarter sessions courts but none of the mayor's courts. In a completely separate jurisdiction, Bryan was commissioned in 1771, and again in 1773, to sit on the court empowered at Philadelphia to try "negroes" accused of crimes. Although common pleas records did not list the names of the presiding justices, Bryan probably sat on that bench more frequently than on the other courts, since those trials dealt with contracts and debts, thereby allowing Bryan to utilize his considerable experience as a merchant.[17]

Bryan's appointment as a judge advanced him into new realms of experience, familiarizing him with the law, court procedures, and the men who dominated the city's legal systems: Thomas Willing, Samuel Mifflin, Samuel Shoemaker, and Isaac Jones. These men represented an established elite of influence and wealth, while Bryan and other recent appointees, James Young and John Bull, were part of a new generation of less wealthy Philadelphians who were wending their way through the city's power structure. By 1776 Bryan belonged to the city's political and legal establishment and consequently was ready to assume a significant share of leadership at the beginning of the revolution.

III

Bryan's initial involvement in America's opposition to Britain was the Stamp Act protest. Philadelphia, already enmeshed in the political turmoil over the petition for royal government, remained fairly calm during the summer of 1765, while New York and Boston reacted violently against the proposed Stamp Act. In June 1765 the assembly speaker, Joseph Fox, received a circular letter from Massachusetts suggesting a convention of all the colonies to protest the tax officially. Fox received the letter favorably and placed the matter on the assembly's agenda in September. The resulting debate and vote revealed deep divisions on the issue within the Quaker party as the House divided fifteen to fourteen in favor of participation in the colonial protest. Among the majority who supported sending delegates to New York were all the New Ticket men and half of the Quakers, while John Hughes, the appointed stamp distributor, led the opposing Quakers against the measure. The following day the assembly chose four of the most vocal opponents of the tax and supporters of the intercolonial protest, John Dickinson, George Bryan, John Morton, and Joseph Fox, to attend the Stamp Act Congress.[18]

Bryan left for New York on 28 September 1765 and arrived in time for the opening session on 7 October. The minutes of the congress fail to mention individual participation, but Caesar Rodney described the work of the Congress as "one of the most difficult tasks" he had ever seen "undertaken." Carefully avoiding any direct challenge to the prerogative of the crown or the power of Parliament, the congress maneuvered between those members who pressed for a more definitive statement of colonial rights and those who preferred a broader statement confirming "principles of freedom." Anxious for unity of action, however, the congress agreed to frame a fourteen-point resolution declaring the Stamp Act to be subversive of the basic liberties and rights of the colonists because it imposed a tax on them without their consent. Parliament was therefore called upon to repeal the detested measure.[19]

By the time of Bryan's return in late October, Philadelphia was in ferment over the impending deadline of 2 November for the implementation of the stamp tax. Angry mobs had threatened to pull down the houses of John Hughes and John Penn, and in early October a self-appointed delegation had visited Hughes in order to "persuade" him to resign his stamp office post. Rather than capitulate, the glib Hughes promised not to put the stamp tax into execution until the other colonies agreed to do the same. An estimated one thousand people assembled at the courthouse and grudgingly accepted his response, the promoters of the protest having cautioned against precipitate action. Menacing crowds patrolled the wharves promising to disrupt the unloading of the hated stamped paper. Twice in December sea captains were brought before Judge Bryan to swear that they were not carrying any of the stamped paper on board their ships. Bryan took one of the oaths that was afterward delivered to the patrons of the London Coffee House, who burned a sample of the offending material amid a delighted crowd of onlookers. Quite probably, Bryan was one of those spectators.[20]

Bryan was one of four hundred merchants who met at the courthouse on 9 November 1765 and declared that they would not import any more goods from Great Britain until the Stamp Act was repealed. The pact, they decreed, would remain in effect until 1 May 1766, when the merchants would consider further steps if the act was still in effect. They took the opportunity to complain of the "restrictions, prohibitions, and ill advised regulations" that the mother country had imposed upon them, and the ways in which those rules had limited their exports, increased their costs, and destroyed their ability to establish a market in specie, which, ironically, would have been used to pay England's customs and taxes.[21] The merchants protested that the province was "heavily in debt to Great Britain" and that Pennsylvania's produce was insufficient to offset its burgeoning imbalance of trade. The taxes of the Stamp Act, they continued, would further inhibit the colony's ability to pay the merchants of Great Britain, or to continue purchasing more goods from them. They established a committee to call upon other traders of the city to comply with the resolves. A week later three hundred retailers signed a similar concord, refusing to buy from "any vendue-master, or other person" any product that was shipped from Great Britain. The retailers deferred to the committee of merchants to determine the products to be proscribed.[22]

Pennsylvanians, like their counterparts throughout the colonies, successfully boycotted British goods and refused to admit the stamped paper on their shores. Governor John Penn wisely ordered the paper to be stored on board the HMS *Sardine* until further notice. The colonists, after some hesitation, adopted John Dickinson's advice to behave themselves "in all things" as if the Stamp Act "did not exist." Newspapers were published on regular, unstamped paper in defiance of the imperial law, and judges convened courts and heard cases but refused to record their official pronouncements on the stamped paper. Although "a degree short of open rebellion," Pennsylvania remained relatively calm during the winter months of 1765–66. Finally, when news of the act's repeal reached Philadelphia in the spring of 1766, the colony believed it had won a major triumph.[23]

Opposition to the stamp tax cut across party lines, and like most members of Pennsylvania's political factions Bryan believed the law to be unconstitutional. Although he apparently was not a member of the Philadelphia Sons of Liberty, and did not participate on the committee that visited Hughes to demand his resignation or the one that enforced the nonimportation agreement, Bryan proved to be a vocal opponent of the tax.[24] Besides attending the Stamp Act Congress, he was, recalled Hughes in 1766, a "red hot presbyterian" in his opposition to the tax.[25] His taking of oaths from sea captains was a public demonstration of support for the opposition and a declaration that in his capacity as a judge he was willing to use the legal system to subvert an unpopular law. Furthermore, along with the other judges, he refused to recognize a parliamentary statute and opened the courts for normal business without the stamps. While not a member of the various local opposition committees, however, he was familiar with those who were members and undoubtedly was a party to their many discussions.

There was an interesting undercurrent to the Stamp Act debates that surfaced during the heated September 1765 assembly session and the October election that followed. The Presbyterians, in the minds of several commentators, were the fomenters of the social unrest over the stamp tax. Thus William Franklin claimed that the Presbyterians were endeavoring to "stir" their "brethren throughout the continent" to take mob action in their opposition to England. John Hughes grumbled that he would have to suffer the "storm of Presbyterian rage" when it became known that he was the stamp distributor, and he further argued that the Stamp Act Congress was "indefatigably pushed forward by the Presbyterians."[26] Admittedly, these sentiments were those of prejudiced partisans of the Quaker party, who had previously experienced Presbyterian hostility. But such comments clearly indicated that the Presbyterians were unique in their opposition—that they, perhaps more than any other group in the colony, were most eager to confront forcefully the authority of imperial Britain. Although his actions were similar to those of other early "whigs" who resisted the Stamp Act, Bryan, the Presbyterians' "city champion,"[27] was undoubtedly viewed by his contemporaries as a "Presbyterian whig," implying that the two terms were synonymous and were intended to distinguish his and his coreligionists' political behavior from other Whigs. Yet, undeniably, the resistance movement cut across ethnic and religious lines. Therefore either Presbyterian Whigs (although fully integrated within the resistance movement) were more vehement than their colleagues in denouncing England, or the characterization was simply the result of lingering prejudices and not of any accurate assessment.

In one demonstrable respect, however, Presbyterian participation in the resistance movement included opposition to measures that specifically concerned them. At the same time that Americans were protesting Parliament's presumed right to tax the colonies, Bryan and his religious peers were further developing and clarifying their opposition to England during the controversy over the establishment of an American bishopric. The episcopacy crisis originated with a plea from Anglican ministers to the king and Parliament for the creation of an American bishop. A small minority in the northern colonies, the Anglicans were attempting to increase church membership but were continually frustrated by inadequate funding, lack of ministers, and an inefficiently structured hierarchy. Their solution was set out in *An Appeal to the Public in Behalf of the Church of England in America,* written by Dr. Thomas Bradbury Chandler and endorsed by the New Jersey and New York ministers at the 1767 Elizabethtown convention of Episcopal ministers from the middle colonies.[28]

Accurately sensing the storm of protest that would fall upon him after the publication of his appeal, Chandler first outlined the necessity of establishing an American bishop and then attempted to assuage the fears of dissenters by stating that the post would not alter the relationship between church and state. The appeal lamented the tremendous inconvenience of sending American-trained ministers to England for their ordination by a bishop but stressed the necessity of such ordination because, unlike other Protestant churches, the Anglican church maintained Christ's "uninterrupted succession."[29] The sole authority to preach the Gospel, argued Chandler, had been successfully transmitted from the savior to his apostles, then to the bishops of the primitive Church of Rome, and finally, at the time of the Reformation, to the Church of England. Therefore, the right to spread the Christian word of God had to be sanctioned by a bishop; otherwise the minister's works and the lives of those who followed him lay in dangerous error. Sending ministers to England for their ordination, however, was time consuming, expensive, and dangerous—several had lost their lives during the Atlantic passage. An American bishop, concluded Chandler, would relieve ministers of that burden.[30]

Hoping to dampen potential objections, Chandler stated categorically that a colonial episcopal establishment "would not interfere with either the civil or religious rights of any." An American bishop, he argued, would serve only to facilitate the administrative needs of the clergy and to provide the church with an ordered form of government. He solemnly declared that the bishop's authority would be derived from the church and not from the state, and that the bishop would "operate only upon the clergy of the church, and not upon the laity nor dissenters of any denomination." Such civil functions of the state, continued Chandler, as the administration of wills, guardianships, and marriages would not be subject to review by the church. Nor would the bishops, he added, sit as "judges of any cases relating thereto." Furthermore, Americans were safe from tithes because only an act of Parliament could order their collection—a circumstance independent of the presence of an American bishop. "The Church of England in America," he concluded, "only requests that proper remedies may be provided for her present sufferings. . . . She asks nothing, but what has been granted to others."[31]

If Chandler anticipated an angry response to his ideas, Philadelphia Presbyterians were eager not to disappoint him. Seething with contempt and cynicism about Chandler's assurances, they openly ridiculed him and tore into his proposal with a vengeance. The establishment of a bishop in America reminded the predominantly Irish community of the hated ecclesiastical courts, tithes, and various test acts of Ireland—all of which stripped dissenters of their citizenship and punished them with fines and imprisonment for their differing religious beliefs. Responding to the perceived crisis inherent in Chandler's appeal, Francis Alison organized a triumvirate of correspondents to refute it. Alison called upon Dickinson and Bryan to join him in creating a series of articles to be published under the pseudonym "Centinel."[32]

The first essay was published on 24 March 1768, and the series regularly appeared until the publication of Centinel 19 on 28 July. Two subsequent publications, Centinel 20 and 21, appeared on 28 November and 8 December, respectively. All of the articles were printed by the Presbyterian William Bradford in his *Pennsylvania Journal*. Four other articles entitled "Remonstrant" were also printed by Bradford in October and November. Elizabeth Nybakken has identified the authors of most of the pieces, concluding that Alison authored Centinel 1 through 5 and the four Remonstrants, that Dickinson wrote Centinel 6 through 8 and 16, and that Bryan was responsible for Centinel 11.[33] The similarity of style and content, however, indicates that Bryan wrote no. 12 as well.

Centinel calmly and methodically undermined Chandler's position, demonstrating that the establishment of an Anglican bishop was ill conceived, ill timed, and contrary to the best interests of the colonists. The authors deliberately set out to discredit Chandler's plans by initially dismissing his promises of a restricted colonial religious establishment, and then by tying them to the recent unpopular acts of Parliament. Alison demanded "substantial proofs" before believing that the "spirit of persecution" was no longer alive in the Episcopal church. He added that until the test act was abolished in Ireland and England, "we must believe, good Doctor, that you not only *would,* but *do* persecute your brethren." Furthermore, asked Alison, "can there be no bishops without establishments; no ordination without act of Parliament?" Moreover, why was the "application made for a bishop at this particular time when the liberties of America are at stake?" What assurances, continued Alison, "are we to have that bishops will be sent over with such limited powers?" Such authority, he warned, contained the "danger of persecutions; which worldly minded men, to gratify their own pride and lust of power, are forward . . . to practice; and which weak men with better intentions, are too apt to be led into."[34]

Dickinson broached the broader subject of the constitutional relationship between England and her colonies, remarking that the issue was not directly about a bishop but rather about the "manner of introducing the bishop, and establishing that discipline in America." If Parliament had the right to establish American bishops without the colonists' consent, Dickinson argued, then Parliament might also pass revenue acts intended for their support, and create ecclesiastical courts to extract submission to their rule as well. "How long shall we enjoy the happiness of this constitution," demanded Dickinson, "if establishments can be imposed on us without our consent."[35]

Continuing Centinel's attack on Chandler's "scheme," Bryan envisaged the easy and insidious way in which the "priestly dominion" would "steal in upon us." The clergy, predicted Bryan, having had "the artifice of making a zeal for orthodoxy, and a regard for their own interests," would overwhelm the local magistrates with their "claims and encroachments" and insulate themselves from reform or redress under the presumption of divine right. Bryan then took a different tack, however, by prompting his readers to assume that Chandler was sincere in his declarations of episcopal passivity toward both the Anglican laity and dissenters. "Let us for a moment suppose," Bryan suggested, that the "bishops would, at first, be sent over with such limited powers"—what could the colonists expect? Bryan foresaw that Chandler's assurances would have little meaning for the bishops of England, and that the potential reaction of the English clergy to the status of their American brethren would pose an immediate threat. The "example of a reduced episcopate in the British Dominions," he warned, would establish a "dangerous" precedent "to their own jurisdiction." The "*successors of the Apostles* in England," mocked Bryan, "whose revenues, dignities, and seats in Parliament, necessarily give them great weight," would use every opportunity "to have every power, every privilege they enjoy, as far as possible, extended to their brethren, the American bishops," and because of "the Inattention of most of our *virtual* representatives, there is too much reason to fear they would succeed to their wishes." Bryan further argued that Chandler's promises would be quickly brushed aside as soon as it was convenient to the church leaders. "Whatever may be promised now, yet reasons of state," observed Bryan, would require "more to be done for this *new-fangled* hierarchy."[36]

As soon as a bishop was settled within the colony the particular nature of the institution, Bryan feared, would begin the process of aggrandizement. He cited Chandler's quotation describing the American church's great necessity for a bishop, and mused that the same plea of "'unprecedented hardship'" would be used to expand the American clergy's powers. After all, Bryan observed, "it cannot be expected that the mother country will maintain the clergy of America," and it would be urged that tithes were well needed for the support of the bishop and the parish minister. Such a decision would then necessitate the "aid of the magistrate" to enforce the powers of the episcopal establishment. In a play on words, Bryan argued that the next demand of the Anglicans would be "that all dissenters" should be "considered as *virtual* churchmen, and made liable" to the church's needs. It would not seem unreasonable, he concluded, that a "*sacramental test* should be extended to America."[37]

While the proposed establishment of an American bishop troubled Bryan the Presbyterian, there was another issue, already a reality, that angered Bryan the merchant, jurist, and nascent patriot. In a separate tract in Centinel 11, Bryan expressed outrage over Parliament's "arbitrary . . . revival of the Admiralty jurisdiction towards Americans," and he described England's exercise of the law as "loose" and "dangerous." Admiralty law and the courts that enforced it, Bryan explained to his readers, found their origins in early England, and their procedure involved civil trials before a single judge without the benefit of a jury. Those courts had never been popular in England, and parliamentary statutes were enacted in the sixteenth century that curbed and qualified "this arbitrary mode of judging." America, however, was not as fortunate, claimed Bryan, because Parliament consistently enforced admiralty jurisdiction over the "subjects *without* the realm, for the benefit of those *within* it."[38] Americans had suffered under, and resisted, admiralty laws as early as William III, but Parliament's recent expansion of admiralty authority and the increase in the numbers of judges and officers who were left to "spunge upon the colonies for a living" had overturned the traditional rights of Americans, exclaimed Bryan. Parliament, upon "assuming a power to tax the colonies," had again attempted to "distress and enslave" Americans through a new exercise of might. "Not content with bringing it [admiralty law] ashore at our sea-ports, and enabling it to scourge our merchants," Bryan fumed, English authorities had also "sent it up into our forests, and directed that the penalties imposed on such persons as shall destroy his majesties pine-trees in New-England, New York, and New Jersey, shall be recoverable in the Admiralty."[39]

Bryan expressed dismay that a court and jurisdiction found "intolerable" in England should be allowed to exist in America. Yet he perceived that such a circumstance could occur because the colonies within "the empire" were by their very definition inferior to the central authority. Colonists were the inevitable victims of official indifference to the legal protections afforded to "distant subjects." Legislatures, argued Bryan, were more scrupulous in the construction of their laws when the subjects and the individual legislators came from the same community. But these men had little interest for the concerns of those "without the realm" and often considered complaints from America as "humoursome, if not factious, and highly inconsistent with the submission and reverence due to the supreme legislature."[40] With this reasoning, Bryan had deliberately redirected his readers away from the straightforward question of the rights of Parliament over the provinces to the issue that struck at the heart of the constitutional crisis between empire and colony. "Can any thing more fully manifest the difference between a *virtual* representative," asked a skeptical Bryan, "and a *real* one?" Falling dangerously close to questioning continued obedience to Parliament and, by extension, to the crown, Bryan wondered whether any "sympathetic affections in these suppositious delegates" existed toward the subjects in America. The recent statute that erected the three or four admiralty courts on the North American continent, he insisted, was yet another "new blow to our rights as Englishmen."[41] Bryan's use of the phrase "rights as Englishmen," however, indicated that he had not yet arrived at a purely "American" view of the potential conflict.

For Bryan, the English common law system and principles were still "the law of the land." Consequently, civil law (as practiced in the admiralty courts) and canon law (as practiced in the ecclesiastical sphere) were severely limited and subordinated to the authority of common law, which provided for trial by jury and the right to a sufficient defense. Trial by jury, reasoned Bryan, was "that happy Mode of administering justice, which having survived the various changes and convulsions of the state, has been preserved and handed down to us." The expanded scope and enforcement of admiralty law would destroy common law, and a jurisdiction that had been treated with "aversion and jealousy" by English ancestors would now have to be endured by their descendants. "GOD grant," pleaded Bryan, "we may be able to transmit to our children" the sanctity of common law and trial by jury.[42]

While Centinel was slaying the episcopal dragon and, via Bryan, the admiralty courts, Philadelphians were involved in another struggle against imperial England: the nonimportation movement of 1768. Thoroughly supportive of the Stamp Act protest three years earlier, many city merchants were now reluctant to oppose the Townshend duties. But under the relentless goading of Charles Thomson, John Dickinson, and other notables, as well as outside pressure from New York and Boston, Philadelphia merchants and tradesmen finally resolved to assume a defiant position against the duties. At a mass meeting on 25 October 1768, over two hundred merchants promised to enter into a nonimportation pact to go into effect in the spring of 1769. On 10 March 1769, with mercantile grievances still pending before Parliament, 250 merchants signed an accord prohibiting the purchase of any English goods until the duties were repealed. Compliance was to be enforced by a committee of twenty merchants who were also to communicate with similar committees throughout the colonies.[43]

Although he did not assume a visible role within the movement, Bryan was an active participant. Given the sensitive nature and explosive potential of nonimportation, Bryan may have preferred to remain an active but anonymous voice in the struggle. While other merchants initially hesitated to support nonimportation, the evidence suggests that Bryan had fully committed himself to the cause of resistance. Bryan's view is detected in an address (probably drafted by John Dickinson) delivered by Charles Thomson to a mass meeting of merchants held 30 July 1768 at the statehouse, protesting the duties and highlighting additional grievances. The address contained a short paragraph relating to admiralty law similar to Bryan's work in Centinel. Dickinson, of course, could have simply borrowed the piece, or he could have asked Bryan to write it; in either case, Bryan and Dickinson most probably consulted together on the protest. More compelling evidence, however, can be found in the letter from Boston merchants to their Philadelphia counterparts on 11 August 1768 announcing their creation of an association. The Boston merchants thought highly enough of Bryan's role in the nonimportation movement to address the letter to him and six others. Bryan signed the nonimportation agreement of 10 March 1769.[44]

The nonimportation agreement survived until the fall of 1770. In May of that year Philadelphians had learned of Parliament's repeal of all the Townshend duties, except that on tea. Many merchants wished to reestablish commercial relations with England immediately, with the proviso that those goods still taxed by Parliament would continue to be proscribed. Radical merchants and tradesmen, however, preferred that the nonimportation agreement continue in full until all the duties were repealed—specifically the tax on tea. The merchants, in short, were no longer unified. Dry goods merchants had suffered tremendously during the embargo as their inventories and sales dropped to precipitously low levels. Not surprisingly they favored the immediate end of nonimportation, while merchants who traded with the West Indies, as well as local tradesmen and mechanics, had fared better and therefore demanded full compliance with the embargo. Other merchants desired revision of the agreement after learning of its abandonment by Newport and New York. As a further complication, Philadelphia Quakers in August 1769 had terminated their association with the project because of a violent incident along the docks involving radicals and suspected importers the preceding July. That decision led to confusion and dissension within Quaker ranks, with some Friends continuing to observe the agreement and others withdrawing from it. In September 1770

the Philadelphia merchant community split openly into competing factions. The moderates, led by Thomas Willing and several principal Quaker
merchants, declared that the embargo (except on tea) was over, prompting
an angry withdrawal from the association by the radical merchants and
tradesmen led by Charles Thomson. The two sides organized new committees, but by 29 September 1770 the embargo was effectively dead as merchants sent their orders for goods to England.[45]

Evidence on Bryan's position vis-à-vis the division of the merchants is
elusive, but given his past involvement he probably favored the more extreme measures. As Richard Ryerson points out, those Presbyterian merchants whose involvement can be identified consistently sided with the
radicals.[46] Bryan, at the center of the Presbyterian political community, was
moving, like many of his peers, toward the patriot party and independence.

IV

The years between 1770 and 1775 were a time of change for Bryan, both
personally and politically. Despite his support for the resistance movement,
Bryan remained partially in the background during the early and mid-
1770s, while others stepped to the fore in leading Pennsylvania against
imperial England. There were, however, pressures at work to keep him out
of the limelight at this time. These years were difficult for Bryan, and they
may also have been unhappy ones. Bryan was declared bankrupt in 1771,
a severe blow to a man responsible for a large and youthful family that was
still to add two more children over the next four years. Besides financial
and, presumably, familial stress, he also suffered serious health problems late
in 1773 that continued well into 1774 and may have restricted his ability
to assume a more significant role in the growing resistance movement.

Personal factors alone, however, do not sufficiently account for Bryan's
decreased visibility during these years. The ethno-religious political structure that served as a platform for Bryan during the mid-1760s collapsed as
the Indian war and the campaign for the transfer of the colonial government to royal authority became less relevant by the end of 1765. Although
the Presbyterian party ceased functioning as a viable entity at that time, the
potential for its return continued to exist as long as political expression in
Pennsylvania was the preserve of the Quaker and proprietary factions. The
emergence of the resistance movement, however, introduced new pressures
that strained and subsequently overwhelmed the existing political institutions, rendering powerless the Quaker and proprietary parties and, by ex-
tention, such ethno-religious movements as the Presbyterians. Like a rock

striking glass, the resistance movement fractured the traditional political landscape of Pennsylvania. As a Presbyterian leader Bryan was isolated, unable to compete effectively with the multitude of new men vying to control and influence the kaleidoscopic nature of the resistance movement. When juxtaposed against Bryan's faltering health, these changes help to explain why his participation in the events leading to the revolution was slight. Not until the winter of 1776–77 would Bryan reemerge on the political stage—this time, however, as one of the state's principal leaders. The controversy surrounding the 1776 constitution had caused the revolutionary factions to split asunder, permitting Bryan and many of his fellow Presbyterians to come to the fore. Once again, as primary spokesman for the Presbyterians, George Bryan had the opportunity to seize the moment, which he did with both hands in order to lead his party and his state to freedom.

Fortunately for Bryan, his earlier participation in the resistance movement had prompted him to examine the nature of representation and its relationship to those who were supposedly represented. This process was a journey that began with his observations about Parliament's ability to represent the colonies and would end ten years later with his vigorous promotion of the controversial unicameral legislature in revolutionary Pennsylvania. In 1767 he argued that all legislation was a response by those who framed the laws to specific interest groups. The further a legislature was removed from its designated constituencies, the greater the likelihood that it would be influenced by interests other than those of the community allegedly represented. Under the constant and effective pressure of English merchants and manufacturers, Parliament could not possibly represent the needs of Pennsylvania, reasoned Bryan; furthermore, he concluded that members of Parliament would be more inclined to protect their own rights and liberties than those of distant subjects. By 1777 his line of reasoning had taken him to a conclusion that he could not avoid: that the validity of representation was undermined not only by unreasonable distances, that is, the 3,000 miles from Philadelphia to London, but also by constitutional mandates decreeing which citizens were more qualified to serve as representatives.

Strongly supportive of the resistance movement and lacking any faith in Parliament's right to govern any aspect of American life, George Bryan was inexorably drawn by the impending crisis to its dramatic denouement, becoming at its occurrence an ardent revolutionary. In 1775 he believed that the colonies had been "forced into an open war" with the British, and that the ministry continued to be "obstinate like the Pharoeh of old." Colonial representatives had met in the Continental Congress in 1774 and 1775 and increasingly challenged both colonial and imperial rule. After the skirmish at Lexington in which blood was shed, the colonies organized armed forces to repel British armies. Bryan eagerly reported to John Ewing that, in response to the battle of Bunker Hill, Pennsylvania would raise a 4,500-man militia and organize a committee of safety.[47] "What times are we fallen into?" Bryan asked rhetorically in 1775, as if to acknowledge that the dramatic events unfolding before him had a momentum of their own, but with uncertainty as to the outcome. Bryan could not foresee it, or perhaps did not wish to see it at that time, but within twelve months the colonies would declare their independence and Pennsylvania's proprietary government, which had lasted for almost a century, would be terminated—events that would dramatically alter his life and propel him from the shadows of relative anonymity into public prominence and leadership.

5

THE YEARS OF POWER
Revolution and the Pennsylvania Constitution

DURING THE LATE WINTER and early spring months of 1777 George Bryan's political career catapulted into sudden prominence. Between 1777 and 1780 he served as Pennsylvania's vice president and acting president, as a Philadelphia city assemblyman, and finally as a supreme court justice. He emerged as one of the principal spokesmen and leaders of his political party, as well as one of the driving forces behind the success of Pennsylvania's revolutionary government. Totally committed to the success of the revolution, Bryan established three goals during his occupancy of public office: support of the state's war effort against the invading British army, the subjugation of the state's Tories who opposed independence, and the successful establishment of the state's controversial revolutionary constitution. The development of an opposition to this agenda, however, complicated Bryan's political goals. In particular, Bryan and his partisans had difficulty distinguishing between the activities of the Whigs who opposed their plans and the Tories. The inability to view their opposition as a legitimate participant in Pennsylvania's early democratic experience and the impact of a tottering economy combined to force Bryan and his party out of power in late 1780.

II

Pennsylvania in 1776 was on the brink of chaos. Proprietary government had lost control of the actual operations of authority as the momentum toward revolution increasingly pushed the direction of public policy into the hands of extralegal committees. One such entity, Philadelphia's Council of Safety, increasingly assumed more power—organizing a city and county militia and navy, encouraging its counterparts throughout the colony to prepare for war, and spending hundreds of thousands of pounds in the process. The city streets were filled with marching militia units, while extralegal committees of safety and inspection searched the wharves and warehouses for violators of the council's decrees. In the spring of 1776 Philadelphia patriots who were pressing for independence (and who were known as Whigs) secretly conspired with delegates from the Continental Congress to overthrow Pennsylvania's few remaining vestiges of royal authority. The result was a mass meeting on 25 May of thousands of city residents outside the doors of the colonial assembly, demanding an end of allegiance to King George III. Inside the assembly stood the remnants of the Quaker party, representing the last legitimate form of authority blocking the Whig push for independence. But the colonial assembly was no longer a respected force in revolutionary Pennsylvania and was easily bypassed by the Whigs, who gathered in a provincial conference in late June for the purpose of calling a constitutional convention. On 15 July ninety-six elected delegates from the eleven counties and the city of Philadelphia convened upon the authority of the provincial conference and set about the task of establishing a free and independent state of Pennsylvania.[1]

The Pennsylvania Constitutional Convention of 1776 began auspiciously, with the delegates pledging to sever their relationship with England, to cooperate with the Congress in supporting the United States army by sending the state's militia to Amboy, New Jersey, and to write a republican frame of government. The inability of the delegates, however, to accommodate competing ideas on the way to construct a republic quickly "split the whigs into pieces."[2] Within the convention a form of Whiggism emerged that was considered too radical by some of the convention delegates. This new political philosophy, however, was embraced by a majority, setting into motion one of the most unique experiments in republicanism during the revolutionary period. The underlying force girding the new political tenet was the belief that the interests of society, that is, the people at large, could only be served by a government that was directly responsible to the citizenry. The proponents of this philosophy maintained that within the construction of government there could be no distinction between the source of sovereignty, the people, and the actual seat of power held by those who governed.[3] This theory contradicted the more traditional view, which suggested that people were sovereign but that legislatures, in their own right, were also sovereign. The differences may seem subtle, but the two views implied two totally different perceptions as to the roles of the public and the legislators. In the traditional view, legislators were granted a greater degree of latitude and were held less responsible to the public in making decisions that affected public policy. This argument was justified, in part, because legislators were considered more knowledgeable than the average citizen on the affairs of government. The more radical view, however, held that the assembly must be a direct reflection of the will of the people. Because people inherently wished to be free, the argument followed that the greater degree of indivisibility between the governed and those governing, the greater the check against possible tyranny. Governments, therefore, should be constructed in the simplest form, eliminating institutions that distanced themselves from the people.

Despite the vigorous protests of the minority, the convention majority, led by Timothy Matlack, James Cannon, and David Rittenhouse and prompted by the advice and influence of Thomas Paine and Dr. Thomas Young, rejected traditional political theory, rejecting in the process a bicameral legislature and a strong executive.[4] These radical Whigs, as historians have identified them, devised an all-powerful unicameral assembly and reduced the executive to an administrative, elected council that was powerless to initiate or veto legislation. The assembly was to have "all other power necessary for the legislature of a free state," including the right to enact any law it desired, to sit on its own adjournment, and to appoint most of the state's officers. The assembly could not, however, alter the constitution. To ensure that the assembly would continue to represent the will of the people and remain free from corruption, the constitution provided for annual elections of assemblymen, restricted the terms of legislators to four out of any seven years, and ordered all legislative debates open to the public. Furthermore, a Council of Censors was to meet every seven years to judge whether the constitution had been violated. Finally, suffrage was extended to all taxpaying males twenty-one years old and over. On 28 September 1776 the convention adjourned, proclaiming the radical 1776 constitution as the new sovereign authority of the commonwealth.[5]

The constitution of 1776 was instantly controversial. "Good God!" remarked a shocked John Adams, "the people of Pennsylvania in two years will be glad to petition the crown of Britain for reconciliation in order to be delivered from the tyranny of their constitution." One critic likened the convention delegates to the "fool in the Gospel, who built his house upon the sand," while another observed that the "history of all countries" proved that there was as much "mischief when lodged in the hands of *one* assembly" as when "lodged in the hands of one man."[6] Deferential Pennsylvania in the eighteenth century shuddered at the concept of a government based so heavily upon the "democratical order." The government, the constitution's critics argued, should be divided into an upper and lower house, with a single governor having the power to veto objectionable legislation. The second house in the assembly should, in fact, serve as a social check on the lower house. "Demophilus," representing the opposition's opinion, stressed that the people of the country were common farmers untutored in history, law, or politics. Although they were honest, he continued, they would decide issues by what appeared right to them, "never weighing so critically the probable consequences of any proposed measure." What they needed, he concluded, was an upper house, representing the "*wisdom* of the most learned and experienced members of the state."[7] A bicameral assembly with a governor, the opposition believed, would provide both a political and a social solution to the uncertainties of democracy and revolution. "Had the governor and council . . . a negative upon the proceedings of the assembly," observed Benjamin Rush, the government would have "safety, wisdom, and dignity."[8]

George Bryan did not participate in the writing of the constitution or significantly influence those who did, although there is some debate surrounding that issue. Alexander Graydon believed that Cannon, Matlack, and Bryan were the authors, whereas Benjamin Rush identified the authors as Cannon, Matlack, and Young, with "Reed, Bryan and Parson Ewing" as the constitution's defenders. Graydon's observation, however, was made some fifty years after the event; Rush, on the other hand, was in Philadelphia in 1776 and was deeply involved with revolutionary events of the spring and summer of that year. Rush, therefore, is more likely correct.[9]

Equally intriguing is the supposition that Bryan was Demophilus, author of *The Genuine Principles of the Ancient Saxon, or English Constitution,* a thoughtful and clever pamphlet published shortly before the convening of the 1776 constitutional convention that urged the delegates to return to the golden age of Saxon England as their example when composing the state's constitution. While some of his suggestions found their way into the 1776 constitution, especially the Council of Censors, Demophilus also argued for a governor and an upper legislative house as well as a lower house, propositions that Bryan would not have supported.[10]

Although not its author, Bryan was, as Rush suggested, the constitution's tireless champion. In the spring of 1777, under the pseudonym "Whitlocke,"[11] Bryan defended the constitution against the criticism of Benjamin

Rush, writing under the nom de guerre "Ludlow." Rush argued that the state was in danger of losing its newly proclaimed liberties because all the power of government was lodged in a unicameral legislature. Such a practice, he maintained, was equivalent in its dangerous ramifications to one-man rule. Furthermore, the constitution presumed that all members of society were equal when, in fact, they were not. Observing that where there was wealth, there was power, and that the poor were always overmatched when confronted by the rich, Rush reasoned that the best system permitted the two groups to be represented separately, thereby enabling each to possess a check on the other and thus preserving their freedoms. An upper council reserved for men of greater learning and wealth would act as a buffer against a lower house reserved for the less wealthy. The upper house would also provide, Rush stated quite frankly, a more intelligent leadership in government than would the lower house.[12]

By challenging Rush, Bryan (at that time the state's vice president) was taking a stand against a body of ideas circulating throughout the nation, an emerging set of constitutional theorems that were products of the revolution and that represented a broad spectrum of political thought. These ideas centered on the manner in which a republican government should be constructed. Bryan was certainly in the vanguard of republican ideals, but he and Pennsylvania's proconstitutionalists differed significantly from their peers on several crucial issues. Unlike Rush and John Adams, for example, Bryan and his colleagues believed that sovereignty lay completely with the people and that it could not be abridged or parceled between the governed and those governing. They suspected that checks and balances in the guise of upper legislative councils and strong executives were a sinister intrusion upon the will of the people, and they resented the implications behind the assumption that the wisest and most virtuous individuals were invariably the wealthiest members of society. The last point was especially insulting. Besides conveying the supposition that the wealthy were smarter, such ideas also lumped together on an equal footing people like Bryan, who no longer enjoyed the prosperity of earlier times, and society's lowest orders. That was not the vision Bryan had of himself. Yet that was the secondary conclusion of Rush's republicanism, and it helps to explain Bryan's motivation, as a man who took his social status seriously, to become the egalitarian champion of the poor against the rich.

Writing as Whitlocke, Bryan went on the offensive, seeking first to defend the constitution and then to turn the argument against Rush. He began by dismissing Rush's strictures as inconsistent and as a misunderstanding of the strengths of the 1776 constitution. He rejected the criticism that the unicameral assembly was all-powerful, repeatedly arguing that the government was divided wisely among a legislature, an executive, and a judiciary—a model that conformed as nearly as possible to the "ancient habit and custom" of the colonial charter. As previously noted, the significant difference was the removal of the veto power from the executive: "No man who wishes to possess so much power can be safely trusted" with that power, observed Bryan, nor was it "consonant to reason," he continued, "to set up the judgment of one man above all the people." Following through on his argument, Bryan observed that since the king, through the proprietary, was formerly the executive, the new constitution replaced him with "*the commonwealth*." Instituting a governor for the executive with the authority to veto legislation, however, would have reversed the progress of the revolution, creating instead a "monstrous disproportion in the distribution of power."[13]

Bryan then rejected Rush's criticism that the constitution was dangerously flawed because it failed to provide for a Senate composed of the wisest and most virtuous of the citizenry. Rush erred, noted Bryan, in his belief that the constitution omitted an upper house because the document supposed a "perfect equality, and an equal distribution of property, wisdom, and virtue, among the inhabitants." Such an observation, Bryan continued, might as well pretend that the constitution assumed that all citizens were "*equally* tall, *equally* strong, and *equally* handsome." Such assumptions were ridiculous. Bryan further observed that recognition of differences existing within society was not the purpose of the constitution. As in all elections, reasoned Bryan, "choice presupposes an inequality, for there can be no choice where things are equal." However, he countered, all men were equal in their inherent freedom and independence, and in their eligibility to hold public office: "It belongs to those who choose to distinguish, in their choice, virtue and wisdom." Therein lay "the *grand* cause of discontent with the constitution." Seizing upon Ludlow's words that all power was derived from the people but not necessarily seated in the people, Bryan reformulated Rush's observation to state that the people might delegate power, but they might not retain it. Bryan then pressed forward the question: "Pray, who have we in Pennsylvania besides the people? and if they are not to be trusted with the care of their own interests who can?"[14]

Having posed the question to Rush, Bryan then answered it for him. He argued that for Rush and his colleagues the only possible measurement to distinguish the wisest and most virtuous individuals was wealth, and that, concluded Bryan, was the real purpose for an upper house in the legislature. For "good reason," Bryan contended, property was not made a "title to government," since rich men enjoyed such a substantial "share of power at all times" that the constitution should not award them with "the addition of governmental powers." Among the populace there was a "predilection to the great," and consequently the people were "ever fond of bestowing the highest offices" upon the wealthy. Yet to give them their own branch of the government, as Ludlow would suggest, was to invite oppression of the poor and the middling classes. Riches were the "inheritance of wise men and fools," Bryan noted, further observing that "wisdom and virtue alone" should serve as the marks of distinction among the people's governors.[15]

Seeking to expose the weakest link in Rush's argument, Bryan attacked the assumptions and implications of the supposed superior qualities of an upper house. Rush wished to gather the men of "middling fortunes" into a lower house, observed Bryan, while reserving an upper house for the men of "overgrown fortunes." But by gathering in an upper house with "controul" over the men of middling fortunes, the rich would have gained unrestrained power. Bryan was appalled. "By this," he exclaimed, "you *fix an aristocracy at once,* and to guard against an *uncertain event,* you propose a *certain evil.*" Bryan concluded with dismay that the government, rather than "being composed of the wise men of Pennsylvania, . . . would, in that case, consist of the rich men of Pennsylvania."[16]

But the ultimate folly according to Bryan was to pretend that there was a significant difference in the quality of leadership between the men of either house. He complained that the opponents of the unicameral system continuously stressed that legislative councillors or assemblymen of an upper house would be "possessed of nothing but wisdom and virtue," and collectively would be "possessed of coolness and deliberation." Correspondingly, continued Bryan, the constitution's critics tirelessly referred to the lower house members as men of "passion, prejudice, ambition, and self interestedness" or called them "frail, ignorant," and "foolish," arguing that their proceedings in the assembly would be "hasty" and "absurd." These assumptions, intentionally or not, unfairly contrasted the presumed defects of the nonwealthy with the virtue and wisdom of the rich and converted this social analysis into political theory. Bryan treated it with ridicule. "What good natured creatures must these councilors be," mocked Bryan. Were they "descended from the same race of beings" as mere assemblymen, he asked, or were they descended from "*gentlemen* of overgrown fortunes, whose hearts are so satiated with every thing this world produces, that they have been long since tired of every pursuit, but the public good." Bryan questioned where to find "these cool, wise, deliberate and disinterested gentlemen?" If they were in Pennsylvania they should be put into the assembly, Bryan observed, but if they were not in the state a "legislative council would not create them."[17]

Bryan concluded that arguments over relative virtue within the polity were a distraction. What mattered was that government, reflecting in its composition the society it served, maintained its own collective sense of virtue and wisdom. The genius of republican government, argued Bryan, was not its freedom from mistakes or immorality, a purity that was impossible to attain, but rather its ability to correct itself. "Passion in the conduct of life," insisted Bryan, was the real motivation behind human behavior, despite the "judgment of philosophers" who thought behavior should have been "directed by reason." Human nature, Bryan conceded, was "governed by interest, or apparent good," and consequently governments would make errors or, as history demonstrated, deliberately conspire in evil. In order to offset these inevitable tendencies, the *"best constitution,"* therefore, must be that "which makes the interest of the legislator and the common interest perfectly coincident." Under those circumstances, "what affects one must equally be felt by the other; and the people can no sooner perceive an evil, than it becomes the interest of the legislator to remove it." Whereas Rush argued that a bicameral government would serve as a check against those errors, Bryan concluded that such an assumption was an error in itself: the safety of a republican government would not be guaranteed by "a legislature perfect in wisdom from any combination of assemblies." That was impossible. The "excellence of every good government" would only exist when the constitution, as in Pennsylvania, united "the common interest and that of the legislator." Ultimately, concluded Bryan, "no government, instituted by so short-sighted a creature as man," could "effectually prevent evils from happening; its perfection must ever consist in a disposition to remove" the evils "as soon as they do happen."[18]

Throughout the ensuing years, the arguments of the two sides would change subtly as they evolved gradually within the context of the development of an American constitutional ideology. As presented by Rush and Bryan in 1777, neither perspective would completely prevail. What emerged was a coherent body of ideas that accepted several of the principle tenets of both views. Within thirteen years, for example, Pennsylvanians accepted Bryan's argument that constitutionally mandated distinctions among the electorate violated the spirit of political equality and that representation within a republican government was to be based upon democracy. By the same token, the concept of checks and balances as a means of protecting government from the interest groups within the legislature were also accepted by the public as legitimate safeguards. For the proconstitutionalists, however, the "common interest" that Bryan assumed would emerge as a superior force to that of self-interest proved to be illusory, in part because the term itself was defined only in vague generalities and in part because common interest was itself a contradiction to the politics of self-interest, a reality that Bryan ironically recognized as one of the main elements behind human behavior.

By 1777, however, the lines for and against the controversial constitution were tightly drawn, and neither Bryan nor Rush would concede the argument. Thus originated the political dispute between those who favored the constitution, originally called the Whig Society and later the Constitutionalist party, and those who opposed the constitution, known initially as the anticonstitutionalists and later as the Republican party. This fundamental dispute would not be resolved until the 1790 state constitutional convention, when a new frame of government abolished the powerful, unicameral assembly and replaced it with a popularly elected bicameral legislature and chief executive.

III

Bryan was not a member of the 1776 constitutional convention, nor did he directly help in drafting the document. But he clearly was a well-known and trusted friend of the Whigs in 1776; in a letter to John Ewing written in the previous year, Bryan anticipated war and left little doubt as to which side he supported. Why he was not elected or appointed to the many extralegal committees and councils during 1774 and 1775 remains a mystery, but through conversation and acquaintance he probably staked out his position and consequently was called upon to serve the resistance and independence movement in several ways. On 5 June 1776 he was commissioned by the colonial assembly as port officer of the Delaware River for Philadelphia. Having enacted wartime regulations along with the Council of Safety, the Continental Congress wished to ensure that all vessels that entered and cleared the city's port were observing those regulations, and it urged the assembly to take the necessary steps. Bryan was selected because he was a trusted Whig judge who could take bonds for good behavior from sea captains, and presumably because he possessed a technical knowledge of the port itself, stemming from his 1763 appointment to oversee its repair.[19] Two months later, on 1 August, the constitutional convention—having closed the colonial courts while deliberating on the new constitution—authorized seven men, including Bryan, to release debtors and other inmates from prison upon security for the city and county of Philadelphia, and further appointed Bryan and thirty-six others on 3 September to act as justices of the peace for the city and county of Philadelphia until the courts were reorganized.[20]

The turning point for Bryan, however, was his election to a three-year term as Philadelphia's representative to the state's Supreme Executive Council in February 1777.[21] From this point forward, Bryan became one of Pennsylvania's central figures during the war and one of the state's leading politicians until his death fourteen years later. His election that February, however, was a direct result of the protracted struggle between the opponents and the supporters of the constitution, as anticonstitutionalists attempted to sabotage the state's new government by refusing to participate in it. Thus, opponents who were elected to the assembly and the executive council in November 1776 refused to attend, hoping to prevent a quorum. Other anticonstitutionalists refused to accept county positions or militia appointments. Mass meetings were held in Philadelphia and Carlisle protesting the new constitution and demanding the immediate convening of a second convention to establish a more acceptable frame of government. A temporary truce between the two sides was effected in late 1776 and early 1777 when fears arose that Gen. William Howe's British forces might invade Philadelphia from their position in New Jersey, but when Howe drew back to New York the two factions returned to their antagonistic strategies. The deadlock was broken in February 1777 when the proconstitutionalists in the assembly ordered new elections for the vacant seats of the absent anticonstitutionalist legislators. The anticonstitutionalists snubbed these elections, and consequently the proconstitutionalists won a sweeping victory, electing four of their previously defeated candidates in Philadelphia.[22] The assembly and the executive council, having fallen under the control of the radical Whigs, moved quickly to organize the government. On 15 March 1777, six months after the publication of the constitution, the Supreme Executive Council and the assembly in a joint ballot elected Thomas Wharton, Jr., and George Bryan as president and vice president, respectively, of the executive council. Timothy Matlack was appointed secretary of the council.[23]

The election of Bryan and Wharton to the top positions had significant political ramifications. Both men were residents of the city and consequently were available to attend the council and to assume the often time-consuming and irksome tasks required for public administration. Wharton, however, was a political moderate and, while generally supportive of the proconstitutionalists, was never particularly active on the party's behalf. Bryan, on the other hand, was an ardent partisan, and his position as vice president gave him high visibility and authority. With his election, Bryan emerged as one of the principal leaders of his political group, a circumstance partly resulting from the lack of known leaders among his faction. A leadership crisis, in fact, plagued the radical Whigs as early as the summer of 1776. "They are mostly honest well meaning country men," observed the Rev. Francis Alison about the convention delegates, "but entirely unacquainted with such high matters."[24] By 1777 Charles Thomson and Thomas Paine were employing their talents in the service of the Continental Congress and army, while John Dickinson had retired to New Jersey rather than serve under the 1776 constitution. Other leading citizens such as Benjamin Rush, James Wilson, and George Ross became anticonstitutionalists. At one point, the desperate proconstitutionalists asked Timothy Matlack to return from his militia service in New Jersey to resume his duties as clerk of the assembly.[25] Bryan's assumption of political power in March 1777, however, would prove to be an enormous triumph for the supporters of the new constitution. Quick-witted and perceptive, he threw his tremendous energies behind the radical Whigs' cause, and in doing so managed to secure the 1776 constitution to a firm foundation.

When Bryan took office in the spring of 1777, the situation was bleak. Philadelphia had been in a state of panic since December 1776, daily expecting an attack by Howe. So chaotic had city life become during that month that Gen. George Washington ordered Gen. Israel Putnam to assume military control of the city. Normalcy had not returned by spring, and in April 1777 when the city lay under the threat of yet another invasion the Continental Congress seriously considered restoring order through military intervention. Furthermore, anticonstitutionalists throughout the state inaugurated an unrelenting newspaper and pamphlet attack on the constitution while continuing their strategy of noncooperation. To complicate matters, the courts and county governments were not yet organized, city and state defenses still needed to be planned, and the government was running out of money.[26]

The Supreme Executive Council moved swiftly to establish order. Wharton undertook to organize and coordinate the movements of the militia, while Bryan attempted to revitalize the county courts and governments. His success was initially limited because many of the anticonstitutionalists continued to disdain proffered appointments. Moreover, some county officials refused to release court records and documents to the incoming appointees. Though such tactics were illegal and effectively disrupted the opening of the courts, Bryan preferred to wait out the obstruction of the opposition, while strengthening the positions of the council's appointed officers.[27] By late 1777 the strategy seemed to have succeeded— the county governments were operating, the courts were open, and many of the county leaders were now proconstitutionalists or allied with that faction. Drastic action, however, was needed on some occasions. For example, having suffered for some time the impertinence of the anticonstitutionalist Thomas Smith, former prothonotary of Bedford County, Bryan ordered his arrest and incarceration without bail in November 1777 until all the records of his office were relinquished to the new officer. Faced with imprisonment, Smith complied.[28]

Although many men continued to refuse office under the new constitution, organization of the state's government proceeded relatively smoothly.[29] Bryan and the council were able to fill provincial positions fairly quickly throughout the spring and summer of 1777. The council offered Joseph Reed, who originally opposed the constitution, the position of chief justice of the state supreme court in March 1777, but after some hesitation he declined the offer in June. A London-trained lawyer married into a prominent family and a popular figure during the resistance movement, Reed was friendly to the Whigs, and Bryan would work patiently to bring him into the fold. He was also a Presbyterian whom Bryan knew from Philadelphia. Bryan and the council then turned to another Presbyterian and prominent resistance leader, Thomas McKean, who accepted the chief justice's post on 28 July 1777. Bryan offered the positions of assistant justice and attorney general to the Presbyterians John Evans and Jonathan Dickinson Sergeant, respectively, both of whom accepted.[30] Ironically, had the anticonstitutionalists initially filled the posts offered to them by the government and then remained in their elected positions, they probably would have commanded a majority and could have forced a second convention. But their tactics, perhaps gratifying for the moment, allowed Bryan and his party to recruit partisans and entrench them into civil and military positions throughout the state. In the event, Bryan turned to many of his coreligionists to flesh out his government. That strategy was no accident; these were the people he knew and trusted. At some point, however, the Constitutionalist party became identified in the public mind with Presbyterianism and with the German Reformed church, a fellow Calvinist faith. Why that identification occurred remains unclear. That Bryan would be responsible for that image is unlikely; however, he may have unwittingly helped it along by relying on his friends to fill government posts.

In July 1777 Philadelphians learned that Howe had landed at the head of the Chesapeake and was marching north toward the city. Guns, wagons, and blankets had to be procured immediately, and the county militia had to be called out and marched to Chester County. Wharton and Bryan turned their attention toward coordinating the state's armed forces, as well as cooperating with the Continental army.[31] The threat of invasion, however, heightened political tensions, and in the sudden emergency forces within the Continental Congress and the council decided to remove from the city "disaffected" persons "inimical to the cause of America." In early

August congress ordered the removal of former royal officials from Pennsylvania and then, led by John Adams, Richard Lee, and William Duer, broadened the list to include many prominent Quakers. While Pennsylvania and congressional authorities wrestled over responsibility for evacuating and maintaining the prisoners, the congress—after Bryan's continued prodding—ordered the arrest and removal to Stanton, Virginia, of John Penn, Benjamin Chew, and other individuals, mainly Quakers.[32]

Bryan's precise role in the arrest and internment of the Quakers and the royal officers remains unknown for lack of specific evidence, but he apparently was instrumental in the seizure and confinement of the "disaffected."[33] Although their arrest lacked any legal cause, Bryan focused only on their potential for treason; in his mind, legal niceties at such a juncture were outweighed by strategic considerations. Commenting on the arrest of Penn and Chew, Bryan revealed that he considered them "subjects of the state of Britain," and believed that they had been given enough time to either retire or renounce the king. Yet here they were, observed an incredulous Bryan, "going at large among us, in short, as adherents of the enemy." For Bryan, those men should be "liable to restraint as prisoners of the war." Rather harshly, Bryan doubted that they were "entitled to the privileges of the constitution."[34] With this viewpoint, therefore, and acting upon the resolve of congress, Bryan ordered the arrest of forty individuals, many of whom hurriedly swore an oath to secure their release. Twenty Quakers, however, true to their principles, refused the oath, and Bryan ordered their seizure and imprisonment at the freemason's lodge in Philadelphia. The twenty men appealed but were informed by Bryan that their complaint would not be heard. On 9 September the council ordered the immediate removal of the prisoners to Reading and from there to Virginia. Thomas McKean issued writs of habeas corpus, but on 6 September 1777 the assembly removed the last obstacle to their banishment by suspending their right to habeas corpus. Bryan ordered the militia along the route to Virginia to provide every assistance to the prisoners' guard.[35]

Despite the obvious legal injustice in the summary arrest and removal of the Quakers, there was little outcry over their fate; Bryan was certainly not alone in his attitude toward potential treason. The state's president, Thomas Wharton, Jr., supported the measures even though his cousin Thomas Wharton, Sr., was one of the twenty men transported. Many members of congress were openly hostile to the plight of the Quakers, and the prisoners recorded that angry and insulting crowds greeted them frequently on their march into exile. Congressional delegate James Lovell recalled that "Israel and the tribe" had been willing to assume military measures against the Paxton marchers but now pretended to pacifism while seeking relief from a constitution they opposed.[36] Yet despite the heightened antagonism caused by the frenzied chaos of war and invasion, many Whigs, including Bryan, feared that the opposition to independence and the war on the part of the Quakers could still undermine the course of the revolution. Only two years before, the Quaker party, and the wealthy Quaker community that supported it, controlled the government and society—as they had for eighty years. Their arrest and exile represented a critical shock to the political power of the Quaker party, and subsequent legislation requiring affirmations of loyalty forever ended any potential for a resumption of that party's former status. No doubt Bryan's personal animosity toward the Quakers conveniently meshed with the necessities of the war, but even so he significantly contributed to Pennsylvania's successful internal revolution as well as to its separation from the imperial crown. In the event, the exiles remained in Virginia until the following spring, when they were released upon orders from congress. The detainees had petitioned the executive council, which in turn recommended to congressional authorities that the exiles be discharged.

On 13 September 1777 Philadelphians read Washington's grim report that the battle of Brandywine had been lost. The town crier hastily pleaded with citizens to close up their homes and shops, but panicked residents and wounded soldiers converged onto the streets in an effort either to escape or to hide from the advancing British. Congress abandoned the city for York, while the executive council quickly followed suit and headed for Lancaster. Bryan gathered his family and made for Lancaster, stopping en route in Reading to visit the Rev. James Sproat, his friend from calmer days.[37]

Between March and September 1777 Wharton and Bryan had attempted to stabilize a state government under unremitting attack from the anticonstitutionalists. Between October 1777 and June 1778 they would contend with the continued obstructionist tactics of their political opponents while the state's principal city was in enemy hands.

IV

Bryan proved to be one of the Constitutionalists' primary leaders, providing direction and influencing important members of the community to join the radical government.[38] Yet in practical terms, his influence within the party itself was confined by the limitations of the Constitutionalists. Loosely organized, the Constitutional Society, established in the winter of 1779 and an outgrowth of the Whig Society begun in March 1777, was more of a faction than a "party," lacking as it did a central governing authority and consisting mainly of small cliques of men intersecting on a variety of common levels. The legendary tenacity that characterized the political behavior of the Constitutionalists during the 1780s was principally a feature of the western counties and developed after the party had been shorn of significant support from the southeastern portion of the state.[39] During the late 1770s, however, as the party encompassed partisans from throughout the state, political consensus was more difficult to achieve. Constitutionalist assemblymen from 1776 to 1779, for example, were united on specific legislative issues, but in their overall voting patterns they revealed a very loose affiliation.[40] Bryan's role in the party, therefore, was as one voice, albeit a significant one, among many voices; he was nearly always highly supportive of many of the controversial features of the Constitutionalists, but at the same time he appeared to exert a moderating influence among his peers. That role was reminiscent of his years in Presbyterian politics; in the First Presbyterian Church and with the Constitutionalists, he was very partisan for their growth and expansion, yet he also envisioned himself as the voice of moderation, anxious to form a common ground upon which all participants could stand. This enigmatic aspect of his personality was almost schizophrenic, for he perceived himself as able to maintain both unbridled zeal and reasoned compromise—to be, in effect, the outspoken partisan and the quiet negotiator. The effect of this dichotomy was mixed, but in any case Bryan brought the full force of his dynamic personality to Pennsylvania politics, giving it shape during the turbulent period of the revolution.

A glimpse into Bryan's political leadership can be caught through his role in two significant issues, the imposition of loyalty oaths and the calling of a second constitutional convention. In each of these episodes the Constitutionalists were confronted with tremendous pressures, reflecting heightened anxiety over the war and conflicting political philosophies among the populace and the politicians. The party waxed and waned on both issues, however, as it attempted to conform to outside forces and internal pressures. The end result was Constitutionalist vacillation.

The first crisis over loyalty oaths began with the constitutional requirement that assemblymen take an oath to support the government and to avoid "any act or thing whatever, that shall have a tendency to lessen or abridge their rights and privileges as declared in the constitution."[41] Anti-constitutionalists immediately complained that the oath prevented assemblymen from working for the adoption of a new constitution. The Whig response was equivocal: some partisans readily agreed with the opposition, and demanded compliance or resignation,[42] while others believed that the oath was not an impediment to any assemblyman's wish to work for a new frame of government.[43] Desperate for a quorum, however, the Constitutionalist-dominated assembly in 1777 and 1778 allowed the anticonstitutionalists to take an oath other than the one prescribed by the constitution.[44] Although the need for a quorum prevailed, those Constitutionalists who objected to the compromise and yielded the point did so grudgingly, less as a measure of moderation than as an act of restraint.

The test laws provided a similar challenge to the Constitutionalists. The premise behind the prescribed declarations of loyalty was the assumption that "allegiance and protection" were "reciprocal," and that tests were intended to ensure that those who did not "bear the former" would not be "entitled to the benefits of the latter." On more practical terms the acts were also intended to eliminate from the electorate those who did not support the revolution. The first Test Act, passed in June 1777, demanded that citizens swear an oath or make an affirmation of allegiance to Pennsylvania and disavow any loyalty to the king.[45] Those men who refused to take the test were barred from holding public office, sitting on juries, suing for debts, purchasing land, or voting. In response to the disturbingly visible signs of Toryism during the occupation of Philadelphia, however, and as a result of the painful and costly war, the Constitutionalist-controlled assembly in April 1778 passed a harsher Test Act.[46] In addition to the previous restrictions, double taxes were imposed on nonjurors; furthermore, those men who continued in their refusal were to forfeit their real estate to their heirs and be banished from the state forever. In addition, nonjurors who were employed in education, medicine, or the legal profession were to be fined £500 and forced out of their positions. The 1778 Test Act no longer confined itself to ensuring the success of the revolution, but sought to punish those who would not, or could not for religious reasons, conform to the standards of loyalty demanded by the Constitutionalists. Under pressure, however, from the anticonstitutionalists, who despised the test acts, the Constitutionalists in November 1778 agreed to a series of compromises, including the abolition of double taxes, banishment, and fines for holding certain occupations.[47] Determined forces within the Constitutionalist party, however, refused to accept the compromise and began agitating for its retraction. Emblematic of their internal dissension, the Constitutionalists in October 1779 partially abandoned their commitment to the compromise and imposed a final deadline for all citizens to take the oath or be barred for life from the benefits of citizenship.[48]

The Constitutionalists reacted in the same ambivalent manner over the calling of a second constitutional convention. In March 1777 the party agreed, under pressure, that in October 1777 it would "take the sense of the majority of electors throughout the counties" as to whether or not a new convention should be convened. The position was endorsed by the Whig Society. But in September Howe was rapidly closing upon Philadelphia, and the assembly under Constitutionalist control suspended the October referendum, leaving little indication that it would be revived under more favorable circumstances.[49] During the period of compromise in November 1778 the two sides agreed on a March 1779 public vote on a proposed constitutional convention, but in February 1779 forces within the party flooded the assembly with petitions demanding the cancellation of the March ballot. The assembly, overawed, acquiesced by a sizable majority.[50]

Bryan faithfully supported the justification offered by the Constitutionalists for the test acts, and he was an ardent champion of the 1776 constitution. The difficulty for Bryan, however, was to balance his own partisan support for those measures while seeking accommodation through compromise. Although he defended the necessity of the test acts and supported banishment from the political society of those who refused to uphold the revolution and independence, he also favored leniency in the execution of the acts. After the passage of the April 1778 Test Act, Bryan advised county lieutenants to use caution and not to harass Moravians, Mennonites, and Schwenkfelders, who had consistently refused to take the test. Their opposition to the tests was based on their refusal to renounce previous oaths of loyalty to the king until they were specifically released from that obligation by the king himself. Although irritated with the religious societies, castigating them as "ignorant" and stressing that the law stated clearly that they could not be excused from taking the oath, Bryan hoped that the disaffected elements would become "better satisfied of the establishment of our cause," and that their objections would "gradually wear away." That could not be made to happen, argued Bryan, by throwing them in jail or seizing their property. Furthermore, as those pacifist sects were "not to be feared, either as to numbers or malice," and as continued prosecution of them would result in the charge of "cruelty" against the "state," Bryan made it perfectly clear that county officials were to leave them alone. Moreover, Bryan was quick to threaten officials with punitive action if they misapplied the legal sanctions against nonjurors.[51]

In one instance, however, Bryan's advice angered the county lieutenant of Northampton, John Weitzel, who insisted that all citizens be treated equally under the law. Shortly after Weitzel's reply to Bryan, Northampton County officials offered the oath to members of one of the county's Mennonite communities. Motivated by their religious principles, the Mennonites refused the oath, as county officials anticipated. Twelve Mennonites were subsequently ordered to leave the state and surrender their property to their heirs. Despite Vice President Bryan's previous order to leave the Mennonites alone, the council on 1 July ordered the sheriff of the county to execute the law against the twelve offenders. The order of the council may have reflected a divided opinion among its members, with Bryan in the minority, but more probably it reflected the sense of the council that the law, once put into operation by the Northampton County officials, had to be executed for fear of embarrassing the state.[52]

Bryan proudly defended the Test Act of 1779, noting that the Constitutionalists had "relaxed" the various penalties imposed on nonjurors "as far as was thought prudent," while Maryland and Virginia, by comparison, continued "stiff in treble taxes" in their punishment of the disaffected. Arguing for toleration of the nonjurors, Bryan recalled that "twenty years relaxation and kindness to the Highlander sects did more to bring them over to the house of Brunswick" than did former measures of "severities." By contrast, he added, the Irish Catholics were still "internal foes" to England because "the laws make them so, as new generations rise."[53]

Bryan drew a strict line, however, between those who refused to take an oath of allegiance for religious reasons and those who betrayed their allegiance to the state, or supported the enemy. Angered at the rampant Toryism in Philadelphia during the occupation, Bryan with other party leaders believed that it was the paramount duty of the government to punish some of the more notorious offenders as an example to others. As acting president of the state, Bryan signed a proclamation condemning more than one hundred men for treason and declaring their properties forfeited to the state of Pennsylvania. In another instance, six men were accused of deserting the state's navy, four of whom were subsequently convicted of desertion and aiding the enemy. The council was heavily petitioned to spare the condemned, but Bryan argued that it was impossible for the state and citizenry to be expected to continue to support the revolution if "examples" were not made of some of the traitors. "Whatever the feelings the members of council may have as men," responded Bryan, the councillors were "bound by their station to perform some of the arduous duties of magistrates." The death penalty was removed for two of the convicted, but petitions of mercy for the remaining two were denied. They were executed.[54]

The position of Bryan vis-à-vis the test acts and the treatment of traitors is revealing. Bryan attempted to establish a moderate policy within the general construct of the test acts. While upholding the right of a state at war to ascertain the loyalty of its inhabitants and to take punitive actions against those who refused to cooperate, Bryan personally believed that toleration toward the disaffected would ultimately ensure their obedience. But by upholding the state's right to enact test acts, he indicated clearly that at some point they also had to be enforced. Consequently, for individuals outside the parameters of the Constitutionalist party Bryan's moderation remained indistinguishable from extremism. Yet within the party, Bryan's position ironically reflected more accurately the opinions of an eastern, urban politician more comfortable with diversity and open to compromise. The western wing proved to be less conciliatory. As John Armstrong explained, Bryan's desire to relax the penal laws might have been a good idea, but he doubted that the western counties would be so receptive.[55] By 1785 Bryan was arguing for the repeal of the test laws while recognizing the difficulty in persuading other Constitutionalists to agree.[56]

In the compromise of November 1778, both parties in the assembly had agreed to elect Joseph Reed and George Bryan as president and vice president, respectively, for the following year in exchange for a March 1779 plebiscite on a constitutional convention.[57] Presumably both Reed and Bryan, city politicians, agreed to the compromise, but the petitions that ended the agreement were principally from the western counties.[58] A growing rift was developing between urban and rural Constitutionalists over the extent to which each group perceived the need to compromise. The eastern Constitutionalists were more flexible regarding a second convention, but a Lancaster party member announced that many people there were considerably unhappy over the assembly resolves and intended to oppose them. Furthermore, he continued that those of the western parts of the state "would think ourselves very happy if the good people of the city of Philadelphia would act in concert with us."[59] This disagreement did not suggest that the party in 1778 was in a weakened position; quite the contrary, its harsh stance against the Tories and the disaffected during the war contributed significantly to its popularity throughout the state. But apparently the leadership of the Constitutionalists was not always unified, and consequently the party would lack consistency—for which it would ultimately suffer.

6

THE YEARS OF POWER
War and the Politics of Revolution

WHILE PARTISAN POLITICS OCCUPIED much of his attention, Bryan was thrust into the core of the war crisis by his membership on the executive council. Besieged by enemies on many fronts, Bryan and the council struggled to keep armies in the field, to maintain law and order, and above all to keep the revolution alive.

Between 1 October 1777 and 20 June 1778 Pennsylvania's government, like the Continental Congress, was forced to conduct its business in the crowded confines of Lancaster, while Howe's army enjoyed the comforts of Philadelphia. Huddled in their various temporary headquarters, state politicians, militia officers, federal delegates, and Washington's tattered army watched and waited while the capital lay occupied. Tempers flared as frustrations mounted. Many in Pennsylvania were discouraged after the humiliating defeats at Brandywine and Germantown, doubting whether Washington's army was capable of victory. Believing that Washington could have done more to dislodge the enemy, Bryan, Christopher Marshall, and others (including the anticonstitutionalist Benjamin Rush) flirted with the idea of creating a state army for the purpose of recapturing Philadelphia. Perhaps the stark realization of what such a move would entail sobered them; in any event, Bryan, Marshall, Rush, and the others never consummated the idea, and Bryan and his fellow state leaders grimly accepted their desperate circumstances.[1]

To meet the emergency, the Supreme Executive Council on 17 October 1777 expanded its membership and powers and transformed itself into a Council of Safety until the assembly could convene in early December. Bryan regularly attended council meetings, except for two months between late February and late April. Bryan's absence for those two months remains a mystery. Given his bouts of ill health at various points in his life and the tremendous stress he was under, Bryan may well have been ill, but evidence of his whereabouts is elusive. Under Wharton's presidency Bryan was a principal participant, forming part of an inner circle of council leadership. In May 1778, however, Wharton became seriously ill, and he died later that month. According to the constitution Bryan, as second officer of the government, was authorized to assume full control, which he did with little difficulty, although he continued to style himself as vice president. Because of Bryan's extensive legal and recent executive experience, he moved swiftly and easily into leadership of the state, displaying a comfortable disposition in the exercise of power. The transition to chief executive went smoothly, except for the innocent but tactless inquiry of Thomas McKean to Bryan: "Why did not the General Assembly choose a new president?"[2]

Bryan was confronted immediately with the expansion of the war in the western and northern counties. Indians and their British allies struck at the frontier settlements of Cumberland County in May 1778, and in June the Indian war spread to Northumberland and Northampton counties.[3] Fortunately for Pennsylvania and Bryan's government, the British army, commanded now by Sir Henry Clinton, had decided to evacuate Philadelphia and return to New York.[4] Pennsylvania had escaped a two-front war. "As soon as General Clinton goes off," Bryan assured the lieutenant of Northumberland County, "assistance will be sent from the main army." Bryan added that an attack was planned "against the Indian towns," and that troops were being levied for the purpose.[5]

The effort to defend the frontiers, however, fell victim to the usual difficulties that plagued the local and federal war effort. Money and supplies were scarce. Bryan suspected that congress was reluctant to assume any responsibility for the protection of the frontiers and sharply reminded congressmen that because the Indian invasion was a part of British strategy Pennsylvania should be supported "by the force & money of the United States." He demanded to know whether or not "Congress mean to pay & victual the militia, necessarily embodied on the western frontiers." He badgered the Continental army's board of war for more supplies, believing that previous shipments were "insufficient" and that since Pennsylvania could not possibly supply the requisite number of guns congress had to intervene with arms from its stores.[6]

Despite these efforts, supplies and arms remained difficult to obtain. Even when obtained, there were difficulties. The board of war complained that powder previously sent had been wasted by the local militias, and that cartridges distributed to the men earlier were missing when the militia appeared for duty in the spring. "It would be a most valuable acquisition," Timothy Pickering of the board advised, if Bryan could "devise some measure to put a stop to this fatal mischief."[7] Other problems hampered the defense effort. The initial calls for militia proved to be ineffective because only a few men, predominantly weaponless, reported. Also, the militia's pay was often late, and there were personality clashes over command appointments.[8]

As the Indians pressed forward, the defenses of the counties collapsed. "More arms and ammunition," pleaded the lieutenant of Northumberland County, would be "very necessary to quiet the minds of the people, as there is a great many more that will use arms in their own defense than we have enrolled in the militia."[9] Despite Bryan's effort to mobilize the state's forces, however, he could not offset the reality of reduced resources and manpower. "The accounts you give of your situation, and of the horrid murders of the savages are truly affecting," consoled a despondent Bryan, but while regretful that "the country and the public stores" were so unfurnished of weapons "in this exigence," he could only comment: "but so it is." Bryan hoped that the removal of Clinton's army would relieve the militia of the eastern counties for duty in the north and west.[10]

Relief would not come soon enough, however, to save the northern tier of Northumberland and the Wyoming Valley. Alarming dispatches arrived daily describing the advances of the Indians and the British Tories. By 14 June 1778 the council learned that communications had been cut off between Fort Augusta and Lycoming, and that the inhabitants were fleeing their homes. In early July the council was stunned to hear that Wyoming had been destroyed and that those inhabitants unable to escape had been slaughtered.[11] With Clinton out of Pennsylvania, the council and the board of war finally agreed on a plan of action. On 14 July Bryan notified the county lieutenants that Continental troops under Colonels Hartley and Brodhead were marching toward Sunbury, Northumberland County, and that it would be necessary to augment those troops with local forces. Bryan consequently ordered out the militia from Cumberland, Northampton, and Berks counties in anticipation of an attack on the Indians in August; but, typical of the difficulties in organizing the actions of the state militia, Hartley's advance into Indian territory would not occur until October.[12]

The war along the frontier would not end until 1782, although the fiercest attacks by the Indians took place in the spring and summer of 1778.

Neither the state nor the Continental forces were very effective against the Indians, and they were unable to sufficiently reverse their early losses. Settlers slowly returned to their farms, but often after the loss of family, friends, or property. Bryan, as acting president and as vice president under Reed, would continue to organize the supply of provisions and arms to the northern and western front. In July 1779 generals John Sullivan and James Clinton led Continental forces into Wyoming and as far north as New York in order to break the spirit of the Indians. But their success was modest at best. Not until the British were defeated, as Bryan anticipated in the summer of 1778, would the Indian war come to an end. If the British could be reduced by force, Bryan had commented, it would "undoubtedly be attended with the most salutary effects in removing the enemy from the frontiers; as it cannot be doubted that they must see the impossibility of their . . . success."[13]

Nor was the war the only business impinging upon Bryan's time and energy. His executive council served in many cases as a clearinghouse for processing information to the county and provincial officers. Bryan was also frequently called upon to define the specifics of legislative enactments, although he once confessed that the "construction of acts of assembly" required a "greater knowledge of the law" than members of the council could "pretend to." The arresting of traitors and the seizing of their estates, the provisioning of Washington's army, and the endless other details of administration consumed much of the time of Bryan and the council.[14]

In August and November 1778 Bryan and the council formally laid before the assembly various proposed measures. Bryan argued for the establishment of an admiralty jurisdiction and a court of errors and appeal, the reestablishment of the provincial courts in Philadelphia, and laws to secure titles and deeds and to cope with other technical matters. He also argued for more money and for the more efficient collection of those taxes already levied. Although suggesting that money raised through fees from taverns, sales of forfeited estates, and fines for refusing to serve in the militia would provide some relief, Bryan admitted that such incremental revenues would not compensate for all the state's debts or those of the confederation, which Pennsylvania was bound "jointly with them to extinguish." Without increased taxation, observed Bryan, all schemes "to restrain or cure the depreciation of the paper-money" would be in vain. The assembly was collecting its $620,000 quota assigned by congress in 1777, but Bryan asked the legislators to prepare yet another tax bill for new quotas to be imposed. "Honor, interest & duty, urge us to perform our share," pleaded Bryan, especially as congress was releasing more bills of credit to support the

"common defense." In the following April the assembly passed a new revenue act.[15]

Bryan understood, however, that Pennsylvania could scarcely afford to
add to its burden of the war effort. Not only had Pennsylvania supplied its
quota of men and money to the Continental army, but it was also furnish-
ing more than its share of provisions. "Exhausted as we are, the main federal
army cannot depend on the middle states for its sustenance," Bryan announced to the assemblymen, adding that the army should seek its supplies
from the Chesapeake area or New England. In fact, insisted Bryan, rather
than increasing its contribution, Pennsylvania should consider prohibiting
"the distilling of all sorts of corn for six months," in order to prevent further
depletion of the state's dwindling grain supplies.[16]

Trying to administer a war program with decreasing resources, Bryan
was further hampered in his relationship with the national government by
intense partisan politics. During 1779 factionalism within the Continental
Congress was mirrored spiritedly by the state's political parties. The Constitutionalists supported the Samuel Adams–Arthur Lee faction, while the
anticonstitutionalists (called the Republicans in 1779) backed the Governor Morris–Silas Deane group.[17] As the principal officers of the state,
Reed and Bryan initially attempted to maintain a nonpartisan attitude with
Congress relative to the differences, but they were eventually, willingly or
not, drawn into the fray.

The lightning rod of Constitutionalist discontent was the aristocratic
Gen. Benedict Arnold. Timothy Matlack, secretary of the council, engaged
in hostile exchanges with Arnold shortly after the general assumed military
command of the city of Philadelphia.[18] Constitutionalists perceived Arnold
as haughty, patronizing, and insulting and were angered over his deliberate
social associations with known Tories. During the winter of 1779 Bryan,
Matlack, and the council attempted to discredit Arnold, complaining to
congress that he had seized wagons in the name of the military for the
transportation of his personal property and that he had issued passes to
individuals to travel to British-held New York City despite specific denial
of such authority by the council.[19] Bryan leveled other charges as well and
desired congress to court martial the beleaguered general, which, had it
taken place, would have altered the course of history. But congress was
initially unsympathetic to Bryan's pleas, and in a flurry of exchanges in
February and March Bryan and William Paca of Maryland, chairman of
the congressional committee investigating the council's allegations against
Arnold, accused each other of partisanship and political machinations.[20] By
recalling past unpleasantries that had occurred between state and federal

officers, Bryan attempted to bolster the state's charges against Arnold. Exasperated, Bryan then outlined a series of perceived insults against Pennsylvania from an imperious federal government. One recollection included a minor confrontation between Bryan and Charles Thomson over a confiscated house. Thomson, upset over this line of argument, admonished his friend Joseph Reed, president of the council, for allowing anger toward Arnold to distort better judgment.[21] Arnold was eventually cleared of all charges except that involving his misuse of the wagons. He was officially reprimanded by Washington, after which the entire matter was dropped.[22]

Bryan's goals during this period were to meet the needs of local, state, and federal governments and to ensure the success of the revolution while invading armies fought along the northern and western frontiers and throughout southeastern Pennsylvania.[23] The level of social dislocation during the late 1770s was dangerously high. The occupation, the ravages by the Indians, the seizure of wagons and provisions from private citizens by the militia and Continental troops, the militia service for adult males, and the imminent collapse of the economy were some of the centrifugal forces working to pull Pennsylvania apart. Many of the events that occurred in the two and a half years Bryan served as vice president and acting president were beyond his control. Yet despite seemingly insurmountable problems, Bryan (along with Timothy Matlack and several other pivotal council regulars) held the state together and kept the momentum toward independence alive.[24]

II

During 1779 the political tension between the Constitutionalists and the Republicans precipitated an unprecedented crisis. Responding to the anger of Philadelphia militiamen (the core of Constitutionalist support in the city), to a devastated economy, and to the continued partisan assault of the Republicans, Bryan, Reed, and Matlack became fierce defenders of their government and party.

Paper currency repeatedly issued by both the state and federal governments was depreciating at an incredible pace. Prices soared as the value of money plunged.[25] The Reed-Bryan government was initially at a loss for a strategy to resolve the developing catastrophe, but the Constitutionalists were certain about who was responsible for the crisis. In a January 1779 proclamation Reed and Bryan declared that forestallers and engrossers were driving up the prices of all commodities, including bread and "other necessaries of life." Branding such practices as "odious" and "heinously criminal," the council announced that it had commenced prosecutions against offenders and that more prosecutions would be forthcoming.[26] At the height of the crisis in May 1779 several Constitutionalists organized mass meetings to promote extralegal price regulations and to compile lists of suspected profiteering merchants. Encouraged by the popular Constitutionalist orator Daniel Roberdeau, the assembled crowd at one of these gatherings elected a committee to establish fair prices for retail goods and to ensure via extralegal visitations that the fixed prices were not exceeded by the city's merchants and artisans.[27] Enforced price regulation was the Constitutionalist remedy for inflation.

Throughout the summer of 1779, however, tensions rose dramatically as prices continued to soar, scarcity of goods increased, and the value of printed currency collapsed. More meetings were held in July, where the extralegal restrictions on prices and exports were reaffirmed and "The Citizens Plan" was adopted: city residents were to voluntarily contribute money to the congress in order to stablilize paper money. The program was apparently sanctioned by Reed and Bryan, although neither one of them participated in the mass meetings and price-fixing committees.[28] Both men at various times during 1778 and 1779 had declared an embargo on such basic staples as salt and flour and had continued to prohibit their export despite angry complaints from merchants, who pointed out that embargoes, like price fixing, were ruinous to the economy. In the event, Bryan was unsympathetic to the merchants' complaints, Reed acquiesced with his fellow Constitutionalists, and both approved of the extralegal committee's seizure of goods scheduled to be transported out of the state.[29]

By September, however, opposition to the price-fixing committee was substantial, particularly in light of its failure to stabilize the economy. The Constitutionalists were forced to abandon their extralegal committees and price-fixing plans, leaving the economy in no better shape and the citizenry angrier over worsening conditions. Ironically, the summer efforts of the Constitutionalists to provide economic relief held in check the simmering discontent of the laboring and artisan poor and the militia. As it was, the year 1779 had been ushered in by a defiant sailors' strike that was subdued by the presence of federal troops, and between May and August menacing crowds eagerly sought out suspected monopolizers and forestallers to either ridicule or "arrest" them.[30] Increasingly apparent, however, was the fact that the Constitutionalists were not in control of these ungovernable crowds.

The turbulence of street demonstrations and extralegal activity culminated in the October "Fort Wilson" riot, which resulted in several dead and wounded. On 4 October disgruntled militiamen from Germantown marched into the city, seized several merchants, and paraded them through the streets to the beat of the rogues' march. Constitutionalist leaders Charles Willson Peale, Dr. James Hutchinson, and Alexander Boyd had initially attempted to dissuade them from their march but then disassociated themselves from the malcontents when it became apparent that their advice was going unheeded. The militiamen, whose spirits were emboldened by liquor, marched (according to one unsubstantiated source) to the homes of Bryan and Reed to give them three cheers.[31] They then decided to head toward the house of the prominent and outspoken Republican James Wilson, who, along with his friends inside the house, heatedly warned the marchers to leave. An exact account remains elusive, but shots were fired on both sides, and several militiamen broke down Wilson's front door, where further shooting occurred. The fighting continued until President Reed and Timothy Matlack arrived with troops to disperse the hotheaded militiamen. Wilson, however, fled the city and other Republicans retired into the country or maintained a low profile for fear of reprisal.[32]

The Fort Wilson riot in many respects was another significant symbol of the limitations of the Constitutionalists in power, which would ultimately cost them their support from the artisans and less prosperous laborers. After all, the party's economic programs (both legislative and extralegal) had failed to stop the reeling economy, the war and its heavy demands continued seemingly unabated, and now the militia—once the proud symbol of the Constitutionalists—had become a mob force immune to the blandishments of their leaders and in need of restraint. The Constitutionalists in the city appeared therefore as a party no longer in control. Although they had argued willingly for an equitable distribution of the burden of militia duty and relief for the poor, who suffered the most during the war, the Constitutionalists could not sanction the violence demonstrated by the militia on 4 October. Both their inability to control the mob and their ultimate reliance on troops to rescue a prominent Republican leader exposed the limits of their radicalism. In the short run, the Constitutionalists would survive, but in many ways the Fort Wilson riot marked the turning point for the Constitutionalist party in Philadelphia.[33]

The immediate effect of the riot, however, was the very opposite of what eventually happened. Although the militiamen in the riot were suppressed by Reed and Matlack, the anger among many of the people over their wartime conditions was still focused on perceived enemies of the Constitutionalists. With many leading Republicans maintaining a low profile during the uneasy days after the riot, and with loyalty oaths continuing to bar many anticonstitutionalists from voting, the Constitutionalists—still supported by the militia, who cowed the opposition—won a sweeping victory in the assembly elections held several days after the incident. The 1779 election resulted in the largest number of Constitutionalists ever to sit in the assembly.[34] Under these circumstances Bryan, whose council term had expired and who had remained curiously disengaged from the entire Fort Wilson affair, was elected as a representative from the city.[35]

Bryan's prominence within the party was demonstrated clearly by his role in the Fourth General Assembly. He was assigned to a variety of committees, including those that brought in bills for the collection of $2.3 million for the state's contribution to congress, and for the establishment of a high court of errors and appeals, a court for admiralty jurisdiction, and a new land office.[36] The creation of the two higher courts was particularly important to Bryan, who had argued for their establishment as early as 1778.[37] Bryan was also involved in several major pieces of legislation that were of paramount importance to the Constitutionalists: the alteration of the charter of the College of Philadelphia, the seizure of Penn's proprietary lands, and the gradual abolition of slavery.

The College of Philadelphia and the proprietary lands of John Penn were both primary targets of the Constitutionalists. While John Penn's right to govern was effectively terminated in 1776, James Cannon in the constitutional convention that year unsuccessfully attempted in the name of the commonwealth to relieve him also of his vast estates. The delegates, however, rejected his proposed clause to the Pennsylvania Bill of Rights, which had stated that "enormous proportion of property vested in a few Individuals" was "dangerous to the rights, and destructive of the common happiness of mankind," and that the state had the "right by its laws to discourage the possession of such property."[38] Nonetheless, the Reed-Bryan government encouraged the Third General Assembly of 1778 to initiate divestiture proceedings against Penn. While exempting his personal manors, the government claimed that proprietary land was not Penn's private property but rather that of the king and was only under the "administration" of the Penn family. The bill for divestiture was left uncompleted until the sitting of the next assembly.[39]

Bryan voted with the overwhelming majority in the fourth assembly to approve the state's assumption of the proprietary lands. He joined, however, several other Constitutionalists in disagreeing with the majority's position that landowners who still owed money to the proprietor for lands purchased should, under the new law, pay their debts to the state. Observing that the Penn family was to receive compensation of £130,000 sterling one year after the conclusion of the war, Bryan and the minority argued that those debts prior to the passage of the law were "indisputably" the property of the Penn family and further suggested that the proposed compensation was due immediately. Although Bryan and a minority of his party lost the point, the defeat of this view was insufficient to prevent his voting for the bill's final passage.[40]

The College of Philadelphia was the next victim on the heated agenda of the Constitutionalists. The collapse of the November 1778 compromise and the economic crisis beginning in early 1779 stimulated a full-scale partisan war. The college's provost and former nemesis of the 1764 Presbyterian party, the Rev. William Smith, incautiously attacked President Joseph Reed in the newspaper. The college had remained politically neutral throughout the late 1770s, although it was suspected correctly that Smith and many of the school's trustees were either unhappy about independence or were staunch Republicans. The underlying antagonism, however, was the long-standing resentment by Presbyterians toward the predominantly Anglican institution, or, as Reed described it, the "preeminence given to some societies in prejudice to others equally meritorious."[41]

Despite a protesting memorial from William Smith, Bryan and the assembly overwhelmingly voted to gut the college's charter and replace it with a drastically altered version, while also appointing new trustees and officers. The assembly declared that oaths required of the college officers under the previous charter were "totally inconsistent with the independence and constitution" of the state and charged that the trustees corrupted the charter's original intent of a "free and unlimited catholicism." The assembly struck at the college with a vengeance, and Bryan played an integral role in the plan of attack. Several prominent Presbyterians and Constitutionalists, including Bryan, were appointed to the newly styled University of Pennsylvania as trustees, with Reed the new president of the board, the Rev. John Ewing the new provost, David Rittenhouse the new vice provost, and Bryan the new treasurer.[42]

Unity among the Constitutionalists was easily maintained over the clearly partisan issues of the college and Penn's lands, especially as there were so few Republicans in the assembly to oppose them. But the Constitutionalists were less unified over the problem of depreciating paper money and the amending of the militia laws. As previously observed, the paper money emissions of congress began to fall in value at the end of 1778, trading at eight dollars to one dollar specie. By September 1779 the exchange rate was twenty to one, and in January 1780 it fell to forty to one. At the end of 1780 the rate was one hundred Continental dollars to one dollar of specie—if specie holders were willing to make an exchange.[43]

While Republicans blamed the staggering amount of paper currency, the Constitutionalists continued to believe that skyrocketing inflation was the fault of greedy merchants. Bryan perceived that the regulation of prices throughout the entire Union was the answer to the economic crisis. Nor was Pennsylvania alone in this concern. A convention was proposed by seven states, to include all the states as far south as Virginia and to be held in Philadelphia in January 1780, to discuss nationwide price control, and Bryan was at the center of organizing Pennsylvania's participation. On 15 November 1779 a three-man committee in the assembly headed by Bryan examined the convention scheme and on 22 November reported favorably on the plan. The assembly elected Bryan, along with four others, to attend the convention as the commonwealth's commissioners.[44] Benjamin Rush, however, speaking for the Republicans, sarcastically commented that the anxiously anticipated convention would produce "all the miracles of transubstantiation, and all the mysteries of alchemy," and that the commissioners talked "of the appreciation of our paper into real Spanish dollars, as a matter to be performed as easily as . . . by a single resolution of Congress."[45]

The convention was scheduled to meet on 5 January 1780, but by the fifteenth Bryan sensed that something was amiss, for the expected commissioners from other states had not yet arrived.[46] Finally on 22 January the attending delegates concluded that the absent members were not coming and adjourned—the convention was a failure. Plans for a February conference were discussed, but they too proved fruitless.[47]

By the spring, however, Bryan had shifted his position. Discouraged over the deepening economic crisis, many Constitutionalists realized that price regulations were not the answer. In March 1780 Bryan prepared a bill to repeal laws prohibiting monopolizing and forestalling. Furthermore, party leaders from the city noted the lack of enthusiasm for price control among their western allies. Bryan and the Philadelphia Constitutionalists were also no longer in agreement with many of their partisans over the maintenance of "tender" laws, which demanded the legal acceptance of money at face value. The spiraling dollar undermined any attempts to set a firm exchange, and congress was forced to fix the dollar officially at a rate of forty to one while encouraging the states to suspend their tender laws. Many Constitutionalists, however, were upset at congressional actions, insisting that tender legislation remain intact. Those members were adamant against further depreciation and continued to believe that the value of the dollar could be artificially maintained. But Bryan led the argument against them, claiming that debt "contracted without idea of depreciation" was an "outrage on common honesty and common sense." Finally, on a third roll call, enough assemblymen from the center counties sided with the city party members to approve the suspension of the tender laws, a victory for Bryan.[48]

Dissension among the Constitutionalists was also evident over the revamping of the militia laws. On this issue a split occurred between the

Philadelphia members and the assemblymen from the central counties of York and Lancaster. Bryan favored four amendments, all of which were defeated—the exemption of legislators from militia duty, the banning of hired substitutes, the imposition of higher fines for those men neglecting to serve, and the levying of discriminatory penalties on wealthier citizens for nonattendance.[49] Bryan was still reflecting the views of the militant city militiamen, who for the past several years had been protesting their grievances. That those views were defeated by western and central county Constitutionalists boded ill for the party in the city.

The division within the party over the militia and tender laws reflected a more serious crisis that was developing among Constitutionalists. The price regulation movement of 1779 had been a total disaster, both on the local and national level. The city Constitutionalists believed that price controls would solve inflation and at the same time solidify the party's base of support. In fact, the opposite occurred. Price regulations drove the artisans out of the party: they complained immediately that ceilings on prices would bankrupt them because they had no control over the costs of the goods they purchased.[50] Although Bryan and the party reversed themselves on price controls, the political damage had already occurred.[51]

As the economic crisis worsened, many voters lost faith in the party's leadership, and in a stunning defeat city residents in the October 1780 elections voted out all of the Constitutionalist representatives, replacing them with Republicans. Such prominent Constitutionalists as Peale, Hutchinson, and William Hollinshead were ousted in favor of Robert Morris, Sharp Delaney, and F. A. Muhlenberg. In Philadelphia County, the voters reduced by half (from six to three) the number of Constitutionalist assemblymen. Only in the western and central counties did the Constitutionalists maintain their strength. For the next six years the balance of power would shift several times between the two parties, but Philadelphia city would be effectively in the hands of the Republicans.

Bryan did not remain in the assembly long enough to taste defeat like his compatriots. In an apparently preconceived strategy, President Reed and the executive council on 3 April 1780 took into consideration "the state of the supreme court" and concluded that another associate justice was required. Bryan was offered the position, which he accepted immediately, receiving his commission on 5 April.[52] Having become a passionate devotee of the law, the forty-eight-year-old Bryan had achieved his greatest judicial honor by becoming the high court's fourth justice. Ironically, had he not become a state supreme court justice his political career would probably have been terminated, the Republicans dominating Philadelphia politics throughout the 1780s.

III

While a member of the assembly, Bryan had brought to the fore the issue of slavery in Pennsylvania. Perhaps no other achievement in his political career was more significant than his unrelenting determination to abolish slavery in the state. Describing the freeing of the slaves as an act of "justice," Bryan observed that "humanity and policy" were advanced while destroying an institution that was "disgraceful to our nation."[53] Through his untiring efforts, the Pennsylvania assembly on 25 March 1780 passed a law providing for the eventual elimination of slavery in the state, the first of its kind in America.[54] Bryan's authorship of the law and his labors to secure its passage were verified by his friend and political ally, the Rev. John Ewing. Amid the "rage and clamour of party," the "tumult of war and invasion," and "despite innumerable prejudices," recalled Ewing, George Bryan "planned and executed the 'act for the gradual abolition of slavery.' "[55]

In this goal, Bryan was motivated by revolutionary ideology—the steadfast belief that slavery was totally incompatible with the rhetoric of the natural rights of man. Yet Bryan knew he had to manipulate the political process skillfully in order to achieve abolition. An adroit politician, Bryan understood that timing was the essential factor in the success of his endeavors. As acting president in August 1778, Bryan speculated that because the assembly and the executive council were controlled by the Constitutionalist faction, the time was propitious for introducing abolition. He hinted at his motives when he advised the assembly of the many "mischiefs" resulting from "the importation of slaves" into the state and of the reasonable expectation that the "scarcity of labourers" would be relieved by the "flow of new comers from Europe."[56] A member of the assembly, acting in concert with Bryan, introduced in August 1778 an abolition bill, but because it was late in the session the bill was tabled. Returning to the proposal in November 1778, Bryan urged the new assembly to consider his plans for abolition. Arguing that gradual emancipation would be an "easy mode" for ending Negro servitude, he pointed out that the bill did not "meddle" with the "present slaves, most of whom were scarcely competent of freedom." Bryan stressed to the legislators that the time was right to end slavery in Pennsylvania: "This or some better scheme would tend to abrogate slavery, the opprobrium of America, from among us, and no period seems more happy for the attempt than the present, as the number of such unhappy characters, ever few in Pennsylvania, has been much reduced by the practices & plunder of our late invaders."[57]

Demonstrating his belief that abolition was not only practical but morally correct, Bryan reminded the assemblymen that abolition offered to "God one of the most proper and best returns of gratitude for his great deliverance of us and our posterity from thraldom." Bryan hoped to intimidate those whose revolutionary sentiments were less firm by observing that Europeans were astonished to see "a people eager for liberty holding negroes in bondage."[58] Additional pressure from Bryan and the executive council in February 1779 resulted in the establishment of a house committee, which brought an abolition bill to the assembly floor in the following March.[59]

The proposed bill granted freedom to those slaves born after a specified date—for females after they had reached the age of eighteen, for males after age twenty-one. The bill also mandated that all slaves were to be registered by their owners with the county government within six months of passage of the bill; otherwise the courts were to recognize unregistered slaves as automatically free upon reaching adulthood. Furthermore, the bill repealed the slave code of 1726 and prohibited the further importation of slaves. Mixed marriages were to remain illegal, however, and the practice of binding out unemployed blacks as laborers would be continued.[60]

The third assembly ignored the abolition bill, either because of resistance to abolition or because it was simply overwhelmed by issues of inflation and invasion. Not until Bryan entered the Fourth General Assembly as a representative from the city of Philadelphia would emancipation succeed. He understood that the weight of legislative business was not the only reason for the bill's failure in the previous assembly; sufficient opposition existed against it. But as a recognized leader of the party, Bryan parlayed his power and prestige into constructing a coalition of proabolition assemblymen able to withstand the opposition's disapproval. Heading a new committee to prepare a second abolition bill, Bryan reported a proposal to the house in November 1779.[61]

On 18 November Bryan's abolition bill won an easy procedural vote, thirty-eight to eight, followed by a second victory, forty to eighteen, on a similar motion on 15 February 1780. On 1 March the bill was passed into law, thirty-four to twenty-one.[62] Support for the act had apparently faltered as the opposition steadily grew. Nonetheless, a core group consistently supported the measure—thirty-six members voted in favor on all participating roll calls, while two members reversed their votes from negative to positive. Initially supporting abolition, however, were twelve members who changed their positions and joined the opposition by the third roll call.[63] Of the total number favoring abolition, nineteen proabolition members were Constitutionalists from the southeastern portion of the state (Philadelphia city and Philadelphia, Bucks, and Chester counties), while six assemblymen from Cumberland County also voted steadily for emancipation. For those whose religious affiliations can be identified, nineteen Presbyterians supported abolition while eleven opposed it; only one German Lutheran and one German Reformed assemblyman supported abolition, while four German Lutherans and three German Reformed assemblymen voted in opposition. Perhaps of equivalent or greater significance, of thirty-five proabolitionist members only twelve were slaveholders, while of the twenty-three antiabolitionist members sixteen were slaveholders.[64]

Although no evidence exists to determine which assemblymen's votes were affected, Bryan had made a major concession to ensure passage of the bill. He agreed to extend to twenty-eight the age that a slave of either sex needed to reach before becoming free. The effect was dramatic: the additional time added ten years of servitude for a female and seven years for a male beyond the original proposal of 1779. As if to offset the increase, the law dropped prohibitions against interracial marriages. The slave code of 1726 was repealed, the importation of slaves was prohibited, and the stipulation that only those slaves born after the passage of the act (1 March 1780) would be eligible for freedom was continued from the 1779 bill. Also, slaves not registered by 1 November 1780 were eligible for their freedom upon adulthood, regardless of the date of their birth.[65]

Bryan felt compelled to make concessions to the slaveholding interests, as well as to the prejudices of nonslaveholders, in order to secure the passage of his gradual emancipation law. While the law did not free one single slave at the moment of its enactment it was still a remarkable achievement, particularly since emancipation did not gain for Bryan or his party any political advantages or increased status among the electorate. Although Bryan claimed that abolition astonished and pleased the Quakers, who "looked for no such benevolent issue of our new government, exercised by Presbyterians," he understood keenly that the law would not win any Quaker voters to the Constitutionalists.[66] Bryan, in fact, ran the risk of dividing the Constitutionalists. Although many Presbyterians supported abolition, others did not. As one political colleague advised Bryan: "The law for freeing of negroes hereafter born in my opinion does honor to your House, but perhaps I only think so because I have no slaves, and inclined never to keep any, but such who have them think otherwise. Self interest is a partial judge of things."[67]Another party member and friend to Bryan, however, expressed his dissatisfaction with the final version of the law, querying the moral difference between gradual and immediate emancipation. For a "child to be born the day before the passing of the act" and "to be held in slavery—slavery for life," remarked Bryan's ally, had the "least color of justice."[68]

Presbyterian opposition to abolition concerned Bryan, who set out to convince those of his religious brethren who were antiabolitionist that their zeal was misplaced.[69] The consummate politician, Bryan reminded Presbyterians, most of whom were Constitutionalists, that abolition would become law. The plan had obtained "such an ascendancy over the mind of the public," Bryan advised, that the bill was "secure of success." It was "irksome," however, to discover that those few men who opposed the bill were generally "members of the Presbyterian churches," who were otherwise "remarkable for their zeal, and for their exertions in the cause of freedom."[70]

Bryan was especially annoyed at the Presbyterian memorialists who claimed that perpetual bondage was sanctioned by Moses and therefore was not objectionable to the will of God. "If precedents from the law of Moses were proper in our times," remarked an incredulous Bryan, then adulterers "must be punished by death," the rebellious son would be put to death, wives could be murdered by their husbands, and polygamy, by inference, would be legal. "Yet such inhumanities would be reprobated by everyone," concluded Bryan, who added that those "depravities" were an "atrocious wickedness, such as no cultivated people ever relapsed into at once." Bryan perceived such biblical arguments as anachronistic and contrary to the purpose of revolution. But he realized the depth of such feeling and dedicated three columns of newspaper print to his counterarguments, citing the law of Jesus and the apostles in an effort to show that there was nothing Christian about slavery. For slavery to be permissible by the law of God, declared Bryan, the people must first "erase the great Christian precept; 'do unto others, as you would that they should do unto you.'"[71] Hoping to embarrass his coreligionists, Bryan countered: "What! Shall Quakers, who we think have but clouded views of the gospel, have nearly cleared their society of this opprobrium of America, and shall any Presbyterian continue so void of charity and justice, as to wish and labor for the continuance of it[?]"[72]

Aside from what he viewed as irrelevant biblical arguments, Bryan was also confronted with the supposedly "practical" reasons for slavery presented by the memorialists. On this point, Bryan expanded the scope of his reply to include all antiabolitionists. Responding to the claim that slavery benefited a race of people who were naturally "indolent and helpless," Bryan observed that such an "objection, if good for any thing, would also justify the enslaving of all poor whites of slender understandings and inactive dispositions."[73] More to the point, replied Bryan, slavery destroyed "industry, care and often times every virtue." Servants for life had no incentive for such qualities as "honesty and obedience," and the "whip alone" was the only compulsion for a slave's good conduct. But such an option was as evil for the society as it was for the slave. "Slaves in a free state especially" would be "bad subjects," Bryan reminded his opponents, because they were "held by violence," and therefore would always be "internal enemies." Furthermore, slavery made labor "dishonorable" and transformed "masters and their children" into "lazy, proud, arrogant and cruel" people. Bryan presaged northern abolitionists of the nineteenth century with his comment that a traveler "into the southern states" would be "shocked at the train of mischiefs, moral and political," caused by perpetual servitude. Yet Bryan added dejectedly that he found too many individuals who were "intoxicated" with the "baneful depression of their fellow man."[74]

The ultimate sanction against slavery for Bryan, however, was its incompatibility with revolutionary ideology and the democratic state. The republic should have neither a "nobility" nor "inferior inhabitants," Bryan argued, because the strength of any society lay in "equal privileges" for all citizens, no matter how they differed "as rich and poor." Slavery, like monarchy, violated Bryan's view of the true commonwealth. Envisioning a land filled with "hardy, diligent and enlightened citizens" and a society "established in peace, liberty and safety," Bryan foresaw a Pennsylvania republic dominated by laborers, merchants, artisans, and farmers, all wealthy according to their talents. Ostentatious riches and the arrogant assumptions of power and prestige that accompanied them were as obnoxious to Bryan as slavery. Each evil, in its own way, disturbed the harmony within a society of industrious freeholders. "Among us," observed Bryan, no service was "required of slaves" that could not be done "by the citizens." Furthermore, Bryan predicted that at the conclusion of the war European laborers and artisans, "qualified for every purpose," would stream into America in order to enjoy "the benefits of liberty and independence."[75] A shortage of laborers therefore was not a valid argument. Most important, Bryan was arguing his perception of the development of the American political economy, not through the economies of slave labor but through the increase of European workers who would become America's "middling class." They would be men and women whose experiences would resemble his own.

Bryan put forth other arguments to buttress his views. In his attempt to persuade the populace to accept abolition, he played upon the sensibilities of Pennsylvanians in their own struggle against Britain. "We rejoice that it is in our power," he exclaimed, "to extend a portion of that freedom to others, which we ourselves were tyrannically doomed, and from which we have now every prospect of being delivered." Bryan continued that it was a "peculiar blessing granted to us, that we are enabled this day to add one more step to universal civilization by removing as much as possible the sorrows of those who have lived in undeserved bondage." Further, while Bryan chastised the "few and interested" slaveholders who persisted in their opposition to freedom for the slaves, no matter how gradual the emancipation, he preferred to encourage white society in supporting abolition. Rather than condemn white society for its previous toleration of slavery, Bryan—a former slaveholder himself—claimed that Pennsylvanians would find their "hearts enlarged with kindness and benevolence towards men of all conditions and nations." A theme that often pervaded Bryan's opposition to slavery was the cruelty of an institution that destroyed the family, pulling apart parent from child and spouse from spouse. The Negro had been cast "into the deepest afflictions," wrote Bryan, by the "sale of husband and wife from each other, and from their children, an injury the greatness of which we can only be convinced by supposing that we were in the same unhappy case." Bryan's abolitionism emerged from his revolutionary idealism, proclaimed in section one of Pennsylvania's Bill of Rights, that all men were "born equally free and independent" and had "certain natural, inherent and unalienable rights." Bryan's empathy with the plight of the slave contrasted sharply with his inability to see the plight of the Indian. The difference for him was freedom. The Negro—enslaved, separated from his family, dehumanized—had no choice, while the Indians were free but chose a style of life that would prove fatal. In any event, Bryan's view of slavery in an age when most citizens were indifferent to the "sorrows and hopes" of the slave made his revolutionary fervor unique.[76]

IV

Emerging as one of the principal leaders of Pennsylvania's revolutionary government, George Bryan set out to fulfill specific objectives during his years in power. As we have seen, his immediate concern was the successful organization of the new government and the preparation of the state for military readiness. Concomitant with those ambitions was the ultimate goal, the success of the revolution. On that score, Bryan would never compromise and insisted on full compliance by the citizenry—even at the cost of imprisoning innocent Quakers because they represented a *perceived* threat through their professions of pacifism.

Moreover, Bryan sought to execute a domestic political agenda while he managed the participation of Pennsylvania in the revolution. He tirelessly worked to establish the 1776 constitution as the law of the land and accordingly supported the enactment of legislative measures intended to strengthen that document. Those measures included the test acts, the reformation of the College of Philadelphia, and the seizure of proprietary lands.

To achieve those ends, Bryan mobilized his political party, the Constitutionalists.

The results for both Bryan and the Constitutionalists in fulfilling their goals between 1777 and 1780 were inconclusive. They successfully established the government, helped to keep armies (both federal and state) in the field, and maintained the momentum of the revolution, even during Pennsylvania's bleakest hours. But while successfully blocking the attempts of the anticonstitutionalists to rewrite the state constitution, Bryan and the Constitutionalists did not provide a firm foundation for the document among the people. The constitution, and the legislation enacted by the party, was always jeopardized by a potential Republican election triumph, which ultimately came in 1780, and in this respect Bryan and his colleagues failed.

The reason for that failure lay partly in the organization of the Constitutionalist party. Consisting of various interest groups loosely associated with one another for different reasons, it maintained an outward unity through support of the war and the 1776 constitution and through opposition to the anticonstitutionalists. Those issues were not sufficient, however, to maintain long-term unity, as emerging differences among party members increasingly thwarted their ability to successfully defuse continued opposition to the constitution. Instead, by 1780 Bryan and his colleagues were defending the constitution, the party, and the controversial wartime measures against a growing body of opposition, including their former supporters.

Bryan, a supreme court justice and an acknowledged leader of the state and his party, could not have foreseen the fate awaiting the Constitutionalists in the 1780s. The party that successfully carried Pennsylvania through the war would suffer a serious setback in the election of 1780—partly as a result of its internal failings, partly due to its mishandling of the economy, and partly because of its inability to expand its support among the electorate. Reduced to the role of a minority party leader, Bryan would spend the next decade vainly attempting to save both the party and the constitution.

7

ON THE DEFENSIVE

IN 1780 GEORGE BRYAN and the Constitutionalist party were at the pinnacle of their power, controlling all three major branches of the government. The executive council led by Joseph Reed, the assembly under the speakership of John Bayard, and the supreme court presided over by Chief Justice Thomas McKean represented visible symbols of the party's political dominance. Within the assembly the Constitutionalists vigorously pursued their political goals, enacting a new militia law, confiscating proprietary estates, and proscribing Tories and traitors. Simultaneously, the executive council supplied local and federal armed forces with provisions and men in spite of shortages and a collapsing wartime economy. Above all, the 1776 constitution, the ideological symbol of the party, survived several attempts at revision and remained the supreme law of the land.

The strength of the party in 1780 was in large part due to the efforts of Bryan, who had emerged as one of its principal leaders in the late 1770s. Bryan continued to coordinate policy and personalities through extensive correspondence (of which, regrettably, only a fraction survives) and through his regular visits to the county seats on his judicial circuit. He corresponded regularly with fellow partisans, discussing political developments, mapping strategy, or assessing proposed legislation.[1] His capacity for writing and working at times overwhelmed those colleagues of lesser endurance, at least one of whom apologized: "I have received so many of yours without answering them that hardly remember where to begin."[2]

From 1779 to 1782 Bryan and Reed dominated the party, acting together as a center of communication for the loosely organized partisans who held county and provincial posts. The two men had become good friends and confidants, exchanging information on legal and political matters while keeping the fate of the "Presbyterian interest" foremost among their concerns.[3] Their discussions often touched on sensitive material not intended for anyone else. Reed once described a letter to Bryan as having been expressed "in terms of too much freedom to fall into bad hands."[4] After the appointment of Bryan to the court, Reed feared that his friend would no longer be available for political and policy discussions. "You will please," Reed urged Bryan, "continue your observations & suggest any alterations of men or measures that you think will be conducive to the publick service."[5] Reed's concerns were unnecessary, for Bryan would remain at the center of party activities throughout the decade.

The close political relationship between Reed and Bryan contrasted sharply with their relationships with Thomas McKean. Though all three men were on friendly terms, there was a growing coolness between McKean and his two compatriots. In 1780 McKean and Reed exchanged sharp words over McKean's granting of bail for the suspected traitor Joseph Griswold. On another occasion Reed and Bryan were cautious in their handling of the chief justice on a particular matter, Reed commenting to Bryan that while he had "great respect" for McKean, he believed the latter had an "easiness with which he gives way" to "gentlemen in authority."[6] Reed's caustic comment was prescient, for McKean had already begun his gradual abandonment of the Constitutionalists for the Republicans, whom he considered more socially acceptable.[7]

Believing their popular support was intact, the Constitutionalists confidently anticipated victory in the October 1780 assembly elections. The party had been buoyed earlier, in May, by the easy electoral victory in the city of Philadelphia by Dr. James Hutchinson, the Constitutionalist candidate to Bryan's vacated seat.[8] With few inflammatory articles appearing in print in either September or October, party managers Bryan and Reed believed themselves justified in their optimism over the prospects of their candidates.[9]

Revolutionary Pennsylvania was rarely predictable, however, and both parties were stunned to learn "how great and how important a change" had taken place after the votes of 1780 were tallied.[10] The defection of voters in the city of Philadelphia to the anticonstitutionalists and the successful inroads into Constitutionalist strongholds in Philadelphia and Lancaster counties gave the Republicans a slim majority in the 1780 assembly.

Hoping that such "misfortunes" as the 1780 election would be of service to the party, one Constitutionalist trusted that it would "steer clear of future calamities."[11]

To the dismay of Bryan and the Constitutionalists, however, efforts to reverse their losses were futile. The new electoral alignment proved prophetic; the Republicans repeated their victory in the election of 1781 despite a flurry of partisan propaganda articles by the Constitutionalists.[12] These articles, which stepped up attacks on the policies and personalities of their Republican opponents, were of little advantage as the Republicans reacted with equal venom against the "furious whigs." Symbolic of Constitutionalist frustration was its failure to obtain support from the Muhlenberg family. Hoping to gain the German Lutheran vote, the Constitutionalists had supported Frederick Muhlenberg for speaker of the assembly in 1780.[13] Muhlenberg's father, the influential Rev. Henry Muhlenberg, from Trappe, Pennsylvania, was the most respected leader of the Lutheran community. In a further attempt to ingratiate themselves with the Muhlenberg family, Bryan, Reed, and Ewing through the auspices of the University of Pennsylvania bestowed on another son of the minister the honorary degree of magister, although the title was neither expected nor solicited.[14] But the Muhlenberg family eschewed such offers of friendship by the Presbyterians and by 1782 were decidedly Republican.[15]

As the election of 1782 approached, Bryan and other party leaders considered victory imperative in order to stop the Republican momentum. There was much at stake. Not only had they been reduced to minority status within the assembly, but the Constitutionalists were also threatened with the loss of the presidency because of the expiration of Reed's term in the council. Furthermore, the selection of the Council of Censors was scheduled for the following year, and each party believed that control of the government was essential for a successful result in that election.

Responding to the sense of urgency, Bryan struck hard at the opposition in a significant campaign pamphlet issued immediately prior to the 1782 election.[16] Using the pseudonym "Freeholder," Bryan ridiculed the "unconsequential" work of the previous two assemblies under the Republicans and set out to portray the qualifications of the ideal candidates the voters should choose—a device intended to humiliate the opposition by comparison. But the ultimate purpose of the tract, in Bryan's perception, was to urge the people to support those candidates who steadfastly supported Pennsylvania in its darkest hour during the war, and who remained faithful to the 1776 constitution. In short, Bryan was attempting to reestablish the ideological link that existed between the voters and the Constitutionalist party during the period from 1777 to 1779.

"Anticonstitutionalists," warned Bryan, would always "lean upon the interest" that would "preserve their own power." Men who were "averse to independency" and who hid "themselves in the times of difficulty" by pretending to oppose the 1776 constitution now plotted their return through the restoration of the proprietary faction and the confiscated estates, as well as through the return of the Tories. "The summer of prosperity," a disgusted Bryan charged, "has warmed these insects into life and vigor." They had formerly "disclaimed" all offices "in times of danger," but they now courted them as earnestly as they had once "shunned them." Bryan pleaded with the electorate to vote for patriots of the "genuine stamp"—the "early and persevering whigs," not those "converted by the successes of Saratoga and Yorktown."[17]

Bryan reminded the voters that such men of "questionable patriotism" proved equally unwilling to invest their private property in their revolutionary governments. "They have no certificates of any kind," he observed, and then asked: "Will these men exert themselves to procure honorable payment to the public spirited whigs, their injured widows and orphans, when they are to pay all and receive none?" Bryan doubted it. Those same men, who were quick to depreciate the paper money, made their contracts in specie, carefully ensuring that their private interests were safe while sacrificing the interests of the patriots who served in the revolution and who were paid in paper money. Now, exclaimed Bryan, they "sneer at our credulity" for believing in the credit of the state and federal paper issues.[18]

Not averse to personal attack, particularly where rich and socially powerful opponents were concerned, Bryan maligned John Dickinson, who was an anticonstitutionalist and a candidate for the executive council from Philadelphia County. For reasons of conscience, Dickinson had refused to vote for the Declaration of Independence. Consequently forced out of politics, he had retired for a short time to his lands in Delaware.[19] Bryan and his colleagues especially despised Dickinson, branding him as one of those men who "fled from public assemblies and the field," returning only when "one army had been captured, and the French alliance had taken place." Although that critique was addressed to an unspecified few, Bryan was clearly aiming at Dickinson; "talents in the hands of such men" were like "arms in the hands of cowards," the former useless to the public, the latter dangerous "to themselves." These "timid creatures—these women in breeches," mocked Bryan, would have to wait until they could be trusted by the public before they could hold office, because they had "shared so very little in the toil or danger of the war." Such men, Bryan lamented, really did not understand "the value of our present acquisition."[20]

The same men, Bryan observed, who had recoiled from the danger during the war and had "remained with the enemy, and partook of all their ease and pleasures," were the same men who now sought public trust. A small knot of wealthy elitists, who hated the 1776 constitution as the cause of their downfall from power, were attempting to regain control of the political process. The revolution, Bryan warned, would be rendered meaningless if the freedoms that were denied by imperial England were merely to be surrendered to a handful of greedy, rich men. Bryan was appalled by an argument then circulating among some individuals that men of wealth made preferable officeholders because they served for less salary. Bryan strove, he said, to return the voters to their senses.

> Do we find men of large fortunes less anxious after money than others? No, my countrymen, it is directly the reverse; a certain excess of fortune sets a man above the public opinion, and in an equal proportion makes him despise those who are poor. The charities of this city, and most public spirited designs, . . . are confined to the middling class of people.

Such self-denying zeal was not to be expected in "such a self seeking age." Bryan advised the voters to beware of presumptions of paternalism by the wealthy. "Depend upon it," Bryan warned, "they will pay themselves in some way or another."[21]

In his conclusion, Bryan asked the voters to choose men of "fair moral character" who possessed a "decent regard" for the "duties of religion." Perhaps trying to demonstrate to non-Calvinists that they had a common religious bond with the Presbyterians who had come to symbolize the Constitutionalist party, Bryan sought the means by which diverse ethnoreligious groups could unite. "A man will be less likely to injure and defraud his country, who sometimes reflects that he is not to live here for ever," mused Bryan, because a guilty man could not escape the notice of a higher, "more solemn tribunal."[22] In short, Presbyterians were as God-fearing as were Lutherans and Baptists.

On a more secular note, Bryan reminded the electorate of the improprieties of the Republicans in previous assemblies as well as their having burdened Pennsylvania with an enormous debt, the interest alone equaling the net annual income of the state before the revolution. Finally, Bryan cautioned the voters against candidates who would betray the patriots by attempting to repeal the test laws and by working for the return of the Tories. If the anticonstitutionalists were not stopped, warned Bryan, their measures "if once done" could "never be undone."[23]

In his lengthy and politically charged pamphlet, Bryan revealed as much about himself as he perceived he had about the Republican candidates in the fall 1782 assembly and council elections. The pamphlet's central dynamic tension is the tireless depiction of the opposition ("these insects") as a handful of self-serving miscreants who, during the war's darkest hour, had been cowards, Tories, or both. That they should enjoy the liberties wrought from the hard-fought revolution was insufferable enough, but that they should receive the public trust so soon after the war was intolerable. In Bryan's mind, men such as Dickinson, James Wilson, and Robert Morris were so self-absorbed that it was a fatal error to confide in them the freedoms won during the revolution. Bryan's declaration was a sweeping indictment against the Republican party cabal, with little or no attempt to distinguish with precise accuracy their identification or motivations. Bryan was convinced that those individuals, thwarted in their attempts to prevent the overthrow of imperial England, intended from the beginning to overthrow the 1776 constitution and so return to power.

His analysis, however, relied on one essential proposition: that the opposition consisted of only a handful of individuals whose support for the revolution was directly proportional to their personal ambition and greed. That same theme had pervaded his reasoning as early as 1777, and it remained remarkably intact over the succeeding six years. His repeated references to men of overgrown fortunes were more emotional than rational, for Bryan did not intend to damn by the same brush men like John Bayard, Joseph Reed, and Charles Pettit—perhaps not men of "overgrown" fortunes but wealthy in their own right and, more significant, members of the Constitutionalist party. Despite the class-conflict rhetoric Bryan was referring only to a handful of people whose conspicuous wealth was an outrage and affront because it belonged to individuals leading the political opposition. Their wealth was the symbol of their relentless greed, which in itself explained their political motivation—that is, the absorption of complete power, wherever it should lay and by whatever means.

Bryan's damning view of the opposition may have been convenient to the Constitutionalists, but it contained a critical flaw. Whether Bryan liked it or not, the opposition had scored significant electoral victories, rendering invalid his perception that the political enemy was a small select club. Rather than change his mind, however, Bryan preferred to ignore the facts. Glossing over unpleasant political realities, Bryan concluded that "honest but uninformed electors were made to believe" through "falsehood, malice, and calumny" that the Constitutionalists had failed in their ability to govern. Bryan hoped that his pamphlet corrected that misimpression.

Not content to rely solely on campaign pamphlets, the Constitutionalists attempted to outmaneuver the Republicans by proposing Thomas McKean as a candidate for council from Chester County with the understanding that, if victorious, he would oppose Dickinson (should he win) for the presidency of the state. Reed, in turn, would be nominated for the position of chief justice.[24]

Despite their efforts, however, the election of 1782 proved to be another particularly bitter disappointment for Bryan and his partisans. The Constitutionalists experienced their "last breath," exalted Benjamin Rush, further noting that prominent leaders, including Reed and Bryan, had by their "conduct" exposed themselves to the "general censure."[25] Republicans swept both the city and county of Philadelphia and continued their hold on the assembly. The executive council also fell to the Republicans after a dramatic election for the presiding officer. John Dickinson defeated the ardent Constitutionalist James Potter (Northumberland County), who suffered further ignominy when he was subsequently denied the vice presidency by four votes.[26] The strategy to move Reed to the high court and McKean to the council also failed, as the chief justice showed little enthusiasm for resigning his exalted position for a mere council post—a circumstance that further alienated McKean from Bryan and Reed.[27]

II

In 1783 political tensions soared to new heights. Newspaper readers were horrified, entertained, or both by articles bursting with unprecedented calumny and slander. None were spared as anonymous partisans savaged their opponents in every conceivable way, attacking their personal as well as their public lives. The cause of the excitement was the statewide election of the Council of Censors; if the Republicans could seize the council they could achieve their ultimate goal—the destruction of the 1776 constitution. Bryan and his political friends were once again on the defensive, attempting to thwart the designs of their unrelenting foes.

Epitomizing the radical import of the 1776 constitution, the document's forty-seventh section provided for the septennial gathering of a Council of Censors, perhaps one of the earliest (albeit halting) steps toward the concept of judicial review. This august group was to determine whether or not the constitution had been "preserved inviolate in every part; And whether the legislative and executive branches of government have performed their Duty as guardians of the people." The censors were granted powers of subpoena and were permitted to order impeachments and to recommend to the assembly the repeal of laws contrary to the "principles of the constitution." More significant for the Republicans, if the censors concluded that

defects existed within the constitution and that amendments were necessary, they were empowered to convene a constitutional convention to meet
within two years of their decree in order to make revisions. There were
limitations, however, to the power of the censors. They could not alter
laws or governmental actions deemed unconstitutional, nor could they call
a convention except by two-thirds vote of the total council, which consisted of two elected members from each county.[28]

Bryan and the Constitutionalists believed that the Council of Censors
was one of the principal features of their constitution, representing the
culmination of commonwealth idealism. The "provincial jury," as it was
called, was a built-in, time-delayed mechanism that would serve as a check
against possible political abuse by the government. One of the most innova-
tive additions to revolutionary constitutional ideology, the Council of Censors was the strongest example of the fear harbored by the "radical whigs"
of a good government gone astray.[29] "After all," remarked an apologist, "no
country can be *free* which is governed by an absolute power," whether that
power be an "absolute royal power" or an "absolute legislative power."[30]
Along with the unicameral legislature, the limits on assemblymen's terms,
and the expanded representation, the Council of Censors made the 1776
frame of government the culmination of Constitutionalist ideals.

The framers of the constitution in 1776, of course, perceived the censors
as a means of protecting society against governmental abuses through the
mechanism of reviewing its acts and recommending changes. But partisan
feelings ran high in 1783, and among the embittered politicians the council
became one more political battleground, shorn of its pristine ideology and
recast as yet another forum in which the Republicans and Constitutionalists
could vent their spleen at one another. Bryan and his colleagues found
themselves forced to defend not just the constitution that the Council of
Censors was intended to scrutinize, but the council itself. Republicans
complained bitterly about the Council of Censors, questioning whether
the censors possessed "any power to do good" and whether the legislature
was "bound to obey them." One critic viewed them as simply "an expensive and ridiculous burthen upon the state."[31]

In an unpublished, undated address probably written in 1784 that Bryan
had intended for the public, he sought to legitimize the purpose of the
council, linking it to traditional republican antiquity. He dated the existence of such councils to the "early and uncorrupted times" of Rome and
further referred to Machiavelli, who, Bryan insisted, recognized the "superior advantage" of a similar institution. Through the Council of Censors,
Bryan argued, "the state" would be "peaceably and orderly reformed and
reduced to its first principles," and he suggested that the alternative was the

dependency of the state on chance or potential upheaval in order for society to maintain its freedom. Bryan recognized the concern of the populace that the Council of Censors might be considered a "novelty," but he believed as did "many great writers" that a body like the censors was a necessary check to enable a society to be spared the inevitable advance of tyranny.[32]

Bryan's glowing defense of the censors, of course, presupposed that it would be in the hands of the Constitutionalists. Unfortunately for Bryan and his party, the Republicans captured both the Council of Censors and the assembly in the election of 1783. The Republican's hold on the censors, however, was slight, because representation on that board was in accordance with the number of counties and not by population. Their edge was precariously maintained only by the absenteeism of William Montgomery and Samuel Hunter of Northumberland County and James McLene of Cumberland County, three "radical whigs." In any event, the tenuous advantage the Republicans held over their opponents was insufficient to enable them to fulfill their original goal. Needing a two-thirds majority, or eighteen votes, the fourteen elected Republicans could not call a constitutional convention in order to write a new frame of government.[33]

Nonetheless, the Republicans took advantage of their majority and proceeded to use the council as a forum for condemning the constitution, suggesting their own alternative in its place. During the first session of the council, which lasted from 10 November 1783 to 21 January 1784, the Republicans pushed forward a committee report calling for two separate legislative bodies, a general assembly to sit for one year and a legislative council to sit for three years. Representation would be proportional to the number of taxable inhabitants per county; the executive council would be abolished and replaced by a governor to be chosen annually who would have the power to veto legislation.[34]

Immediately upon adjournment of the first session of the censors, Bryan and the Constitutionalists rushed forward with plans to undo the work of the anticonstitutionalists.[35] James McLene assured Bryan that he would be attending the second session, having reacted with horror over the demand of the Republicans in the council for a governor, or "king, if you please."[36] Believing that the Republicans intended to pressure the other censors into calling a convention, the Constitutionalists responded by collecting petitions countering attempts at constitutional revision. Bryan presented to the Council of Censors remonstrances signed by 443 citizens of the state against calling a convention, while his western colleagues presented similar petitions signed by over eighteen thousand citizens.[37]

The efforts of Bryan and his allies were successful, in part due to Bryan's opportunistic and fortuitous election to the council. Samuel Miles, the Republican censor for the city of Philadelphia, resigned his seat in the spring of 1784 upon the revelation of possible improper financial transactions. In the critical election to replace Miles, Bryan—thanks to a sparse turnout— won handily over William Lewis, a staunch anticonstitutionalist, and Thomas McKean, who may or may not have been a serious candidate.[38] Of equal importance to Bryan's party, Montgomery, McLene, and James Potter (who replaced the deceased Samuel Hunter) began to attend the council regularly, giving the Constitutionalists fourteen votes and the majority.[39]

The impact of Bryan's election to the Council of Censors was presaged by the appointment of his son, Samuel, as council secretary on 7 June. Two weeks later George Bryan took his seat as the city representative to the council.[40] During the second session (1 June until 25 September 1784) Bryan, McLene, William Findley, and John Smilie dominated the proceedings, effectively reversing the efforts of the Republicans during the first session. In an address framed by the Constitutionalists, the council declared to the freemen of the commonwealth that it would not call a convention, nor would it attempt any changes in the frame of government. Charging that the enemies of the constitution were attempting to introduce an "arbitrary government" into Pennsylvania, Bryan and his peers reported that some Republicans, including members sitting on the Council of Censors, "entertained ideas of government" that were "highly pernicious, and utterly inconsistent with liberty." The target of the Constitutionalists was the attempt by the Republicans to scrap the 1776 constitution and replace it with a bicameral government and a governor. The final report reminded the opposition that the purpose of the censors was to investigate whether the constitution was faithfully served by the government's officers, not to alter the constitution. "Whilst one part of us has laboured to purge from the constitution the abuses that have crept in, others," charged Bryan and his colleagues, "have never ceased to hold up the pretended necessity of a convention." The Constitutionalists advised the public that while "it would be great presumption to say that our constitution is perfect," the document nonetheless contained "those great principles of equal liberty, which in our opinion ought never to be endangered."[41]

Bryan's own unpublished address to the citizens underscored the judgment of the council's final report and was probably used as a working draft for one of the Constitutionalists' several reports from the council. Bryan observed that the "charter of liberty" was "misunderstood" by its friends, "debased" by its opponents, and, because of partisan politics, "set at war" against itself. Bryan argued that contrary to anticonstitutionalist perceptions the frame of government was wisely designed to "sever and distribute" its powers among the three branches of the legislative, executive, and judicial departments. Governmental power was thereby checked and the "public safety" secured through the "exact boundaries of authority" prescribed by the constitution.[42]

Bryan was defending from unremitting attack one of the critical elements of the 1776 constitution: the separation of powers as distinct from checks and balances. Through their consistent opposition to Pennsylvania's constitution beginning in 1776, the Republicans by 1784 had developed an effective weapon against the revolutionary document. The polity was fatally flawed, they argued, because it combined all governmental functions within the sphere of the legislature's authority, and consequently it failed to provide any check against abuse of power by the assembly. As early as 1776 an anticonstitutionalist commented that the powers of the government were indeed "separated and distributed into different hands," but there were no safeguards established that would allow one power to "check another." Bryan and his colleagues, however, argued that the accusation was false, for the constitution strictly delineated three separate categories, the legislature, the executive, and the judiciary, while clearly defining the powers and authorities of each. As such, each was theoretically immune from abuse by the other two. Checks and balances were not an alternative desired by the Constitutionalists because they saw in that argument sinister implications: notwithstanding the glowing description by the Republicans, the system of constitutional checks was a ploy by the ambitious and unpatriotic few to insinuate themselves into the polity and hold the government hostage through their exercise of the veto. Yet by the mid-1780s the theory of checks within the government was gaining acceptance by the public, and Bryan and the Constitutionalists found little recourse except to proclaim in their final report of the Council of Censors that they were "firmly persuaded that the constitution of Pennsylvania needs only to be faithfully administered by men" who were "honestly disposed to support it according to its true spirit and intention." Then and only then, Bryan and his fellow partisans declared, would the constitution "be the best system of government in the world."[43]

The final report of the censors was received by the general public in the same spirit as it was written. Proponents and detractors of the constitution had already staked out their positions, and it was highly improbable that the efforts of the censors influenced anyone to be either for or against the 1776 constitution and the partisan factions involved. Although both parties may have viewed their impact differently, each undoubtedly believed that they had, in fact, convincingly demonstrated to the public the correctness of their positions. With the tables turned on them by the election of Bryan to the council, the Republicans shifted ground and dismissed the censors as irrelevant, concluding yet again that "*the government*" as then constituted was "*an impracticable one*." As for Bryan, the Republicans concluded that he had proven the constitution to be either "too straight for the people; or the state too crooked for the constitution." Whichever side Bryan took, they warned, he would prove the necessity of calling a convention.[44]

Bryan, on the other hand, strove to remind or to educate the public of the "two . . . great and strongly marked powers" in the state's government: the "supreme legislature" reserved in the representatives of the people, and a "supreme executive, vested in the president and council." Upon these two pillars rested the wisdom of the constitution, preventing society from devolving into "arbitrary and despotic rule." Convinced of the rightness of his views, Bryan believed that the efforts of the Constitutionalists to save the 1776 document was "supported by the sense of our constituents."[45] For Bryan and his fellow partisans, only time would tell if they were to survive.

The events of 1784 illuminated a significant point in Bryan's political career. His efforts on behalf of the censors revealed an impassioned and highly emotional characteristic that was reminiscent of his efforts on behalf of the First Presbyterian Church of Philadelphia many years earlier, an un-questioned loyalty to the 1776 constitution and the Constitutionalists; also exhibited was an untiring antagonism toward the Republicans, the latter sentiment felt in equal measure by the Republicans toward Bryan. By the time the Council of Censors adjourned, Bryan and his party along with the Republicans had established an uncompromising, absolutist position on the constitution, from which only one side could emerge as victor. Yet there was a profound and not totally discernible shift occurring among the public, which was radically altering its views on constitutionalism and republicanism. Like many of his peers, Bryan apparently did not see that the distinction between separation of powers and checks and balances was slowly being erased—that in fact in the public's perception each axiom was developing a logical dependence on the other. It is true that many anticonstitutionalists, for various reasons, despised the 1776 frame from its enactment; Bryan was correct in observing that among the opposition "very few could agree together what alterations were proper to be made." But the linking of separation of powers to checks and balances was proving increasingly difficult to resist and would provide the Republicans with a common standard on which all could agree. That development was fatal for the 1776 constitution.

III

By the mid-1780s George Bryan stood alone in the public leadership of his party. The emerging party leaders from the western counties, William Findley, John Smilie, and James McLene, as well as other prominent local Constitutionalists such as James Potter and Robert Whitehill, could not yet match the provincial prestige of Bryan or even Joseph Reed. The earlier partisans of 1776 who had dominated the party and the state were slowly disappearing from the political stage.

Timothy Matlack was one of the earliest leaders to fade into the background. At the outset of the 1782 election the Republicans quietly suggested that Matlack, as secretary to the Supreme Executive Council and receiver of the fees collected for marriages and taverns, was responsible for financial irregularities. After the election they pressed forward their charges against Matlack, whom they personally despised. Although the investigation concluded weakly that Matlack was probably guilty of technical violations, the entire house was persuaded to censure him and remove him from office. True to political partisanship, the Constitutionalist-dominated assembly of 1784 reversed Matlack's censure. In personal terms, however, the restoration of Matlack's good name came too late to save his ruined career. In any event, his revolutionary fervor, appropriate in 1776, was probably inappropriate in the 1780s. It was exemplified by his fistfight with the Republican Whitehead Humphreys on New Year's Day 1782, an event that embarrassed even the Constitutionalists. The altercation was probably the result of an unavenged insult. In July 1779 Humphrey had published a pamphlet whose main purpose apparently was to humiliate Matlack.[46]

John Bayard, one of the early and principal supporters of the constitution (although he initially disliked it) from the city of Philadelphia, was another victim of partisan politics. He lost his reelection bid in 1780, and his subsequent election to the executive council in 1781 was clouded by charges of voter manipulation. The Republicans claimed that the militia, while on duty in Newtown, Bucks County, had been ordered to vote for Bayard at a Philadelphia County polling station, resulting in his victory over Thomas Mifflin and John Dickinson.[47] Disgusted by the opposition's attempt to discredit Bayard, Bryan observed that "no proof of force or confinement" of the militia existed. Nonetheless, the election dispute dragged on until the spring of 1782, the council finally asking justices Bryan and McKean for their opinion in the case. Both justices, not surprisingly, replied that the election was legitimate.[48]

Unrelenting in their pursuit, however, the Republicans complained that Bayard was guilty of dual officeholding. Citing his appointment in 1781 by

President Reed as an auctioneer of the city, the opposition argued that Bayard's election to the executive council represented a conflict of interest. Although no law had been broken, Bayard yielded to the pressure generated by the Republicans and resigned from the executive council in the summer of 1782. Forced to choose between the two posts, Bayard decided to remain as city auctioneer—the more lucrative position. If Bayard thought that move would propitiate the Republicans, he was sadly mistaken. Desiring the spoils of the office of auctioneer for themselves, the Republicans who controlled the assembly announced in November 1783 that, contrary to former practice, the House rather than the council would appoint auctioneers. The assembly therefore dismissed Bayard summarily along with Constitutionalist William Brown, and appointed Republicans Arthur St. Clair and James Mease in their stead.[49] Except for his election to the assembly in 1784, Bayard would no longer play a significant role in provincial politics.

Although not a victim of partisan politics, Thomas McKean proved to be another loss for the Constitutionalists. Gradually distancing himself from the party, McKean remained on friendly terms with Bryan as long as he could. Perhaps more skilled in reading the political barometer than either Bryan or Reed, McKean was maneuvering toward the Republican camp and advocacy of a new state constitution. Sensing his disaffection as early as 1781, the Constitutionalists resorted to petty harassment of their erstwhile ally. Taking advantage of McKean's vulnerability to charges of plural officeholding as chief justice and as a representative of Delaware in the confederation, disgruntled Constitutionalists attacked him in the newspapers. Never inclined to suffer any criticism, McKean promptly identified Constitutionalists William Clajon and Jonathan Dickinson Sergeant as his principal detractors. Clajon firmly denied the charge, but Sergeant remained conspicuously silent.[50] At the Pennsylvania Ratification Convention for the federal Constitution in 1787, McKean dispelled any lingering doubts about his political position, openly supporting the Republicans in the convention and in their subsequent drive for a new state constitution.

While all this attrition was traumatic for the party, the most disheartening loss was that of Joseph Reed. After the expiration of his council term in 1782, an exhausted Reed returned to private life. Although his name was mentioned as a possible candidate for several congressional assignments, Reed preferred to stay at home, rebuild his law practice, and remain close to provincial politics. Any aspirations he may have entertained for returning to office were effectively lessened by Republican ascendancy in Pennsylvania and the Congress. Moreover, from December 1783 until September 1784 Reed was in England, hoping that the change of climate would improve his deteriorating health. Shortly after his return to Philadelphia his condition worsened rapidly. He suffered a stroke in January 1785 and two months later he was dead.[51]

The fortuitous appointment of Bryan to the high court left him as the only provincial officeholder of his party, and the death of Reed, the estrangement of McKean, and the victimization of Bayard and Matlack reduced the nucleus of the party leadership to one—George Bryan.[52] By the end of the decade he would be assisted by the western partisans who would fill the roles vacated by earlier party leaders, but by that time the party was only a shadow of its former strength.

Although Bryan showed a remarkable talent for political survival, he was by no means immune or invulnerable to partisan assault. In December 1781 the Republicans, relying on their position of power in the assembly, had launched their first attack against him. The House passed a bill increasing the wages of Chief Justice McKean, maintaining the salary of William Atlee at its former rate, but reducing the salaries of Bryan and John Evans from £500 per annum to £300. Clearing the House on 26 December 1781, the bill was supported solidly by the Republicans in concert with several nonaligned members and was opposed by the Constitutionalists. Bryan's allies in the House bitterly denounced the law, declaring that its passage was "diametrically contradictory to the spirit and letter of the constitution." It was, they contended, a flagrant violation of the separation of the legislative and judicial powers.[53]

The law was blatantly partisan, systematically reducing the salaries of those Constitutionalists remaining in office while increasing the wages of McKean, whose political loyalties were increasingly difficult to define, and of the non-Constitutionalist Attorney General William Bradford. The assembly's revenge also reduced the salaries of Presbyterians William Moore and James Potter, president and vice president, respectively, of the executive council.[54] Like the Constitutionalists within the assembly, Moore was incensed, complaining angrily to the House that the law was unconstitutional as well as morally wrong.[55]

Bryan was aware as early as March 1781 that the Republicans would attempt to strike at the justices by voting them an "insufficient salary." He was startled and annoyed when an assemblyman with whom he had no obvious cause for friction, Alexander Lowrey, "absurdly" suggested that the house should "strike off the 4th justice." Although surprised at Lowrey's verbal assault, Bryan understood that such malice reflected Republican intentions to bully the Constitutionalists out of office.[56]

After the Republicans passed the bill to reduce salaries, an angry Bryan mocked "our very *worthy* legislature" and charged that the assembly had begun its "attack on the characters" of those men who had supported the 1776 constitution. The "indirect attempt to remove the present judges of the supreme court" by reducing them to "low and precarious salaries," Bryan commented to Justice Atlee, "was in manifest contempt" of the constitution. Bryan further reported that the "monstrous" law was to be retroactive to 22 June 1781. The reduced salaries therefore were to be slashed even more until the difference was paid. It was "whispered," noted Bryan, that Evans was "contented" with the new financial arrangements, but he dismissed the rumor as propaganda. Bryan urged Atlee to come to Philadelphia in early January, because both he and McKean intended to protest against the law to the assembly.[57] The loss of salary for Bryan was a cruel but well-aimed stroke by the Republicans; they were aware of his financial woes, which continued throughout the 1780s.

In September 1783 a second attempt was made to oust Bryan from the court when several residents of Chester County petitioned the assembly, arguing that only three judges were necessary to complete court business.[58] Relief finally arrived, however, in 1783 with the appointment to the Supreme Court of Jacob Rush, brother of Benjamin Rush and an ardent anticonstitutionalist. Rush replaced Evans, who had died on 11 December 1783. Determined to provide adequate compensation for their allies, the Republicans restored the salaries of the justices to their 1777 level, magnanimously allowing Bryan to resume his former wage. Nonetheless, his enemies still managed to insult Bryan by deliberately elevating Rush to the third position on the court while leaving the Constitutionalist leader as the fourth justice.[59]

While weathering the machinations of the anticonstitutionalists in the assembly, Bryan was also targeted for a stream of abuse by anonymous detractors in the newspapers. The attacks began in 1783 and achieved their greatest notoriety the following year. Authors condemned him for a multitude of alleged sins—ranging from his failure in business to his doubtful patriotism and questionable integrity. One writer assured his readers that despite Bryan's immorality, the public could be confident that he was not an adulterer, for his "croaking voice and cadaverous appearance" guaranteed his innocence while his "inability of body" prevented him from the "commission of other indictable crimes."[60] Another writer ridiculed Bryan for having "groped" many years in the "Irish trade" before finally resorting to smuggling. Addressing Bryan, the publicist discussed his smuggling career: "A number of merchants employed you as a fit hand for this dark business, your hypocrisy and cant pointing you out as a fit character to go through the same without suspicion, and your want of principle and matchless effrontery to sell the smuggled property under price, and by this means, defraud the fair trader his honest gains."[61] An anticonstitutionalist who was a disgruntled litigant before the Supreme Court declared Bryan to be an enemy to tradesmen and mechanics, as well as a party to a small group of miscreants who conspired "against that sacred of characters, General Washington."[62]

With the retirement of Reed, Bryan became the sole "champion" of the Constitutionalists, prompting the Republicans to deride him as the leader of a "disjointed faction, allured by no motives but the spirit of disappointed ambition." Another antagonist labeled him a "veteran in politics," never striking until he thought himself "secure." Charging that Bryan had "tutored" his "tools" well—men like Charles Pettit, John Whitehill, James McLene, William Montgomery, and John Smilie—the author viewed Bryan as a fomenter of "party schemes" who sacrificed his conscience "to the emolument" of his "dependents." Opponents further criticized Bryan for sitting on the Council of Censors when he was needed on the Supreme Court, likening him to an "ass between two bundles of hay." The Constitutionalists on the Council of Censors "stood motionless," opponents cried, waiting for their leader to arrive from court.[63]

Like most of the articles that slandered political opponents in late eighteenth-century Pennsylvania, the attacks on Bryan were comprised of complete falsehoods or shreds of truth intertwined with distortions. Subtlety was not a virtue for most political propagandists of the period. Fortunately, Bryan had his defenders. One such author dismissed the charges leveled against Bryan's personal life as "childish." Addressing one critic of Bryan, the author commented that no one had charged that critic "with *drunkeness*, . . . but it may be suspected that your piece was not produced from the cool reflections of the morning."[64] Protesting that Pennsylvanians had the right to "speak what they think," one defender nonetheless wondered how much longer the "names of those who have risqued their lives and fortunes" in the cause of freedom would be "prophaned." The author concluded that "if the debilitated lion must be insulted, let it not be with the heels of an ass."[65] One defender of Bryan believed that Benjamin Rush was behind the anti-Bryan articles and addressed an open letter to "Dr. Froth," demanding to know why he had slandered Bryan. Was it, the writer asked rhetorically, because Bryan supported the constitution, or because he was too honest for the good doctor, or because he stood in the "way of your lazy brother?"[66]

Several authors writing in defense of Bryan suggested that many of the perceived criticisms were, in fact, compliments. A "theme of constant abuse," noted one author, was Bryan's "poverty." Yet, the writer continued, "to whom does he owe money," and who were his defrauded "creditors?"

They did not exist, exclaimed the author—quickly adding, however, that Bryan was indeed "poor," as were "many of the honest men in the community." Reflecting a political value often articulated by Bryan, the author further explained that he was not an enemy "to wealth honestly acquired," but that he did despise the "aristocratical junto" who plotted the restoration of proprietary estates and enriched themselves with the spoils of public office.[67]

"Junius" chastised one Bryan critic for his "futile malignity" and reminded his readers that Bryan's call from " 'silent obscurity' " in 1776 was an "envious circumstance." He asked whether Bryan's defamers remembered that "Cincinnatus was taken from the plough to command." The author praised Bryan's merit and observed that he was rewarded for his services to the people with his recent election to the Council of Censors.[68]

One unrelenting enemy of Bryan was Francis Hopkinson. Judge of the admiralty court and a zealot against the Constitutionalists, Hopkinson was at the center of the Republican circle in Philadelphia. Arrogant and intelligent, he seized any opportunity to strike at his judicial superiors—Bryan and McKean. He once charged them with deliberately influencing a member of council to withhold his pay, and he regularly condemned as inefficient and sloppy the law that created the admiralty court—knowing that Bryan was its author.[69]

In January 1783 Hopkinson was able to renew his antagonism toward Bryan and McKean. On 12 October 1782 Chief Justice McKean had issued a warrant for the arrest of Eleazer Oswald, publisher of the *Independent Gazetteer*.[70] Oswald had openly criticized the chief justice for his stiff sentencing of Col. Thomas Proctor, who had physically assaulted an election inspector. Insulted, McKean charged Oswald with libel and summoned a grand jury to order prosecution. But on 1 January 1783 the grand jury returned the bill ignoramus and confirmed that return after McKean angrily ordered a reconsideration. The jurors, rebuked again by McKean and Attorney General Bradford, refused to consider the indictment further and published a memorial protesting McKean's actions.[71] Embarrassed by the boldness of the jurors, McKean and Bryan (who had presided with the chief justice during the Oswald case) replied in kind.

Under the pseudonym of "Adrian," Bryan defended his colleague against the charges of the grand jury. Although the Oswald case had become highly political, Bryan argued the result strictly from a point of law. He outlined the history of the case, from the assault by Colonel Proctor to the refusal of the grand jury to indict Oswald. Bryan pointed out that McKean had not acted arbitrarily in the Proctor case, but that the court had responded to irregularities committed by the grand jury. The latter "had no right to hear any witness, or receive any evidence," Bryan reported to his readers, "unless admitted by the court." Apparently the foreman of the jury had been seen in conversation with participants in the trial, including Colonel Proctor; earlier that day, one of the jurors had told some of the witnesses that they had come to court too late to testify. When McKean pressed the jury for an explanation, according to Bryan, the jurors declared to the surprised justices "that they were sworn not to reveal the secrets of state of their fellows."[72]

Bryan subsequently explained in clear and precise terms the role of the grand jury within the judicial process. While stressing that grand juries were not to be under the undue influence of judges, and that they were "to decide for themselves" the merit of the cause, Bryan did insist that juries must be "held to the rules of law in receiving evidence." Otherwise, their decisions would become "wild and capricious," threatening the sanctity of trial by jury. "If the grand inquest might receive all that offers," Bryan observed, "the most improper and illegal testimony might be received; but then, what would become of those approved rules of evidence, which the wisdom of ages has devised for the safety of the innocent, and the investigation of the truth?" In the case against Oswald, concluded Bryan, the grand jurors transgressed "their bounds."[73]

Bryan hoped the controversy would fade. But he failed to reckon with Francis Hopkinson, who saw the case as another stick with which to beat his two superiors. In a long-winded polemic, Hopkinson argued that grand juries were independent of the judges and "not accountable for their decisions." He further declared that grand juries could order for trial only those who were actually guilty; otherwise they would "serve no other purpose but that of giving a legal sanction to the will of the court."[74] Hopkinson's reasoning was directly counter to that of Bryan, who had argued against the right of a grand jury to determine guilt prior to trial because that concept would prejudice the accused before the petty jury.[75] Perhaps less interested in the technical details of the law, Judge Hopkinson preferred to call Bryan "our new pope" and caustically remarked that "Adrian thinks a man accused and not hanged, is a cause stifled."[76] Not satisfied with prose alone in his pursuit of Bryan as Adrian, Hopkinson resorted to verse as well:

> All this did *Adrian* in his fury,
> Pronounce against a late grand jury;
> And prov'd that *animal rationale*
> With jurymen will never tally;
> Because 'tis plainly to be seen
> A jury's but a *mere machine*.[77]

Bryan, of course, was not Hopkinson's sole target. In "A Full and True Account of a Terrible Uproar which lately happened in a very Eminent Family," Hopkinson added McKean and other members of the Constitutionalist faction as subjects for his satiric wit. The story centered in the household of Lady Pennsylva, a widow whose husband, Patriotism, died shortly after the birth of their son, Independence. In an unseemly squabble between the various servants of the house, Kitty (Eleazer Oswald) tossed a bucket of slush on the scarlet robes of George (Bryan), the understeward. "But George avoided fighting openly, and only pinched his adversaries as opportunities offered."[78] McKean was portrayed as the severe chief steward attempting to maintain order. Hopkinson managed several digs at Reed and Potter as well.

After the Council of Censors issued its favorable report on the constitution in September 1784, Hopkinson acknowledged Bryan's powerful influence among his party members on the council through another satirical article published on 24 November. Hopkinson suggested that a man could preserve his posterity by deeding his land in such a way as to make a self-portrait. He then listed a series of points marked by degrees and directions that, when connected, formed a caricature of Bryan. Hopkinson was mocking Bryan's imprint on the 1776 frame of government.[79]

Although the malignity of the Republicans toward the Constitutionalists seems harsh, the fact is that their behavior was an accurate reflection of the political temperament in Pennsylvania during the 1780s. Partisans from both camps unleashed a torrent of vicious lies and public slanders about their opponents; no one was spared. Perhaps the meanness of spirit was a reaction caused by the assumption shared by each party that the other had violated an implicit value, a value that may have been based more on myth than reality and that pretended to a harmonic unity which submerged the will of the individual to common good within the body politic. Or perhaps the ill-spirited articles and the personalization of political emnity was behavior suitable to an unprepared, immature society frightened by the perceived horrific consequences of unfettered democracy. Freedom is a dual-edged sword, satisfying but also frightening. In any event, Bryan, like most of his contemporaries, was certainly not above the fray, and like his peers he could give as well as he received.

Once during a later libel case (ironically, again involving Oswald) Bryan protested that he could never be "suspected of partiality to libelers," having had his share of their "malevolence." But, he added, "it is true I have not suffered much; for these trifles do not rankle in my mind."[80] Perhaps Bryan had a thicker political skin than Chief Justice McKean and, as a "veteran politician," could handle the cut and thrust of partisan rancor. What he could not control, however, was the continued loss of power by the Constitutionalists.

IV

Bryan never stopped believing that the Constitutionalists represented the majority of the people, and that Republican victories were based on guile and on that party's ability to hoodwink the electorate. He perceived, therefore, that one of the goals of his party was to bring back those voters stolen by Republican propaganda. That task, however, would be formidable, since the Republicans controlled the assembly throughout the decade by varying majorities, with the exception of a temporary setback in the election of 1784 and an evenly split house in 1785. By 1786 Philadelphia City and County, Montgomery, Lancaster, Chester, and Bucks counties were surrendered completely to the anticonstitutionalists, while the Constitutionalists remained strong in the northern and western counties of Cumberland, Northampton, Northumberland, Fayette, Franklin, and Dauphin. Having relinquished control of the numerically superior southeastern Pennsylvania region, however, the Constitutionalists would never be a majority party again.

Why did the Constitutionalists fall from power in the 1780s? Both Robert L. Brunhouse and Douglas McNeil Arnold offer broad explanations, which emphasize a gradual shift of voter allegiance over time. They argue that the voters perceived the Constitutionalists as increasingly incompetent, unable to revive a wrecked economy, and having depleted the resources of the state. Having established a democratic constitution, having stripped the proprietary of its power and land, and having ousted the anticonstitutionalists from the College of Philadelphia, the Constitutionalists, Brunhouse concludes, had "exhausted their ingenuity" and were unable to sustain public support. Arnold believes that despite the Constitutionalist electoral appeal that a vote for the party was a vote for the republic, the party was severely wounded by local controversies, partisan rivalries, the devastated economy, and the need for a national government. Furthermore, the insistence of the Constitutionalists on discriminatory test laws resulted in the formation of a substantial coalition of disaffected voters who in turn supported the Republicans.[81]

Owen S. Ireland provides a different perspective, suggesting that electoral behavior was based more on core groups expanding arithmetically than on changing attitudes. In a detailed analysis of the election results of the 1780s, Ireland demonstrates that the success of the Republicans was based on the triumphant coalition of "Anglicans, Quakers, Lutherans, Baptists and Sectarians" over a substantial Scots-Irish Presbyterian and German Reformed minority, who formed the core of the Constitutionalists. The initial success of the Constitutionalists in the late 1770s was primarily the result of consistently low voter turnout and enforced test laws. Because of the relaxation of the test laws in 1785 and increasingly higher voter participation in the postwar decade, the Republicans were able to establish a secure majority among the ethno-religious groups that either had been penalized directly by the Presbyterians or had other reasons for distrusting them. While recognizing that the Presbyterians were dedicated firmly to the revolution and had often incurred tremendous hardships in the process, Ireland suggests that the intolerance shown by the Presbyterians toward values different from their own alienated large pockets of ethnic and religious constituents, resulting in a "relatively short" reign of power. By 1787 the Republicans were firmly established as the majority party, and in the following year the Constitutionalists slowly began acknowledging their minority status.[82]

For some historians, however, the loss of the artisan vote in the city of Philadelphia was the key to the Constitutionalists' political demise. Eric Foner and Charles S. Olton emphasize that after the debacle of the attempted price controls and enforcement committees of 1779 the artisans and mechanics of the city deserted the Constitutionalists and became active and consistent supporters of the Republicans. Artisans favored a sound currency and protective tariffs against British imports, policies they believed were best achieved under Republican government. The 1784 Constitutionalist victory that captured the city of Philadelphia resulted simply from a sudden but transient loss of faith with the Republicans by the city's artisans because of the unloading of excess manufactured goods on Philadelphia's market by British merchants. Steven Rosswurm describes the breakup of the political alliance between middle-class artisans and lower-class laboring poor after 1779 as the demise of the radical force in Philadelphia city politics. Without that impetus, the Constitutionalists could no longer expect to win the majority vote in Philadelphia.[83]

The truth probably contains portions of all the various explanations—although, generally speaking, expanding core groups influencing voting patterns, rather than shifting voter allegiances, seem to explain more adequately the rise of the Republicans and the concurrent demise of the Constitutionalists in the city and county of Philadelphia. Undoubtedly, the loss of confidence in the Constitutionalists by the artisans was a critical blow to the party, as was its apparent inability to appeal beyond its own ethnic and religious limitations. In the event, it may well be that the Constitutionalists never enjoyed support from the majority of eligible or potential voters throughout the whole state, and in the city and county of Philadelphia particularly. Concomitant with this explanation is the correlation between low voter turnout and Constitutionalist success in Philadelphia. The election of 1784 helps illustrate the point. Despite Republican victories in the city and county of Philadelphia from 1780 to 1783 and from 1785 to 1789, the Constitutionalists scored a stunning victory in the 1784 elections, capturing nearly all of the city and county assembly positions. Supported by the Philadelphia delegations, the Constitutionalists in the assembly awarded all of Lancaster County's seats to candidates of their own party in that disputed election, giving the party a commanding majority. In the following year the Republicans regained control of the Philadelphia delegations, but the assembly was evenly divided between the two factions—in part because of the creation of Dauphin County in the previous year, which returned four Constitutionalists in 1785.

Bryan saw the 1784 victory as a popular reaction against the Pennsylvania Bank (established by the previous Republican assembly) and as a vindication of the work of the Council of Censors. As noted above, some historians attributed to economic conditions a sudden shift in artisan support back to the Constitutionalists in that year. Both analyses involve crossover voting, that is, former Republican voters changing their behavior and voting for the Constitutionalist candidates. The reality, however, may be quite different. The Constitutionalists in the city did only marginally better in votes received in 1785 and 1786 than they did in 1784, indicating that the number of votes for the city Constitutionalists remained relatively constant. Yet only in 1784 did the party win, suggesting that in that year the Republicans did not get out the vote. Charles Pettit, for example, who was the victorious Constitutionalist candidate in 1784, received 1,024 votes that year. In 1785 and 1786 he garnered 1,135 and 1,043 votes, respectively. Thomas Fitzsimons, the Republican candidate who won in 1785 and 1786, received in 1784 a total of 781 votes and in the next two years 1,232 and 1,567 votes. Exact returns for the 1783 assembly elections are not known, but in the city election for two censors held at the same time the Republican candidates (Samuel Miles and Fitzsimons) received 944 and 934 votes each. The Constitutionalist candidates received only 685 and 665 votes. Although the incomplete voting records render all analysis speculative, both parties steadily increased their voting totals in the city from 1781 until 1786. The Republicans, however, consistently received the highest totals except in 1784, when there appears to have been an inexplicable drop in support, not a shift. If there was a shift in voter support in 1784 and again in 1785, the differences in the totals would be reflected in the results of

1785 and 1786. But the totals for Pettit and Fitzsimons, for example, do not reveal such a circumstance. Rather, the total voting pattern for the city indicates that both parties received a steady progression of increased support from 1781 until 1786, with the Republicans receiving the greater share. The only anomaly of the voting pattern is the drop in support for the Republicans for 1784—but with no apparent increase for the Constitutionalists above what they would have normally received that year.

Bryan's own electoral history helps to illustrate the point. In all of his victories, the circumstances were skewed in his favor. He won the seat on council, for example, in the special election of February 1777, in which one critic charged that only seventy voters participated. In Bryan's 1779 assembly victory he was apparently assisted by the Fort Wilson riots and parading militia units, which undoubtedly helped to keep the anti-constitutionalists at home. In the 1783 election of censors for the city of Philadelphia, Samuel Miles and Fitzsimons defeated Bryan and David Rittenhouse by a total of 944 and 934 votes to 665 and 685 votes, respectively. Bryan's election to the Council of Censors in August 1784 was also a specially arranged poll, with Bryan receiving the highest number of votes cast, a total of 350—a remarkably low voter turnout, probably a reflection of the season of the year and apathy for a by-election.[84]

Their surprising victory in 1784 and their evenly divided status in the assembly in 1785 allowed the Constitutionalists to extract close victories in the selections of speaker (John Bayard) and clerk (Samuel Bryan) of the House[85] and buoyed the party's spirits and aspirations unfairly. Not only had the city and county of Philadelphia become Republican strongholds as early as 1780, but other counties that supported Constitutionalist candidates also turned to the Republicans with the easing of the test acts (Bucks and Northampton, for example). By 1787 and the fight over the proposed federal constitution, the Constitutionalists were a decided minority. By the following year their numbers in the assembly were even smaller. Bryan still believed that his party would eventually prevail; unfortunately for him, the death knell of the Constitutionalists would be sounded in 1787 and again in 1789.

8

"CONSPIRATORS AGAINST EQUAL LIBERTY"

RECAPTURING THE GENERAL ASSEMBLY in 1786, the Republicans pressed forward their political goals. Envisioning a grand reformation of state and federal politics, Republicans sought to reorganize the national government as well as to rewrite the 1776 constitution of Pennsylvania. Working in concert with political nationalists throughout the states, Republicans agitated for a stronger, centralized government that would possess the power to raise taxes and regulate commerce without the crippling dependence on the states that characterized the confederation. In 1787 they successfully pressured the Confederation Congress to hold a national convention in Philadelphia for the purpose of amending the Articles of Confederation. Bryan and his colleagues vehemently opposed any major alterations in the articles and feared for the safety of the state constitution. Time was not on their side, however, and they were forced to witness the continued diminution of their political legacies.

II

Like other Constitutionalists, Bryan recognized that the Articles of Confederation required revision. As Samuel Bryan explained to his father, there was a "general disposition in people to vest Congress with efficient powers for the regulation of commerce." The difficulty, he added, was "how to regulate such powers with the individual importance of the several states," and how to prevent Congress from "absorbing all power and influence within their vortex." The Bryans were apprehensive that Congress would seize the moment to obtain "dangerous powers."[1]

But neither the Bryans nor their allies were in a position to demand concessions from the Federalists, and the final draft that emerged from the Philadelphia Convention sent shock waves through the Constitutionalists' ranks. In the final days of the Eleventh General Assembly, and only two weeks after the Philadelphia Convention had adjourned, the Republicans added insult to injury to the Constitutionalists by ramming through the House a resolution calling for a state convention in November for the purpose of ratifying the proposed constitution. In order to ensure a quorum on the day of the vote authorizing the ratifying convention, a mob led by Anthony Wayne seized two Constitutionalist assemblymen and dragged them to the House. Stunned, the Constitutionalist party protested futilely against the heavy-handed tactics of the opposition. With thinly disguised contempt, the Republicans ignored their objections.[2]

The election to the convention was a sweeping success for the Republicans, who were generally also Pennsylvania's Federalists. In the city of Philadelphia, Federalists George Latimer, Benjamin Rush, Hilary Baker, James Wilson, and Thomas McKean were elected easily, while the Constitutionalist-Antifederalist candidates Charles Pettit, David Rittenhouse, and John Steinmetz were thoroughly humiliated.[3] Although John Smilie, William Findley, and Robert Whitehill defended the Antifederalist cause ably in the ratifying convention, the result was a foregone conclusion. The Constitution was approved by the convention members overwhelmingly, making Pennsylvania the second state to approve the document.[4]

Outraged, Bryan and the Constitutionalists charged that the Republicans had rushed the ratification of the Constitution precipitously through the state convention, despite the fact that the majority of the people opposed it.[5] They protested further that the delegates to the convention in Philadelphia never had the authority to draft a new constitution, let alone "annihilate" the confederation. Having been preempted in their ability to mount an effective opposition, the Constitutionalists charged that the Republicans had trampled the rights of the people by not providing sufficient time to examine the proposed scheme.[6] Calling the proposed constitution "damnable" and "vile," one critic expressed relief that "Judge B—n" and others were the only men of "good sense" who understood that the document was an "absurdity."[7]

The swiftness with which the Republicans defeated the Constitutionalists angered Bryan even more perhaps than the Constitution itself. Bryan charged that the Federalists deliberately stopped "news papers from state to state" that criticized the proposed national frame, allowing only favorable accounts of the document's reception in Pennsylvania to be "circulated and re-printed from Georgia to New Hampshire." Reports of popular dissatisfaction were systematically suppressed, complained Bryan, while a series of Federalist tricks were propagated to deceive the nation into believing that there was a "general approbation" of the Constitution. Bryan charged, for example, that in order to influence the Massachusetts ratifying convention a ship was sent to Boston with news that North Carolina had accepted the Constitution, when in fact that state's convention had not even convened. Similar frauds, he claimed, occurred in New Hampshire and Rhode Island. "The conspirators against equal liberty will have much deceit and wicked conduct to answer for."[8]

Bryan was convinced that the Constitution would be rejected ultimately and a second convention called. Otherwise, he predicted, "confusion and bloodshed" would result—"for if nine states" were led into the plan while the "body of the people" remained averse to it, a "civil war" would ensue. As a precursor to such a calamity, Bryan pointed to the disturbances that had occurred in Carlisle. Antifederalist demonstrations there had turned into riots, and officials pressed Chief Justice McKean for warrants to arrest twenty of the alleged ringleaders. Bryan reported, however, that since one of the effigies burned by the Antifederalist rioters was of McKean, the chief justice suggested a possible conflict of interest. He therefore asked Bryan and Atlee to issue the warrants. "I represented the danger of risquing insult to our precept," a coy Bryan commented, and thus he advised McKean instead to delay any decisions, especially "as no hasty steps had been taken to bring the city rioters to justice."[9] Bryan was referring caustically to Federalist rioters in Philadelphia who had not been, and probably would never be, arrested for their behavior.[10]

Bryan believed that throughout the counties the majority of the people opposed the Constitution, and that even in Bucks and Chester counties the Antifederalist movement was increasing. Philadelphia, however, presented a different picture in his view. The Federalist dominance within the city, Bryan claimed, was largely due to the "supreme influence of the Bank, the weight of Mr. Morris," and the "bankrupt and dependent state of the traders." The merchants and traders hoped that a new Congress would be able to stop the influx of British goods and prevent the shipping of American produce in foreign bottoms. But that was a "vain delusion," in Bryan's opinion, fed by the distress caused at that time by too substantial a "consumption of foreign goods." He realized, however, that "all ranks" had been erroneously led to believe that the Constitution "would be a cure for every sore." Moreover, many people remained silent for fear of offending the new order, but Bryan resolved to be "open and avowed" against the Constitution, thereby risking the "malice" of the Federalists. "The common people," he proclaimed, shared his view—but the real culprits were the "*gentlemen mobs*" who had been "active in Philadelphia."[11] Once again, Bryan saw the overmighty rich gentlemen as the true enemy to the Constitutionalists, and by implication to the people.

If the public had any doubt about Bryan's position on the Constitution, that uncertainty was unwittingly rectified in March 1788. Two letters outlining his animus toward the Constitution and its framers were intercepted by Bryan's enemies and printed in the *Pennsylvania Gazette*. Reaction to the letters was swift. "Do you really believe," asked an incredulous "Pennsylvanian," that the postmen had been seduced to "stop all newspapers from state to state?" Were "Gen. Washington, the President Franklin, the vice-president, the supreme court judges, and the majority of the Council, two thirds of our state convention, and two thirds of our assembly really conspirators?" Another writer condemned the "malevolence" of Bryan "in daring to violate the names of the most respectable characters on the continent."[12] Insisting that it was the prerogative of God to bring good out of evil, Benjamin Rush proclaimed that "Heaven" had permitted Bryan to be seen in his "proper colors." Rush viewed Bryan and his ally Ewing as "oxen decorated with ribbons parading the streets," being led "to their destruction." Rush asked a friend if he had seen Bryan's "detested letters," adding that they "infallibly" proved that he was the "author of the 'Centinel.'"[13]

The "Centinel" in question did not refer to the 1768 series against the establishment of an American Anglican bishop and the revival of admiralty jurisdiction to which Bryan had contributed, but rather to the most remarkable of all Antifederalist propaganda pieces. Centinel blasted the Federalists and the Constitution in a series of twenty-four scathing letters printed, ironically, in Eleazer Oswald's *Independent Gazetteer* from 5 October 1787 to 24 November 1788. Rush's hypothesis as to the author, however, was incorrect: it was not George Bryan but his son, Samuel.[14] Centinel contained a basic assessment of Constitutionalist-Antifederalist thought regarding both the proposed constitution and those who drafted it. Centinel also reflected the similarity of thinking between father and son. Samuel Bryan, for example, echoed his father's sentiments accurately when he attacked the "wealthy and ambitious" who thought they had the "right to lord it over their fellow creatures," and when he insisted that a "republican, or free government" could only exist when "property" was "pretty equally divided."[15] It seems probable that George Bryan, his father, and Eleazer

Oswald, his editor, contributed to Centinel, but the extent cannot be determined. Nonetheless, Samuel Bryan was the driving force behind the letters.

Centinel represented the depth to which Antifederalist thinking was pervaded by distrust of all power and by the belief that corruption lay at the root of man's willingness to abuse that power against the people. Therefore, consolidation of authority in any form was a mistake. Warning that "government ought to be cautious" and that it should not "govern over much," Centinel observed that "when the cord of power" was "drawn too tight," it "generally" resulted in its own "destruction." He added that the "opinion of power in a free government" was more "efficacious than the exercise of it." After all, the Swiss cantons were confederated on "weaker ties" than the United States had been by the Articles of Confederation, yet they had held together "for ages without any apparent chasm." Centinel advised his readers that the "power of the future government to levy money at pleasure" and to place the government "independent of the people as to enable the administration to gratify every corrupt passion of the mind, to riot on your spoils, without check or control" would destroy the republic.[16]

Throughout the letters, Centinel exposed what he considered to be the fatal errors of the Constitution—the power of the president to veto legislation, the unrepresentative nature of the Senate as well as its small size, the direct taxation of the people by the Congress, the lack of provision against a standing army, and the absence of a bill of rights.[17] Furthermore, the Constitution was structured deliberately to destroy the sovereignty of the state governments. The proposed legislative power of Congress was "so unlimited," exclaimed Centinel, that it would be the "coup de grace to the state governments," swallowing them up "in the grand vortex of general empire."[18]

Concomitant with the denunciation of the Constitution by Centinel was his vituperative assessment of those who drafted the document. This attack was not mere bombast, but an integral aspect of the Antifederalists' perception of the nationalist movement. As Douglas Arnold has pointed out, "country" ideology, the wellspring of Constitutionalist and Antifederalist thought and to a lesser degree the Federalist viewpoint, contained the fundamental precept that politics was the constant struggle between liberty and oppression, the virtuous and the conspirators. To that extent, Centinel was reiterating a consistent theme expressed by the Antifederalists and also by the author's father, George Bryan, in his published letters.[19] Calling the Federalists "aristocratic juntos of the *well-born few*," Centinel described the manner in which wealthy elites had been "zealously endeavoring" to humble the "*offensive upstart, equal liberty*." Centinel concluded that "such false detestable *patriots* in every nation" had guided their "blind confiding country, shouting their applauses, into the jaws of *despotism* and *ruin*." Centinel's overriding desire was for the "wisdom and virtue of the people of America" to preserve them "from the usual fate of nations."[20]

While such forceful pronouncements were gratifying to the Antifederalists they simply inflamed the opposition, which in April 1788 retaliated. As the printer of Centinel and editor of the only Antifederalist newspaper in the city, Oswald was targeted for particular retribution. Charged with libel by Andrew Brown, editor of the *Federal Gazette,* Oswald was required to post a £1,000 security bond, a considerable sum, and was bound over for trial. Oswald contested his bail and brought his case before Justice George Bryan, who dismissed the bail and released Oswald on his own recognizance.[21]

Since everyone suspected that George Bryan was the author of Centinel, the case against Oswald was intended to pressure and embarrass the Constitutionalist leader, who had become the most conspicuous symbol of the Antifederalist forces in the city. But Bryan and Oswald were not easily trapped. Oswald promptly printed in his newspaper all the material pertaining to his lawsuit, preferring to try his case in the court of public opinion. Chief Justice McKean, not to be outdone, charged Oswald with contempt of court, fined him £10, and imprisoned him for a month. At his hearing for contempt Oswald was represented by Constitutionalists Sergeant and Andrew Bankson, while the prosecution was led by William Lewis, an ardent Federalist; the judges were the Federalists McKean, Rush, and Atlee. Realizing that he was powerless to prevent the justices from ruling against Oswald and refusing to have any part in an action against his political ally, Bryan withdrew from the case, claiming that because he was absent for the initial proceedings he could not participate in the hearing. Lewis sought to force Bryan back into the case:

> Bryan, Justice. I was not here when the complaint was made to the court, when the evidence in support of the motion was produced, or the arguments against it were delivered; I consider myself, therefore, totally incapacitated for taking any part in this business.
>
> Lewis. We can immediately furnish the court with the proofs.
>
> Bryan. Can you furnish me, likewise, with Mr. Sargeant's arguments?
>
> Lewis said, that he had not penetration enough to discover any argument in what had been said for the defendant; and having

again read all the evidence which had been produced, he recapitulated what he had before said in support of the motion.

Bryan. I still say, that not having heard what has been offered in extenuation of the offense, I am incompetent to join in any opinion respecting the punishment. I cannot surely be suspected of partiality to libelers; I have had my share of their malevolence. But it is true, I have not suffered much; for these trifles do not rankle in my mind.[22]

Despite the persistence of the Federalists, Bryan continued to believe that the Constitution could be stopped and a new convention called. To that end, he used his position as leader of the Constitutionalists to organize the Antifederalist movement throughout the state. Suspecting the worst as early as September 1787, before the Constitution was published, Bryan held a meeting at his home with members of his party to plan measures of opposition.[23] While he could not have prevented the coup the Republicans managed in the hurriedly called ratifying convention, he did plan to derail the Federalist movement by creating a substantial and vocal opposition. Consequently, Bryan needed to act before the requisite nine states adopted the Constitution. He advised New York Governor George Clinton that as soon as possible the Antifederalist forces planned "to hold at some convenient point a meeting of delegates" who were to decide "how far the majority of the people of this state" were to abide by the "decision of the violent and tyrannus minority." Bryan continued: "Our action will much depend on the complexion of the acts of those states which we look to hold up the standard of liberty." He requested that Clinton notify him immediately "of the probable action" of New York, and if there was "any change in sentiment" there toward the Constitution.[24]

For whatever reason, however, the proposed meeting failed to occur in time to be of any real threat to the ratification of the Constitution. It was not until after ten states had approved the federal plan that a circular letter appeared in July 1788, issued by a self-appointed committee from Cumberland County, calling for a meeting to be held in Harrisburg on 3 September.[25] The delay might have resulted from Bryan's fruitless attempt to coordinate a national opposition in conjunction with the state movement.[26] He reasoned apparently that if the ratification process could be stalled for a few months only, the Harrisburg convention could have the dramatic impact he envisioned.

By the time of the Antifederalist meeting, however, eleven states had sanctioned the national charter, and further attempts to thwart the Federalists were futile. At Harrisburg forty-three men represented fourteen counties, while five counties—Luzerne, Montgomery, Northampton, Westmoreland, and York—were unrepresented. Bryan was chosen as the presiding officer of the convention, and Blair McClenanhan of the city of Philadelphia was elected chairman of the committee of the whole. After four days the delegates released a statement declaring that the Constitution in its present form contained "principles" that could be "perverted to purposes injurious to the rights of free citizens," as well as "some ambiguities" that were "incompatible with order and good government." Expunged from their rhetoric were the hopeful expressions of resistance to the Constitution, while respectful suggestions were inserted calling for a "peaceable method" for revising the Constitution.[27]

The resolutions drawn up by Bryan, Smilie, and Albert Gallatin proposed a series of adjustments to the Constitution. The suggested amendments would expand the size of the House of Representatives, permit the recall of senators by state legislatures, prohibit Congress from regulating the election of congressmen, eliminate direct taxation of the people by Congress (replacing it with a quota system to be imposed on the states), forbid the existence of standing armies unless two-thirds of both houses consented, reserve the regulation of the militia to the states, limit the power to create federal courts, and include the House of Representatives in the treaty ratification process.[28] Ironically, none of the Harrisburg amendments were presented to the assembly, nor would they form the basis of the Bill of Rights that was added to the Constitution in December 1791. While the Bill of Rights was intended to protect the individual from the excesses of the federal government, the Harrisburg amendments attempted to reduce significantly the power and authority of the national government in favor of the states. Accordingly, the Federalists would never consider them.

Bryan was at the center of Pennsylvania's opposition to the Constitution, aided by his son Samuel, Charles Pettit, and others in the city. John Nicholson, the Constitutionalist comptroller of the state, acted as a clearinghouse for Antifederalist information from the various states, while Constitutionalists Whitehill, Smilie, Findley, and Gallatin led the opposition in the western counties. But despite their spirited efforts, they failed. In fact, the contest against the Federalists in Pennsylvania was doomed from the outset. By 1787 the Republicans were not only in command of the government, but were also the majority party in the state.[29] Although he refused to admit it, Bryan was witnessing the denouement of the cause he had so ardently championed and led.

III

Aside from their dissatisfaction with the confederation, the Federalists were disgruntled with the unrestrained autonomy of local governments and the sudden, unwelcome rise of relatively unknown middle-class politicians. As Gordon Wood has noted, the drive for the federal constitution was inspired as much by the need to reform the state legislatures as to revive the collapsing national government.[30] Having achieved their victory on the federal level, the Republicans turned their attention toward the state.

In Centinel no. 9, Samuel Bryan had predicted that the Republicans, after having triumphed with their establishment of a new national government, would not rest until they had destroyed the 1776 Pennsylvania Constitution.[31] Republicans like Benjamin Rush happily agreed. Rush perceived that the Federalist movement would provide the needed momentum to overthrow the state's "dungcart" of a constitution.[32] On a summer evening at his home in 1789, Rush and other leading Republicans discussed the second phase of their political reformation—the calling of another state convention in order to rewrite the provincial frame of government.[33]

By 1787 the Republicans despised the 1776 constitution thoroughly and refused to consider any political option other than its total destruction. They were distressed with the chaos (as they perceived it) of an all-powerful assembly; legislation that was passed one year could always be repealed by the opposing faction the following year. Their policies therefore were always liable to the vagaries of an assembly chosen annually. As a prime example of such turmoil, they needed to look no further than the Bank of North America.

Founded by the financial czar of the confederation, Robert Morris, the bank had been chartered by both the national and Pennsylvania governments in 1781. Conceived as the cornerstone in Morris's effort to revitalize an economy wrecked by the war, the bank was also perceived by him as the link that would forge a common cause of economic nationalism among America's monied men.[34] No other institution, however, upset Bryan and his party as much as the bank with its monopolistic charter. It epitomized the arrogance of wealth the Constitutionalists believed to be the principal characteristic of the opposition. They pushed for the repeal of the charter as soon as they returned to power in October 1784, and after a year of maneuvering they successfully stripped the bank of its charter despite the protests of the anguished Republicans.[35]

Bryan worked closely with the Constitutionalist assemblymen during the charter debates.[36] Corresponding with friends and allies, he observed that the "general dislike of the bank" had surfaced with a vengeance. Petitions demanding the repeal of its charter flooded the assembly, and an exultant Bryan exclaimed, "never did I see any thing receive such favor." The bank itself contributed to its own demise, Bryan observed, by its opposition to the creation of a second bank and by its initial refusal to honor the paper money issued by the Constitutionalists in the 1784 session.[37] Those actions were "foolish interferences & provocations." The intransigence of the directors to accept paper money particularly angered Bryan, who astutely perceived that the political crisis was whether or not "our paper credit" would be "that of a bank, or of the public."[38]

Bryan's victory over the bank, however, was short-lived. When they resumed control of the assembly, the Republicans reversed the actions of the Constitutionalists and reestablished the charter of the bank on 17 March 1787. Although the law modified certain aspects of the charter to appease the opposition, the Constitutionalists were thoroughly dejected over the bank's revival. Remonstrances furnished by the antibank forces were futile gestures, however, and the Constitutionalists—wearied and dispirited—were once again left to "groan" under the bank's "baneful influence."[39]

The issue for the Republicans, however, was not only reestablishing the bank and their economic policies, but destroying a state government that could arbitrarily undo all their carefully laid plans. Their imperative to eliminate the 1776 constitution therefore was stronger in 1789 than it was at the document's adoption. The establishment of a new state government, equipped with a strong executive and a bicameral legislature with staggered terms, combined with the elimination of the rotation of office clause for assemblymen, would restore the order the Republicans desperately sought. On 20 March 1789 the Republicans in the assembly issued their address *To the Citizens of Pennsylvania,* declaring that the sovereignty of the people was the supreme law and that if the people wished to revise their state constitution immediately, it was their legal right to do so. Happy to oblige the people in their rights, especially when it coincided with their own goals, the Republican-controlled assembly ordered an election for delegates to a state constitutional convention the following October.[40]

Once again Bryan thrust himself into the fray, organizing the opposition against the latest attack on the 1776 constitution. Calling upon his son Samuel and other colleagues throughout the state, Bryan worked to counter the Republicans through petitions and public pressure.[41] Samuel Bryan returned to the press, issuing "Centinel Revived, No. 24," on 27 August 1789 and continuing publication of the Constitutionalist propaganda until 28 October with "Centinel Revived, No. 34."[42] Petitions were circulated, while Gallatin even suggested boycotting the elections. Once again, however, the burst of activity was all for naught, and the Constitutionalists discovered the exposed and weakened state of their party. "The people," explained Findley to Bryan, were "callous to an extreme." While many members of the electorate condemned the "calling a convention by the Assembly," they would not "exert themselves" in opposition. Others, continued Findley, were in a "sullen pit," despising the convention but remaining inactive.[43]

Like the ratifying convention before it, the Pennsylvania Constitutional Convention of 1789–90 was a Republican triumph. Not wishing to repeat the earlier humiliation, Findley sought a compromise and approached James Wilson. If the Constitutionalists accepted a bicameral government and a governor with veto power, Findley inquired, would the Republicans acquiesce in the direct election of assemblymen, senators, and the governor, drop property qualifications for officeholders, and continue Pennsylvania's liberal voting requirements? Fearing a reactionary element within his party and generally sharing democratic aspirations similar to those of Findley, Wilson readily agreed. On 24 September 1790 the state convention announced its new constitution. The 1776 constitution was dead. With the radical frame of government of 1776 no longer to be defended, the Constitutionalists lost their reason to exist.

In an epilogue to the history of the 1776 constitution, members of the Fourteenth General Assembly, the last under the old state charter, were perplexed as to their official status. Seeking a clarification of their role from the supreme court justices, the assemblymen were informed by the jurists that the assembly should not reconvene. The decision of the justices was unanimous, except for one judge who declined to answer. That solitary and suddenly quiet voice was, of course, George Bryan.[44]

CONCLUSION:
Bryan, the Law, and the Protection of Society

IN HIS CAPACITY AS COUNCILLOR, assemblyman, and politician, Bryan attempted to mold the government to standards that embodied his political philosophy. Like the Republicans, Bryan and the Constitutionalists opposed tyranny and sought the means to that end. Unlike the Republicans, however, Bryan believed that strenuous safeguards must be established and maintained to keep the government from falling into the hands of those individuals who would subvert it. Therefore, he opposed the consolidation of the national government into the federation because that would allow too much power to accrue into the hands of the few. By the same reasoning, he opposed the addition of an upper house to the state legislature and of a governor to the polity, because those institutions would present opportunities for unscrupulous men to seize control of the government. He rejected the argument that checks and balances were needed to stabilize the process of making public policy or that the state legislature was "all powerful," but rather believed that the annually elected, unicameral assembly was the most perfect expression of the will of the people and the surest safeguard against tyranny. In short, the state must be protected from forces from within.

Of equal importance to Bryan and for that matter to his party, as well as to the Republicans, was the integrity of the state against such forces that would compromise or subvert its authority. Although heavily imbued with revolutionary ideology, Bryan always prescribed limits to that ideology and its relationship to social behavior. He was intolerant of those who would disregard the state's authority and perceived that the proper role of the individual was, when necessary, to conform to the more pressing needs of the society. Consequently, Bryan strove to maintain the safety of the state through a rigorous interpretation of the law.

His justification for the test acts, for example, proceeded from the assumption that they were necessary safeguards against those individuals who were not fully committed to the revolution. Even when he feared correctly that some officials would abuse the power entrusted to them through those acts, Bryan nonetheless supported the power of the state to execute its laws. His reasoning developed from the perception that the state must maintain its ability to act based on the integrity of its authority. Bryan would not tolerate challenges to that authority.

While most American revolutionaries agreed on what essentially was an issue of law and order and the strength of the state in response to disorder, Bryan differed from his colleagues in his relentless pursuit of order. In 1778, for example, Bryan refused to pardon convicted traitors Abraham Carlisle and John Roberts, while James Wilson, equally committed to the revolution and the defense of the state, defended the two men in court.[1] Wilson was also sympathetic to the petitions of more than seven thousand citizens pleading for the lives of the two prisoners.[2] As one Bryan critic bitterly recalled, there was not "one good reason" why they needed to be executed, for there was "no danger of their conduct being imitated." Indeed, the critic continued, they were men of "good heart" who had been led into treason by "mistakes of their judgment." Nonetheless, Bryan executed them—or as another critic claimed, "rather than pardon them" Bryan would have served as "hangman himself."[3]

Bryan's insistence on the executions of Carlisle and Roberts reflected his uncompromising commitment to the revolution, and his belief that the two men were cognizant of their behavior and of the consequent punishment for treason. But Bryan further justified their sentences by declaring that an example had to be made of them in order to prove the strength of the government.[4]

Bryan adopted a similar stance toward the perpetrators of the Berks County tax revolt in 1780. In that episode, the court indicted 153 rioters protesting their taxes, and Bryan, a supreme court justice, believed that because their behavior was "very high and daring, bordering on treason," the rioters "needed a cheque that would not soon be forgotten." He feared, however, that the evidence against all the participants would be difficult to establish. Yet he refused the request of the counsel for the defendants to submit guilty pleas for some of the rioters, in exchange for the dismissal of the charges against the rest. "It was too serious a business to bargain about," Bryan replied to the defense lawyers, but if all the accused would submit to their guilt the court would reduce their punishments to a substantial fine. The defendants agreed, and Judge Bryan resigned himself to the best result he could achieve under the circumstances. In his description of the rioters Bryan noted that they had been former patriots, all of whom had "taken the oath of allegiance & fidelity" and most of whom had "been active in the marching of the militia." They had been, "in short, tolerable whigs." But despite Bryan's sympathetic perception of the cause of their behavior, he remained disgruntled. "I wish it had been in our power to have come at the leaders, who are in my opinion let go much too early."[5]

In a similar case, Bryan further elaborated his philosophy regarding social order and the rights of the state. In 1788 rioters protesting state taxes in Washington County were charged with seizing the tax collector, holding him hostage, stealing his money, and burning government documents. The case was brought before Bryan and Atlee in a court of oyer and terminer. In his summation to the jury, Bryan revealed his basic fear that society was inherently fragile and always susceptible to those individuals who would deliberately test the cords that bound the community together. "When members of the community" combined against the state, charged Bryan, the "bands of society" were in "immediate danger of dissolution." Those men, he observed, were "incapable of freedom" and had betrayed the "interests of the community." Consequently, they needed to be "punished in the most exemplary manner." After all, asked Bryan, was not their violent behavior against the laws of the people the very "nature of treason?" Would Pennsylvania "permit such doings?" Bryan insisted that it must not be tolerated. The "treasonable licentiousness of multitudes" would always lead to anarchy, which was "the most deadly foe to freedom" because from anarchy, tyrants emerged. Bryan insisted that the prosecution of those men would commence not only the "execution of the excise laws in this county, but of the laws in every other case." All law, he stressed, depended "on the same authority, and if one of these laws may, with impunity, be resisted, the force of the whole is evacuated. Upon what a slender basis then must the safety of the persons and properties of the orderly citizens of this county, depend."[6]

Bryan warned that society had to be vigilant against "combinations, associations of members, either in direst treasons" or in "high handed riots," because their behavior endangered "the whole community." Such evildoers "must by due severity, be saved from themselves, and taught to respect" the law. "Nothing less" would serve. Bryan leaned upon the rhetoric of the

Whigs to support his vision of social justice. "Liberty cannot subsist without public virtue," but public virtue could not exist when the "private will" was "set up against that of the community."[7]

While Bryan fought against the larger threats of riots and treason, he also scrupled to apply the same reasoning to lesser cases as well. In a fascinating example, Bryan was angered at a city grand jury for presenting the Philadelphia County commissioners for matters touching upon prison and judicial reform. The grand jury cited the county commissioners for allowing two defendants to remain in jail because they could not pay the court fees. In late eighteenth-century America, defendants were obligated to pay costs of prosecution regardless of their guilt or innocence; defendants would remain in prison until the fees were paid or were waived by the individual prosecutor and clerk. In the instances cited by the grand jury, a woman who was found not guilty and a mariner who had been found guilty and had finished his sentence remained in prison because they had not paid court costs.

Bristling at the grand jury's presumption, Bryan replied that the fees were the property of the court officers, and they had every right to expect their money. Moralists had always assumed, he declared, that charity to the poor and forgiveness of debts of those who were unable to pay were actions "accountable to the Supreme Being only."[8] No one had ever imagined that the courts were "competent to these investigations" or were "armed with power to punish the sinners." By law, court officials were not obligated to waive their fees, since they were after all a form of income. But the arrogance of the grand jurors, complained Bryan, had led them to present the "cruelty of holding prisoners in gaol for fees due by law to the officers of the court and county." Bryan then discussed the two prisoners cited by the grand jury. The acquittal of the woman who was detained in prison for payment of her fees, he observed, "was derived from the merciful supposition of law that a woman found in larceny with her husband" was to be considered "as under his compulsion and therefore discharged of the indictment." Bryan absolutely believed that the woman was guilty—perhaps not in law, but in fact. He also pointed out that she had a previous conviction of keeping a "bawdy-house." The grand jury was wrong therefore to "censure the commissioners of the county for not hastily relieving a prisoner of infamous character, who might have raised enough to pay for her fees by indenturing herself as a servant for less than a year." As for the mariner who was convicted of stealing an overcoat, Bryan suggested that since the prisoner was a "seafaring man" and "able of body" he could have "long since" obtained "his discharge from jail if he had bound himself for one short voyage to sea."

The court had no business, he argued, interfering with the payment of fees. The sheriff, the attorney general, and the court clerk could be "benevolent" and waive court costs, since they had "a perfect right" to dispose of their own property as they wished. Bryan added, however, that officials of the court occasionally set at liberty "too many villains upon the public by being too ready to remit their due." In the cases cited, Bryan was not only upholding the custom of the court, despite the obvious unfairness of imprisoning innocent citizens for their inability to pay the costs of their own prosecutions, but also clarifying his attitude toward people whom he knew or suspected to be of "infamous character."

Bryan was quick to add, however, that while a member of the assembly he "benevolently laboured" to enact legislation that would have "exonerated" the court fees for any person acquitted by either a grand or a petty jury. He further identified himself as part of a reform movement that sought to restructure the penal system, supporting the suggestions forwarded by Caesar Beccaria, the Italian penal reformer.[9]

The strength of the state, argued Bryan, lay not only in the execution of the laws, but also in the supporting of laws that were injudiciously made. In 1789 the assembly asked him whether or not it had the constitutional right to repeal a monopoly granted by an earlier assembly in order to award the same exclusive charter to another party. Bryan answered that while former acts might have been "obtained improperly," it remained in the community's best interest "to abide by its own legislative grants" unless there existed a "very great necessity" to overturn previous decisions. Bryan rationalized his position by arguing that "if one man" could not "rely on the faith of the government," then neither could "others." For governments to have their "faith suspected" was a dangerous precedent, and states "whose legislative grants" could not be depended upon would "sink into contempt." Bryan admitted that governments often did "foolish things." Yet he concluded that "the wisdom of government cannot be impeached without injury to the state; nor its most absurd grants be revoked, without arraigning at the same time its justice and its wisdom. Tens of thousands of money would be a trifling sacrifice compared to the loss of character of a state."[10]

Bryan as abolitionist, stern jurist, and politician provides interesting contrasts. On the one hand, Bryan agitated for the freeing of the slaves from their unjust servitude, while remaining impervious to the pleas of seven thousand citizens to save the pathetic lives of Carlisle and Roberts. Similarly, Bryan supported penal and legal reforms that would have eliminated court costs for defendants found not guilty while remaining totally unsympathetic to a woman incarcerated for her inability to pay those same fees, going so far as to suggest that because she was probably guilty, her fate was not all that undeserved. Furthermore, his advice in 1789 to the assembly not to reverse itself on monopolies granted by previous assemblies, even if the award was "foolish," directly countered his active support in repealing the state-chartered monopoly of the Bank of North America in 1785.

Yet within the parameters by which Bryan viewed political society, he was not inconsistent. His opposition to slavery ultimately rested on the belief that it undermined society by creating unnatural inequalities within it. Free men within the body politic, however, were capable of making choices, and each decision was either the reward or the punishment for their individual actions. In the case of Carlisle and Roberts, each chose his fate, and Bryan was determined to ensure that the established rules were observed. His philosophy therefore perceived that men and women were free to pursue their individual talents, were equal before the law, and were unencumbered by the morally draining leeches of aristocracy and slavery. But because the society that provided those freedoms was always vulnerable to the machinations of greedy or reckless men, safeguards were needed. While laws may be changed in a republic, such as the law ordering the payment of court fees by defendants, the law had to be obeyed while it existed. Bryan and the Constitutionalists of his generation who shared his philosophy were revolutionaries attempting to maintain order in a disorderly world.

The order that Bryan sought, however, was not always obtainable in a revolutionary society eagerly pursuing a variety of commercial, intellectual, and social goals. While Bryan at times revealed an accommodating spirit, or sought an unofficial relaxation of the enforcement of the test acts and eventually their repeal, he was also at times rather rigid in his thinking, uncompromising on events that perhaps called for more latitude. He defended until the end a state constitution that, whatever its merits, failed to unite Pennsylvanians in their search for a republican government. His support of the test acts, the arrest of the Quakers in 1777, the attempt of the state to impose price regulations during the economic crisis of 1779–80, and the unofficial sanctioning of the price control committees were all drastic measures that Bryan believed were necessary actions to save the state. Yet he was angered at the opposition's continued attempts to thwart his programs. For Bryan, the safety of the society and the success of the revolution were at stake, and he viewed the charges of bigotry and zealousness leveled at him by the Republicans as red herrings intended to hide selfish ambitions. In many respects the uncompromising commitment of Bryan and the Constitutionalists to the war was their greatest strength. They never faltered in their belief that victory would be achieved, and Bryan as councillor, chief executive, and assemblyman was instrumental in bringing Pennsylvania's government and society fully into the war. Perhaps the critical weakness of Bryan and his party was an inability to make the transition from the party of war to the party of peace.

Bryan the abolitionist, jurist, and wartime leader all merged in the politician through his relentless energy, wit, intelligence, and often conflicting values. In some respects his political career was a failure; in many other respects, however, he was a success. Where he failed, men like William Findley had to bring about the reconciliation of the Constitutionalists to the new order of American politics, abandoning the more rigid political philosophy for one that accommodated more fully the nascent political and social needs of the state's expanding democratic society. Findley, like Bryan, promoted the right of men to participate fully in the scramble for economic, political, and social upward mobility without the hindrance of property requirements for voting or officeholding. But unlike Bryan, Findley understood that the development of the political economy and the free state would not occur in the unsettling atmosphere of constitutional upheaval. With the establishment of the 1787 federal constitution and the 1790 state constitution, Pennsylvanians finally achieved a resolution of the debates over republicanism.

II

On 30 November 1789 Mrs. Elizabeth Bryan wrote to her son, George Bryan, Jr., that his father continued to suffer from influenza. "Indeed I have been alarmed for your father, as it clung to him long, and affected his eyes, so that he could scarcely see."[11] Despite his age and increasing debilities, Bryan continued to sit on the supreme court and to organize political affairs for his party. Samuel Bryan even attempted to create a movement to elect his father to the newly created gubernatorial position in 1790. "The idea of running my father," he announced, had been received "with a warmth and unanimity that was quite unexpected, and the dormant spirit of the old whigs" appeared to have been "roused with its former vigor."[12] But such plans were unrealistic. The candidate for governor preferred by most Constitutionalists and Republicans was Thomas Mifflin, who overwhelmingly defeated his opponent, Arthur St. Clair, 27,725 votes to 2,802 in the fall 1790 elections.[13] Men like Mifflin and Washington, generals of the revolution, were the new heroes, not the revolutionary zealots who had brought about the destruction of the old order and its violent replacement by "radical" republicanism. Despite the ambitions of Samuel Bryan, the political world of George Bryan had vanished. The adoption of the 1790 state constitution represented a new era.

Bryan sat during the supreme court's January term, which ended on the twenty-second. That was the first session of the court under the new state charter, which had gone into effect officially on 7 December 1790. But soon after his return from the January session, Bryan fell ill. On 27 January 1791 he took his last breath.[14] Four days later, with Bryan barely in his grave, Justices McKean, Rush, and Atlee petitioned the assembly for support for his widow, Elizabeth, noting that her late husband "died very poor, leaving an aged widow and seven children." In the twenty-five years of his public service, the petition continued, Bryan had received "very small compensation," and despite the "most rigid economy" he had been unable to save any money for a "future day." The petitioners observed that as widows and children of men who served in the military received a pension, the same should hold true for those in the "civil life." While the plea was well intended, the assembly had little incentive to initiate such a precedent, and they referred the plan to the governor's office, where the idea was quietly dropped. Elizabeth Bryan died on 5 January 1799 at the age of sixty-six.[15]

Bryan's death marked the passing of an era in American political culture. The political vision that he and the Constitutionalists had put into practice in 1776 briefly held sway over a society at war. By 1790, however, the Constitutionalists were no longer a political force, and Bryan alone continued to carry the torch. It was ironic that Samuel Bryan, who showed flashes of brilliance in his political analysis of contemporary society, would suggest his father as a gubernatorial candidate in 1790, objecting to Thomas Mifflin as not worth half a penny to the "whig interest." Leaving aside the improbability of George Bryan being elected, he was unlikely to have condescended to accept a constitutional position that he believed to be the antithesis of republican government. Yet the time had come for American society to resolve the outstanding differences of the revolutionary period and form a national consensus. Bryan's moment was in 1776, and by the time of his death in January 1791 the democratic society he had helped to create was leaving him behind.

Notes

Introduction

1. *Pennsylvania Gazette*, 29 September 1784, "A Citizen of Pennsylvania." The author of the allegation hated Bryan, so he may have fabricated the story to either embarrass Bryan or fool future Bryan historians.

2. Oswald Seidensticker, "Frederick Augustus Muhlenberg, Speaker of the House of Representatives in the First Congress, 1789," *Pennsylvania Magazine of History and Biography* 13 (1889): 200. (hereafter *PMHB*).

3. *Independent Gazetteer*, 5 November 1785, "A Physiognomist."

4. George Bryan to Elizabeth Bryan, 4 July 1777, James Tyndall Mitchell Papers, Historical Society of Pennsylvania (hereafter HSP).

5. *The American Magazine*, first half of 1791, 81–82. The following are based on articles written shortly after Bryan's death and were written by his friends, who were casting the most favorable light on his life.

6. *American Advertiser*, 31 January 1791.

7. *The American Magazine*, first half of 1791, 81–82.

8. *Independent Gazetteer*, 5 November 1785, "A Physiognomist."

9. *American Advertiser*, 31 January 1791.

10. Alexander Graydon, *Memoirs of His Own Time, with Reminiscences of the Men and Events of the Revolution* (Philadelphia, 1846), 287.

11. Even though he was a judge and possessed an excellent knowledge of the law he once told Grace Galloway, who was about to lose her house during forfeiture proceedings against declared traitors, that he would inquire into her fate, although he protested that he was "no lawyer." Raymond C. Werner, ed., "Diary of Grace Growden Galloway," *PMHB* 55 (1931): 45.

Chapter 1

1. Burton Alva Konkle, *George Bryan and the Constitution of Pennsylvania, 1731–1791* (Philadelphia: W. J. Campbell, 1922), 17–19; deposition of Eliza and Anne Bryan, 4 March 1786,

Bryan Papers, HSP. Konkle lists Elizabeth, Nancy, Arthur, and Samuel as Bryan's siblings, but according to the deposition of 1786 there is a William (who identifies himself as George Bryan's brother in another correspondence in the Bryan Papers, HSP), and an Anne as well. Konkle possibly misidentified Eliza as Elizabeth.

2. Konkle, *George Bryan*, 17–19.

3. John J. McCusker, "Ships Registered at the Port of Philadelphia before 1776: A Computerized Listing," compiled 1970, HSP.

4. For excellent descriptions of eighteenth-century merchants in Philadelphia, see Thomas M. Doerflinger, *A Vigorous Spirit of Enterprise: Merchants and Economic Development in Revolutionary Philadelphia* (Chapel Hill: University of North Carolina Press, 1986); Arthur L. Jensen, *The Maritime Commerce of Colonial Philadelphia* (Madison: State Historical Society of Wisconsin, 1963); Harry D. Berg, "The Organization of Business in Colonial Philadelphia," *Pennsylvania History* 10 (1943): 157–77. See also Grace H. Larsen, "Profile of a Colonial Merchant: Thomas Clifford of Pre-Revolutionary Philadelphia" (Ph.D. dissertation, Columbia University, 1955); and Mark M. Egnal, "The Pennsylvania Economy, 1748–1762: An Analysis of Short-Run Fluctuations in the Context of Long-Run Changes in the Atlantic Trading Community" (Ph.D. dissertation, University of Wisconsin, 1974).

5. Jensen, *Maritime Commerce*, 12.

6. McCusker, "Ships." See also "Ship Registers for the Port of Philadelphia, 1716–1775," *PMHB* 24 (1900): 510.

7. R. J. Dickson, *Ulster Emigration to Colonial America, 1718–1771* (London: Routledge & Kegan Paul, 1966), 82; Maldwyn A. Jones, "Ulster Emigration, 1783–1815," in E.R.R. Green, ed., *Essays in Scotch-Irish History* (London: Routledge & Kegan Paul, 1969), 56.

8. Samuel Bryan to George Bryan, 23 September 1752, copy in the Bryan Papers, HSP.

9. *Pennsylvania Gazette*, 27 August, 30 November 1752; Samuel Bryan to George Bryan, 23 September 1752, copy in the Bryan Papers, HSP. See also Thomas M. Truxes, *Irish-American Trade, 1660–1783* (Cambridge: Cambridge University Press, 1988); and Jensen, *Maritime Commerce*, 86.

10. Doerflinger, *Vigorous Spirit*, 99–100.

11. McCusker, "Ships"; *Pennsylvania Gazette*, 11 June 1752–12 September 1754 passim, customhouse entries, and 30 November 1752–27 June 1755 passim, advertisements under Wallace and Bryan. Also, for reference on the topics of flax seed, see Truxes, *Irish-American Trade;* and Philip White, *The Beekmans of New York in Politics and Commerce, 1647–1877* (New York: New York Historical Society, 1956). On trade with the West Indies, see Mark Egnal, "The Changing Structure of Philadelphia's Trade with the British West Indies," *PMHB* 99 (1975): 156–79.

12. *Pennsylvania Gazette*, 14 September 1752.

13. Diary of George Bryan, 15 May 1753, LC. The diary of George Bryan is attributed to Bryan by the archivist of the Library of Congress. The content, context, and style of the material is definitely similar to Bryan's other works.

14. Jensen, *Maritime Commerce*, 12.

15. *Pennsylvania Gazette*, 10 October 1754, 4 February, 4 and 11 March 1755. James and Thomas Wallace were partners from approximately 11 March 1755 to 26 February 1756.

16. *Pennsylvania Gazette*, 4 March–30 October 1755 passim; William Bryan to George Bryan, 10 August 1756, Bryan Papers, HSP.

17. Doerflinger, *Vigorous Spirit*, 100.

18. McCusker, "Ships"; *Pennsylvania Gazette*, 16 December 1756–2 August 1759 passim, under customhouse entries.

19. McCusker, "Ships."

20. Ibid.

21. Doerflinger notes that although there was depression among dry goods merchants in the early 1760s, trade with the West Indies was very strong. Consequently, large sums of money were made in shipping or the sale of ships (*Vigorous Spirit*, 174). For further discussion on shipping, see Simeon J. Crowther, "The Shipbuilding Output of the Delaware Valley," *American Philosophical Society Proceedings* 117 (1973), and John J. McCusker, "Sources of Investment Capital," *Journal of Economic History* 32 (1972).

22. Leonard Labaree, ed., *The Papers of Benjamin Franklin* (New Haven: Yale University Press, 1963), 6:438.

23. William Gilliland to George Bryan, 7 April 1762, Bryan Papers, HSP.

24. James D. Anderson, "Thomas Wharton, 1730/31–1784: Merchant in Philadelphia" (Ph.D. dissertation, University of Akron, 1977), 79–80.

25. George Bryan to Joseph Shippen, Jr., 5 April 1760, Reed Papers, New York Historical Society; William Gilliland to George Bryan, 7 April 1762, Bryan Papers, HSP.

26. Doerflinger, *Vigorous Spirit*, 94–95, 133. See also Mary M. Schweitzer, *Custom and Contract: Household, Government, and the Economy in Colonial Pennsylvania* (New York: Columbia University Press, 1987), chap. 5.

27. *Pennsylvania Gazette*, 26 February 1756.

28. Unsigned [Samuel or Arthur Bryan] to George Bryan, 24 and 31 March 1767, Bryan Papers, HSP.

29. William Bryan to George Bryan, 10 August 1756, Bryan Papers, HSP; Truxes, *Irish-American Trade*, 44; Jensen, *Maritime Commerce*, 130–31.

30. William Gilliland to George Bryan, 6 February, [n.d.] April 1762, Bryan Papers, HSP.

31. Receipt of Baynton, Wharton, & Morgan from George Bryan, 13 August 1764, James T. Mitchell Collection, HSP; Rubin Gardner to George Bryan, 10 May 1765, unsigned [Samuel or Arthur Bryan] to George Bryan, 24 and 31 March 1767, Bryan Papers, HSP; Cadwalader Collection, Thomas Cadwalader Section, Custom House Tonnage Books, 1765–1775, bk. A, 38(2), 50, 57, 61; *Pennsylvania Gazette*, 14 May 1767.

32. *Pennsylvania Journal*, 6 September 1764?; *Pennsylvania Gazette*, 9 July 1767, 20 March 1766.

33. William Otis Sawtelle, "Acadia: The Pre-Loyalist Migration and the Philadelphia Company," *PMHB* 51 (1927): 280, 283–84.

34. Conveyance of Realty, West New Jersey, Liber T, 378–80, Liber U, 211–12; "A Map of two Tracts of Land . . . ," undated, Bryan Papers, HSP.

35. Conveyance of Realty, West Jersey, Liber Z, 219–23.

36. "1769 Tax List," microfilm, HSP; Phila. Deed Bk., H, 12:489–91, and D, 29:24–26; *Pennsylvania Gazette*, 19 September 1771.

37. George Bryan to Elizabeth Bryan, 4 July 1777, James T. Mitchell Papers, HSP.

38. Konkle, *George Bryan*, 78–79; Records of the First Presbyterian Church, 1701–1856, HSP; Records of the Second Presbyterian Church, 1745–1833, HSP. Their children were: Sarah (b. 1758), Samuel (b. 1759), Arthur (b. 1761), Francis (b. 1764), Mary (b. 1765), George (b. 1767), Elizabeth (b. 1769), William (b. 1771), Thomas (b. 1772), and Jonathan (b. 1774).

39. *Pennsylvania Gazette*, 20 March 1766, 14 May 1767.

40. Hannah Benner Roach, ed., "Taxables in the City of Philadelphia, 1756," *Pennsylvania Genealogical Magazine* 22 (1961): 21; "1765 Tax List," microfilm, HSP.

41. Hannah Benner Roach, ed., "Taxables in Chestnut, Walnut and Lower Delaware Wards, Philadelphia, 1767," *Pennsylvania Genealogical Magazine* 22 (1961): 180; "17th Eighteenth Penny Provincial Tax, 1769," microfilm, HSP. Bryan's 1769 assessment included one Negro, presumably a slave.

42. *Pennsylvania Gazette,* 2 February 1791. Konkle cited a letter written by a Philadelphian in Dublin in 1786, which suggested that the cause of George Bryan's failure lay with his brother in Ireland. Unfortunately, Konkle cited neither the location of the letter nor the identity of the correspondents (*George Bryan,* 88).

43. "17th Eighteenth Penny Provincial Tax, 1774," microfilm, HSP.

44. Doerflinger, *Vigorous Spirit,* chap. 1.

45. *Votes and Proceedings of the House of the Representatives* (Philadelphia, 1774), 5:424.

46. Minutes of the Corporation for the Relief of Poor and Distressed Presbyterian Ministers, and of the poor and distressed Widows and Children of Presbyterian Ministers, 1759–1797, 12 October 1773, typed copy, Presbyterian Historical Society (hereafter PHS).

Chapter 2

1. Samuel Bryan to George Bryan, 23 September 1752, copy in the Bryan Papers, HSP.

2. Guy S. Klett, ed., *Minutes of the Presbyterian Church in America, 1706–1788* (Philadelphia: Presbyterian Historical Society, 1976), 340–42.

3. Francis Alison to Ezra Stiles, 10 December 1762, 10 July 1761, PHS, typed copy.

4. Howard Miller, *The Revolutionary College: American Presbyterian Higher Education, 1707–1837* (New York: New York University Press, 1976), 22–29; Francis Alison to Ezra Stiles, 22 October 1773, PHS, typed copy; Elizabeth Ingersoll, "Francis Alison: American Philosophe, 1705–1779" (Ph.D. dissertation, University of Delaware, 1974), 441–44; Klett, ed., *Minutes,* 377, 381–82. See also Charles Hodge, *The Constitutional History of the Presbyterian Church* (Philadelphia: Presbyterian Board of Publication, 1851), 312–16.

5. Klett, ed., *Minutes,* 381; the ministers relocated in the Second Philadelphia Presbytery were: Robert Cross, Francis Alison, John Ewing, John Symonton, and James Latta. In 1763 the presbytery licensed Patrick Alison (no relation to Francis Alison).

6. Ibid., 516–20; Francis Alison to Ezra Stiles, 22 October 1773, PHS, typed copy.

7. Diary of George Bryan, 5 July 1758, LC. Bryan was making a pun. Every Friday evening New Side communicants would gather at the Second Presbyterian Church and pass out tokens, or medals, to those who had been saved and were subsequently eligible for communion. On Sunday those with the tokens received communion. The tokens were returned until their distribution on the following Friday. J. Thomas Scharf and Thompson Westcott, *History of Philadelphia, 1609–1884* (Philadelphia, 1884), 2:1262–64.

8. Dietmar Rothermund, *The Layman's Progress: Religious and Political Experience in Colonial Pennsylvania, 1740–1770* (Philadelphia: University of Pennsylvania Press, 1961). See also Perry Miller, "Jonathan Edwards and the Great Awakening," in Daniel Aaron, ed., *America in Crisis* (New York, 1952), 3–19; Martin E. Lodge, "The Crisis of the Churches in the Middle Colonies, 1720–1750," *PMHB* 95 (1971): 212; and Marilyn J. Westerkamp, *Triumph of the Laity: Scots-Irish Piety and the Great Awakening, 1625–1760* (New York: Oxford University Press, 1988).

9. Presbytery of Philadelphia to Dr. Samuel Chandler, 15 March 1755, First Presbyterian Church Minutes, 1755–1772, PHS.

10. Ibid.

11. Leonard J. Trinterud, *The Formation of an American Tradition: A Re-examination of Colonial Presbyterianism* (1949; reprint, Philadelphia: Westminster Press, 1970), 150.

12. Dr. Samuel Chandler to the Philadelphia Presbytery, 6 April 1756, First Presbyterian Church Minutes, PHS.

13. First Presbyterian Church Minutes, 25 November 1757, PHS.

14. Ibid., 28 July 1758, PHS.

15. Ibid., 18, 21 September 1758, PHS.

16. Ibid., 10 August 1761, PHS.

17. Ibid., 10 August 1761, 17 August 1764, 4 July 1765, 24 and 25 June 1765, PHS.

18. First Presbyterian Church Minutes, George Bryan, William Allison to the Second Presbyterian Church in the City of Philadelphia, 1 July 1765, PHS.

19. Ibid.

20. Ibid.

21. First Presbyterian Church Minutes, Answer of the Second Presbyterian Congregation in Philadelphia to the foregoing Letter and Proposals, 1 July 1765, PHS.

22. Ibid.

23. First Presbyterian Church Minutes, 8 and 16 January 1766, PHS.

24. Trinterud, *American Tradition,* 213; Ingersoll, "Francis Alison," 494–95; Francis Alison to Ezra Stiles, 4 December 1766, PHS, typed copy.

25. John Maclean, *History of the College of New Jersey, from Its Origin in 1746 to the Commencement of 1854* (Philadelphia: J. B. Lippincott and Co., 1877), 23–60; Ingersoll, "Francis Alison," 498–500.

26. The discussion surrounding the delegation's proposals and its first visit with the trustees of Princeton is based, in part, on the account provided by Ingersoll, "Francis Alison," 498–500; Maclean, *College of New Jersey,* 288–89; Francis Alison to Ezra Stiles, 4 December 1766, PHS, typed copy.

27. Maclean, *College of New Jersey,* 288–89; Francis Alison to Ezra Stiles, 4 December 1766, PHS, typed copy.

28. John Wallace to Archibald Wallace, 4 December 1766, Whitaker Collection, Dartmouth College; William Wallace to John Wallace, 3 August 1774, Wallace Papers, HSP. See also Ingersoll, "Francis Alison," 504–5; Maclean, *College of New Jersey,* 291–94.

29. Ingersoll, "Francis Alison," 502–7. Ingersoll also notes that the actions of the trustees were only an attempt to stall and that the conciliatory attitude was "a meaningless sop." According to the Rev. Asbel Green, no one seriously expected that the proposals "would ever be carried into effect." (507).

30. Francis Alison to Ezra Stiles, 4 December 1766, 4 June 1768, PHS, typed copy.

31. Ibid., 4 June 1768, 22 October 1773.

32. Ibid.

33. First Presbyterian Church Minutes, 5 March 1767, PHS.

34. Ingersoll, "Francis Alison," 493, 498–99.

35. First Presbyterian Church Minutes, 21 January 1768, PHS.

36. Ibid., 10 and 16 February 1768, PHS.

37. Ibid., 1 March, 15 and 18 April 1768, PHS.

38. Ibid., 25 April 1768, PHS.

39. Klett, ed., *Minutes,* 455; Second Presbyterian Church Minutes, 2 January 1769, 1 April 1772, PHS; Records of the Second Presbyterian Church, Philadelphia, Marriages, Burials, Baptisms, 1745–1833, PHS.

40. Francis Alison to Ezra Stiles, 12 December 1767, PHS, typed copy.

41. Francis Alison to Great Britain and Ireland, 4 March 1760; "Minutes of Corporation for Relief of Poor Ministers," *Journal of Presbyterian Historical Society* 30 (March 1952): 128 (hereafter *JPHS*).

42. Ingersoll, "Francis Alison," 278–82.

43. Of the original twelve members, five were ministers (two Old Side, three New Side) and seven were prominent merchants and landowners long active in the church. Four were

from the First Church and three were from the Second Church. Of the second group, six were ministers, six were merchants, one was a doctor, and one unknown. Five were from the First Church and two were from the Second Church. "Minutes of Corporation for Relief of Poor Ministers," 20; Alexander Mackie, *Facile Princeps: The Story of the Beginning of Life Insurance in America* (Lancaster, Pa.: Lancaster Press, 1956), 70–75.

44. Minutes of the Corporation for Relief of Poor and Distressed Presbyterian Ministers, and of the poor and distressed Widows and Children of Presbyterian Ministers, 1759–1797, 7 and 8 February 1760, 1:24–25, PHS, typed copy.

45. Minutes of the Corporation, 10 December 1766, 1:118, PHS, typed copy.

46 Ibid., 16 November 1762, 1:81, PHS, typed copy.

47. Ibid., 27 and 29 May 1767, 1:124–26, PHS, typed copy; John Baird, *Horn of Plenty: The Story of the Presbyterian Ministers' Fund* (Wheaton, Ill.: Tyndale House, 1982), 38–39.

48. "Corporation," 27 May 1767, 1:124–26, PHS, typed copy.

49. Ibid., 23 May 1771, 2:171, PHS, typed copy.

50. Ibid., 2 November 1763, 14 February, 25 May, 16 December 1767, 1:106, 120, 122, 129, PHS, typed copy.

51. Baird, *Horn of Plenty*, 48–49.

52. First Presbyterian Church Minutes, 27 February 1772, PHS.

53. Third Presbyterian Church Minutes, 12 March 1772, PHS; First Presbyterian Church Minutes, 26 March 1772, PHS.

54. First Presbyterian Church Minutes, 2 and 22 June 1772, PHS. Bryan agreed to inquire if a Reverend Howe of New England would be interested in a call to the Third Church. Nothing came of it.

55. Third Presbyterian Church Minutes, 27 June 1772, PHS; Hughes Oliphant Gibbons, *A History of Old Pine Street* (Philadelphia: John C. Winston Co., 1905), 39–40.

56. Third Presbyterian Church Minutes, 21 June 1772, PHS; Klett, ed., *Minutes*, 503.

57. Klett, ed., *Minutes*, 523–24.

58. Gibbons, *History*, 54.

59. Ibid., 47–48.

60. First Presbyterian Church, Minutes of the Meetings of the Committee for regulating Pews, 1774–1786, PHS; "Journal of Reverend James Sproat, D.D.," 3 April 1778, HSP.

61. Second Presbyterian Church, Pew Rent Book, 1779, 1781; First Presbyterian Church, Minutes of the Meetings of the Committee for regulating Pews, 1774–1786; Records of the Second Presbyterian Church, Philadelphia, Marriages, Burials, Baptisms, 1745–1833, PHS.

Chapter 3

1. Samuel Purviance to Ezra Stiles, 1 November 1766, in Francis B. Dexter, *Itineraries and Correspondence of Ezra Stiles* (New Haven: Yale University Press, 1916), 557.

2. James H. Hutson, *Pennsylvania Politics, 1746–1770: The Movement for Royal Government and Its Consequences* (Princeton: Princeton University Press, 1972), 211–13.

3. Scotch-Irish Presbyterian immigration to North America and Pennsylvania is discussed in the following: Wayland F. Dunaway, *The Scotch-Irish of Colonial Pennsylvania* (1944; reprint, Hampden, Conn.: Archon Books, 1962), 29, 41; James G. Leyburn, *The Scotch-Irish: A Social History* (Chapel Hill: University of North Carolina Press, 1962), 170–75; and Marianne Wokeck, "A Tide of Alien Tongues: The Flow and Ebb of German Immigration to Pennsylvania, 1683–1776" (Ph.D. dissertation, Temple University, 1983), chap. 6.

4. The following table shows the discrepancy between actual representation and representation based on the province's taxables by county.

	Actual Members	Members by Taxables
Philadelphia City	2	4
Philadelphia County	8	8 (base)
Chester	8	7
Bucks	8	4
Lancaster	4	8
York	2	5
Berks	1	4
Northampton	1	3
Cumberland	2	2

Source: Brooke Hindle, "The March of the Paxton Boys," *William and Mary Quarterly*, 3d ser., 3 (1946): 463 (hereafter *WMQ*).

5. "Circular Letter and Articles of some Gentlemen of the Presbyterian Denomination in the Province of Pennsylvania, 24 March 1764," in Joseph Galloway, *Historical and Political Reflections of the Rise and Progress of the American Rebellion* (London, 1780), 49–50, Library Company of Philadelphia (hereafter LCP).

6. Prerevolutionary Pennsylvania politics has been thoroughly discussed by several historians. Theodore Thayer, *Pennsylvania Politics and the Growth of Democracy, 1740–1776* (Harrisburg: Pennsylvania Historical and Museum Commission, 1953), depicted the Quaker party as the protagonist of early democracy against neo-feudal rule. William S. Hanna, *Benjamin Franklin and Pennsylvania Politics* (Stanford, Calif.: Stanford University Press, 1964), concluded, however, that colonial politics was not the result of a fundamental drive for democracy. Rather, Pennsylvania was ruled by a Quaker oligarchy, who viewed attempts to change the political order as a threat to their security and to the best interests of the colony. John J. Zimmerman, "Benjamin Franklin and the Quaker Party, 1755–1756," *WMQ* 17 (1960): 291–313, observed that the "crux of the dispute" was constitutional: whether the Quaker party or the proprietor was to control the colony. The Quakers emerged as victors, but only through the leadership of Benjamin Franklin and the restructuring of the party (291). Alan Tully, *William Penn's Legacy: Politics and Social Structure in Provincial Pennsylvania, 1726–1755* (Baltimore: Johns Hopkins University Press, 1977), saw the Quaker and proprietary leaders as the elites of Pennsylvania society but held that while the latter was never able to establish any real permanent ties to local institutions in the province, the Quaker party, by providing inexpensive government, represented more thoroughly the will of their constituents.

7. Ralph Ketchum, "Conscience, War, and Politics in Pennsylvania, 1755–1757," *WMQ* 20 (1963): 434–35.

8. Thayer, *Pennsylvania Politics,* 11.

9. Hanna, *Benjamin Franklin,* 18–20.

10. Tully, *Penn's Legacy,* 98.

11. Winfred Trexler Root, *The Relations of Pennsylvania with the British Government, 1696–1765* (1912; reprint, New York: Burt Franklin, 1969), 293, 302–4.

12. See Jack D. Marietta, *The Reformation of American Quakerism, 1748–1783* (Philadelphia: University of Pennsylvania Press, 1984), 150–86.

13. Hanna, *Benjamin Franklin,* 101. The alliance between Franklin and Norris must have been uncomfortable for Norris and those remaining Quakers, as military legislation continued to be a question of conscience for them. In 1757 pacifist Quakers were lamenting their dis-

placement: "Our Country People seem already to repent Friends being out of the House of Assembly. And if we do not use much precaution it will be next to impossible to prevent a majority of them [Franklin's people] being chosen next year" (John Pemberton to Dr. Samuel Fothergill, quoted in Hanna, 120).

14. Robert S. Hohwald, "The Structure of Pennsylvania Politics, 1739–1766" (Ph.D. dissertation, Princeton University, 1978), 114–26; Leonard W. Labaree, ed., *The Papers of Benjamin Franklin* (New Haven: Yale University Press, 1963), 6:14–27, 307–14; Franklin was memorialized for his wagon effort in a contemporary poem entitled "Musing Near a Cool Spring," in Thomas P. Haviland, "Two Epitaphs for Ben," *PMHB* 65 (1951): 198; also, Whitfield J. Bell, Jr., and Leonard W. Labaree, "Franklin and the 'Waggon Affair,' 1755," *American Philosophical Society Proceedings* 101 (1957): 551–58.

15. *Pennsylvania Gazette*, 2 September 1756.

16. *Pennsylvania Journal*, 18 and 25 September 1755; *New York Mercury*, "Supplement No. 168," 27 October 1755. Bryan's participation in the creation of Humphrey Scourge is discussed in Joseph Shippen to Edward Shippen, 13 December 175[5], in Thomas Balch, *Letters and Papers relating chiefly to the Provincial History of Pennsylvania* (Philadelphia, 1855), 169.

17. *Tit for Tat, or the Score wip'd Off*, by Humphrey Scourge, Esq., Philadelphia, 1 November 1755, LCP. The Quakers were no more amused with Scourge than was Governor Morris. The Philadelphia Monthly Meeting promptly condemned the article as a "virulent, seditious and scandulous libel." *Pennsylvania Gazette*, 1 January 1756.

18. *Tit for Tat*.

19. *Votes and Proceedings of the House of the Representatives* (Philadelphia, 1774), 4:509, 523 (hereafter *Votes*); *Pennsylvania Colonial Records* (Harrisburg, 1852), 6:724, 735; *Pennsylvania Gazette*, 24 February 1756; the militia law was favorably explained in Benjamin Franklin's publication of "A Dialogue between X, Y, and Z," *Pennsylvania Gazette*, 18 December 1755; Richard Peters to Richard Penn, 1 June 1756, Penn Papers Official Correspondence (hereafter PPOC), 8:95, HSP: "If the new Governor does not bring over with him a repeal of the militia law all will be to no purpose." Under proprietary pressure, the Militia Act was disallowed by the Board of Trade. Pennsylvanians learned of its termination in October 1756 (*Votes*, 4:631).

20. *Tit for Tat*.

21. William Peters to Richard Penn, 4 January 1756, and Richard Peters to Richard Penn, 17 February 1756, PPOC, 8:3, 29, HSP; *Colonial Records*, 6:769.

22. *Pennsylvania Gazette*, 25 December 1755; Labaree, ed., *Franklin Papers*, 6:389; Richard Peters to Richard Penn, 17 February 1756, PPOC, 8:29, HSP. Perhaps a consolation for Bryan was his sale to the militia of 757 shirts, grossing a considerable £391 14s. 4d. Labaree, ed., *Franklin Papers*, 6:438.

23. *Pennsylvania Gazette*, 25 March 1756. The eight men were William Bradford, George Bryan, John Rhea, Thomas Smith, Matthew Clarkson, Josiah Davenport, Thomas Bourne, and George Brooks. All but Bryan and Brooks were from the New Light Second Presbyterian Church.

24. *A Brief State of the Province of Pennsylvania* (London, 1755), LCP. William Allen to Thomas Penn, 26 October 1755, PPOC, 7:137, HSP.

25. *Pennsylvania Journal*, 10 June 1756, Depositions of William Smith and Daniel Roberdeau, and 17 June 1756, Deposition of Daniel Roberdeau.

26. Gilbert Tennent, *The Happiness of Rewarding the Enemies of our Religion and Liberty, Represented in a Sermon . . . February 17, 1756, to Captain Vanderspiegel's Independent Company, at the request of the Officers* (Philadelphia, 1756), LCP.

27. *Pennsylvania Journal*, 10 June 1756, Deposition of Nathaniel Grubb; Richard Peters to Thomas Penn, 30 October 1756, PPOC, 8:181, HSP.

28. Richard Peters to Thomas Penn, 16 September 1756, PPOC, 8:165, HSP, and Diary of George Bryan, 13 April 1764, LC; Hutson, *Pennsylvania Politics,* 211n. Marietta, *Reformation,* 140, 204, discusses the blurred image of the religious Friends and the political Friends.

29. John Elder to Richard Peters, November 1755, and Edward Biddle to James Biddle [c. November 1755], *Colonial Records,* 6:704–5; Thayer, *Pennsylvania Politics,* 53–54.

30. *London Chronicle,* 20–23 October 1764.

31. Charles Thomson to Benjamin Franklin, 18 December 1764, in Labaree, ed., *Franklin Papers,* 12:521–24; Benjamin Franklin to Jared Eliot, 1 September 1755, and to Ezra Stiles, 1 September 1755, ibid., 6:175–78; Francis Alison to Ezra Stiles, 15 April 1764, PHS, typed copy.

32. Norman S. Cohen, "The Philadelphia Election Riot of 1742," *PMHB* 92 (1968): 306–19; William Allen to Fernando John Paris, 25 October 1755, in Lewis Burd Walker, ed., *The Burd Papers, Extracts from Chief Justice William Allen's Letter Book* (Pottsville, Pa., 1897), 25; and William Allen to Thomas Penn, 25 October 1755, PPOC, 7:137, HSP.

33. John Armstrong to Thomas Penn, 5 November 1759, PPOC, 9:122, HSP; Bryan's Diary, 13 April 1764, LC.

34. Bryan's Diary, 16 February 1758, 9 February 1764, 5 July 1758, LC.

35. Ibid., 5 July 1758.

36. Ibid., 13 April 1764. On the death of the frontiersmen and their families, Bryan wrote, "Some think the Quakers are not displeased at this, as it reduces other people not of their society to come [into] proportion with them."

37. Ibid., 9 February 1764, 27 April 1764.

38. See, for example, John Chester Miller, *The Wolf by the Ears: Thomas Jefferson and Slavery* (New York: The Free Press, 1977), for Jefferson's view of the Indians.

39. For accounts of the Paxton boys' massacre at Lancaster, and their subsequent march on Philadelphia, see, James E. Crowley, "The Paxton Disturbance and Ideas of Order in Pennsylvania Politics," *Pennsylvania History* 37 (1970): 317–39; Brooke Hindle, "The March of the Paxton Boys," *WMQ,* 3d ser., 3 (1946): 461–86; Herbutis M. Cummings, "The Paxton Killings," *Journal of the Presbyterian Historical Society* 44 (1966): 219–43 (hereafter *JPHS*); and Peter A. Butzin, "Politics, Presbyterians and the Paxton Riots, 1763–64," *JPHS* 51 (1973): 71–84.

40. Hindle, "Paxton Boys," 476; Marietta, *Reformation,* 189–92; *The Quaker Unmask'd, or Plain Truth,* reprinted in John R. Dunbar, ed., *The Paxton Papers* (The Hague: Martinus Nijhoff, 1957), 211–12, sarcastically noted that "if any of their Fellow Subjects become obnoxious to their mild and peaceful Rage, by opposing any of their arbitrary Measures, we then see the Quaker unmask'd, with his Gun upon his Shoulders."

41. According to Marietta, *Reformation,* 327, many of the tracts ascribed to the Quakers by historians like James Hutson were, in fact, by non-Quakers, a point that annoyed contemporary apologists for the Paxtonites when they found "they had no Quakers to debate and that no opponents even professed to be Quakers."

42. *A Dialogue Containing some Reflections on the late Declaration and Remonstrance, of the Back-Inhabitants,* 122, and *A Looking Glass for Presbyterians,* 246, in Dunbar, ed., *Paxton Papers.*

43. *The Cloven-Foot Discovered,* 85–86; and also *The Apology of the Paxton Volunteers addressed to the candid and impartial World,* 189, in Dunbar, ed., *Paxton Papers.* The author of *The Cloven-Foot Discovered* added:

> Pray, worthy FRIENDS! observe the text,
> Get money first, and virtue next.
> In many things change but the name,
> Quakers and the Indians are the same; . . .

But those who th' Indians cause maintain,
Would take the part of bloody Cain,
And sell their very souls for gain.

44. Benjamin Franklin to John Fothergill, 14 March 1764, in Labaree, ed., *Franklin Papers,* 11:102–3; Edward Shippen to James Burd, 9 February 1764, in Balch, *Letters,* 204; *Pennsylvania Archives* (Harrisburg, Pa., 1852), 1st ser., 4:148–49 (hereafter *Pa. Arch.*); Bryan's Diary, 9 February 1764, LC.

45. Bryan's Diary, 9 February 1764, LC; John Ewing to Joseph Reed, 1764, in William B. Reed, *Life and Correspondence of Joseph Reed* (Philadelphia, 1847), 35.

46. Bryan's Diary, 19 March 1764, LC.

47. William Allen to Thomas Penn, 25 September 1764, PPOC, 9:270, HSP; Hutson, *Pennsylvania Politics,* 153–55.

48. *Votes,* 5:334–37; *Cool Thoughts on the Present Situation of our Public Affairs* (Philadelphia, 1764). The assembly officially instructed its agents to present to the king its petition for royal government on 26 May 1764. Franklin's description of his relationship with Penn was succinctly stated. "You know," Franklin mused, "I don't love the Proprietary, and . . . he does not love me" (Franklin to Dr. Fothergill, 14 March 1764, in Labaree, ed., *Franklin Papers,* 11:103). See also 11:199–200.

49. Bryan's Diary, 13 and 26 April 1764, LC.

50. John Stanley Murzyn, "Principles and Politics in Pre-Revolutionary Pennsylvania, 1756–1776" (Ph.D. dissertation, New York University, 1969), 83–84; Israel Pemberton to David Barclay, 6 November 1764, Pemberton Papers, HSP; *Pa. Arch.*, 8th ser., 7:5688–89.

51. Rev. Hugh Neill to the Secretary, 25 June 1764, in William Stevens Perry, ed., *Historical Collections relating to the American Colonial Church* (1871; reprint, New York: AMS Press, 1969), 2:360–61.

52. Richard Peters to Richard Penn, 1 June 1756, PPOC, 8:95, William Allen to Thomas Penn, 25 September 1764, PPOC, 9:270, William Peters to Thomas Penn, 4 June 1764, PPOC, 9:226, HSP; Revs. William Sturgeon and John Hughes to the Secretary, 23 March 1765, in Perry, *Colonial Church,* 2:375; *An Address of Thanks to the Wardens of Christ Church and St. Peters . . . in the name of all the Presbyterians in Pennsylvania* (Philadelphia, 1764), LCP.

53. Dietmar Rothermund, "The German Problem of Colonial Pennsylvania," *PMHB* 84 (1960): 17–20.

54. William Allen to David Barclay and Sons, 25 September 1764, in Burd, ed., *William Allen's Letter Book,* 56–57.

55. "Circular Letter," in Galloway, *Rise and Progress,* 49–53.

56. Samuel Purviance to James Burd, 10 September 1764, in Balch, *Letters,* 204–6; James Burd to Samuel Purviance, 17 September 1764, Shippen Papers, 6:109, HSP.

57. *Pennsylvania Journal,* 27 September 1764; Labaree, ed., *Franklin Papers,* 11:390–93.

58. Milton E. Flower, *John Dickinson, Conservative Revolutionary* (Charlottesville: University Press of Virginia, 1982), 42.

59. *Pennsylvania Journal,* 27 September 1764. Apparently, Franklin ran on both the county and city slate in order to defeat Dickinson in the county elections. Labaree, ed., *Franklin Papers,* 11:390; William Allen to Thomas Penn, 21 October 1764, PPOC, 9:282, HSP.

60. Hugh Roberts to Benjamin Franklin, 12 October 1765, in Labaree, ed., *Franklin Papers,* 12:312.

61. Wokeck, "A Tide of Alien Tongues," 152.

62. *Pennsylvania Journal,* 27 September 1764.

63. Charles Pettit to Joseph Reed, 3 November 1764, in Reed, *Correspondence,* 36–37;

John Penn to Thomas Penn, 19 October 1764, PPOC, 9:274, HSP.

64. Edward Shippen to James Burd, 6 October 1764, in Balch, *Letters*, 206–7; Benjamin Franklin to Richard Jackson, 8 October 1764, in Labaree, ed., *Franklin Papers*, 11:395; Charles Petit to Joseph Reed, 3 November 1764, in Reed, *Correspondence*, 36–37.

65. *Votes*, 5:375; John Penn to Thomas Penn, 19 October 1764, PPOC, 9:274, HSP; Benjamin Chew to Thomas Penn, 5 November 1764, PPOC, 9:286, HSP.

66. *Votes*, 5:379–80.

67. Ibid., 5:380–83; *Pennsylvania Journal*, 1 November 1764. A remonstrance protesting Franklin's appointment was presented by the "citizens of Philadelphia" to the assembly preceding the published protest. The remonstrance was similar in detail to the minority's protest.

68. *Pennsylvania Journal*, 1 November 1764; also Labaree, ed., *Franklin Papers*, 11:408–12. The protest was signed by John Dickinson, David McCanaughty, John Montgomery, Isaac Saunders, George Taylor, William Allen, Thomas Willing, George Bryan, Amos Strettle, and Henry Keppele. Though he voted with the minority, Joseph Richardson, as a member of the Quaker party, could not sign such a blatantly anti-Franklin article.

69. John Dickinson to Isaac Norris, 24 October 1764, Norris Letter Book, HSP; William Allen to Thomas Penn, 27 February 1768, PPOC, 10:140, and 11 March 1765, PPOC, 10:1, HSP; *Votes*, 5:381, 384.

70. *Votes*, 5:374–76.

71. Ibid., 5:385–430, passim.

72. Ibid., 5:386–87, 396–97, 406, 408; James T. Mitchell and Henry Flanders, eds., *Statues at Large of Pennsylvania, 1682–1801* (Philadelphia, 1896), 6:432–40.

73. Ibid., 5:37–38, 419–21. John Hughes to Benjamin Franklin, 8–17 September 1765, in Labaree, ed., *Franklin Papers*, 12:265. Hutson (*Pennsylvania Politics*, 198–202) argues that the Quaker party was practicing the politics of ingratiation with the ministry. With their petition pending, the Quakers were caught off balance with the Stamp Act protest. Objecting to the revenue acts, yet fearful to offend the home government, the Quakers backed themselves into a stalemate.

74. *Votes*, 5:420. The committee was Dickinson, Bryan, Morton, Giles Knight, Saunders, McCanaughty, Allen, and Taylor. Morton and Knight were from the Quaker party.

75. *Votes*, 5:499–504; Thomas Wharton to Benjamin Franklin, 5 October 1765, Thomas Wharton to Benjamin Franklin, 7 November 1765, in Labaree, ed., *Franklin Papers*, 12:292, 12:356–57.

76. Samuel Purviance, Jr., to Ezra Stiles, 1 November 1766, in Dexter, *Itineraries*, 555.

77. Alan Tully, "Quaker Party and Proprietary Policies: The Dynamics of Politics in Pre-Revolutionary Pennsylvania, 1730–1775," in Bruce C. Daniels, *Power and Status: Officeholding in Colonial America* (Middletown, Conn.: Wesleyan University Press, 1986), 103–4.

Chapter 4

1. George Bryan to Rev. John Ewing, 8 July 1775, in *PMHB* 23 (1889): 405–6.

2. William Allen to Thomas Penn, 12 November 1766, PPOC, 10:70, HSP; Horace W. Smith, *Life and Correspondence of the Reverend William Smith, D.D.* (Philadelphia, 1879), 1:414.

3. Historians have generally agreed that during the late 1760s and early 1770s the proprietary and the Quaker party cooperated more than they contended on policy. The Quaker party, observed Tully, dominated politics, stood for popular issues, and remained visibly faithful to its popular heritage into the late sixties when imperial issues cut across party lines and undercut its strength. Alan Tully, "Quaker Party and Proprietary Policies: The Dynamics of Politics in

Pre-Revolutionary Pennsylvania, 1730–1775," in Bruce C. Daniels, ed., *Power and Status: Officeholding in Colonial America* (Middletown, Conn.: Wesleyan University Press, 1986), 75–105. Both Hanna and Hutson specifically related the Quakers' loss of strength to their rapprochement with Penn. William S. Hanna, *Benjamin Franklin and Pennsylvania Politics* (Stanford, Calif.: Stanford University Press, 1964), 189, 191; James H. Hutson, *Pennsylvania Politics, 1746–1770: The Movement for Royal Government and Its Consequences* (Princeton: Princeton University Press, 1972), 236, 238. Hutson cited the fear of the Presbyterians as the principal motive for the Quaker-Penn reconciliation.

4. *Pennsylvania Colonial Records* (Harrisburg, Pa., 1852), John Penn to the Assembly, 8 February 1768, 9:461, the Assembly (Joseph Galloway, Speaker) to the Governor, 20 February 1768, 9:473, and the Assembly (Joseph Galloway, Speaker) to the Governor, 5 February 1768, 9:457.

5. *Colonial Records,* 9:325, 385, 408–12, 416–20, 430–36, 447, 454–58, 554–55, 645–46, 684–85, 708, 709–10, 10:70, 75, 130–33, 142–44, 196–97; William Allen to Thomas Penn, PPOC, 10:174, HSP; John Swift to Jasper Yeates, 1 January 1772, Balch Papers, Swift and Willing Papers, HSP. See Thomas M. Doerflinger, *A Vigorous Spirit of Enterprise: Merchants and Economic Development in Revolutionary Philadelphia* (Chapel Hill: University of North Carolina Press, 1986), chap. 4, for a description of the economic fluctuations during the 1760s.

6. Hutson, *Pennsylvania Politics,* 238–40; Richard Alan Ryerson, *The Revolution Is Now Begun: The Radical Committees of Philadelphia, 1765–1776* (Philadelphia: University of Pennsylvania Press, 1978), 22.

7. William Allen to Thomas Penn, 8 October 1767, PPOC, 10:116, James Tilghman to Thomas Penn, 30 January 1773, PPOC, 11:61, 28 October 1773, PPOC, 11:107, and 31 March 1774, PPOC, 11:123, James Tilghman to Henry Wilmot, 22 June 1774, PPOC, 11:153, HSP.

8. Alan Tully, *William Penn's Legacy: Politics and Social Structure in Provincial Pennsylvania, 1726–1755* (Baltimore: Johns Hopkins University Press, 1977), 111.

9. 2 March 1761, Court Papers, Philadelphia County, 1749–1821, HSP. The justices removed were Thomas Yorke, John Hughes, Rowland Evans, Samuel Wharton, and John Potts; John Penn to Thomas Penn, 17 March 1764, PPOC, 9:216, HSP; *Colonial Records,* 19 November 1764, 9:204–5.

10. *Colonial Records,* 19 November 1764, 9:204–5; Samuel Wharton to Benjamin Franklin, 23 November 1764, and Joseph Galloway to Benjamin Franklin, 23 November 1764, in Leonard W. Labaree, ed., *The Papers of Benjamin Franklin* (New Haven: Yale University Press, 1963), 11:472, 468. Wharton was mistaken—Huston was not commissioned; *Colonial Records,* 23 May 1770, 9:672, and 27 April 1772, 10:45–46.

11. Frank M. Eastman, *Courts and Lawyers of Pennsylvania: A History, 1623–1923* (New York: American Historical Society, 1922), 1:255–57, 266–67; *Colonial Records,* 9:204–5, 393, 672, 10:31, 45–46; 2 March 1761, Court Papers, Philadelphia County, 1749–1821, HSP.

12. Eastman, *Courts and Lawyers,* 1:266–67; M. Carey and J. Bioren, eds., *Laws of the Commonwealth of Pennsylvania* (Philadelphia, 1803), 1:169–87. Governor's commissions are listed in the minutes of the Provincial Council, and some of the actual commissions are stored in the court records, Philadelphia County, HSP. Also, in the colonial and revolutionary period the justices of the peace held the same legal position as judges. In 1790 the state constitution divided the two into separate authorities.

13. Replevin was an action whereby the owner could recover goods or chattels wrongfully detained or possessed by another (*Black's Law Dictionary*).

14. Carey and Bioren, eds., *Laws,* 1:169–87. For an excellent review of existing court

records: Marylynn Salmon, "The Court Records of Philadelphia, Bucks, and Berks Counties in the Seventeenth and Eighteenth Centuries," *PMHB* 107 (1983): 249–91. Beginning in the eighteenth century, the assembly began reorganizing the courts in order to distinguish their role more clearly, as well as to accommodate the colony's growing population. The 1722 act for establishing courts of judicature separated minor criminal cases from common pleas, and relocated them in quarter session courts. Though the orphans' court was established in 1683, experience proved it to be only partially successful, and the assembly in 1705 and 1713 reorganized it by explicitly stating its jurisdiction. In 1727 and 1759 the assembly attempted to reorganize the county courts further, but those laws were repealed by the king in council. In the 1759 revision the assembly prohibited county justices from sitting on quarter session courts, but the law's repeal returned the county justices to their former authority. Only supreme court judges could sit on the supreme court and courts of oyer and terminer. Carey and Bioren, eds., *Laws,* 1:169–87; Lawrence Lewis, Jr., "The Courts of Pennsylvania in the Seventeenth Century," *PMHB* 5 (1881): 155, 143–49; John Bioren, *Laws of the Commonwealth of Pennsylvania, 1682–1801* (Philadelphia, 1810), 1:31–32; James T. Mitchell and Henry Flanders, eds., *Statutes at large of Pennsylvania, 1682–1801* (Harrisburg, Pa., 1897), 4:84–95, 5:462–65, 7:107–10; Staughton George, Benjamin M. Nead, and Thomas McCamant, eds., *Charter to William Penn, and laws of the Province of Pennsylvania, 1682–1700* (Harrisburg, Pa., 1879), 131, 346–51.

15. 6 June 1772, Meeting of the Commissioners, Minute Book of Commissioners and Assessors of Philadelphia, Pa., 1771–74, HSP.

16. 2 December 1761, Philadelphia Mayor's Court Docket, 1759–64, City Archives, Philadelphia.

17. Philadelphia Orphans Court, Bks. 7–11 passim, microfilm, HSP; Philadelphia Quarter Sessions Dockets, 1761–66, 1766–70, 1773–80, passim, City Archives, Philadelphia; Philadelphia Mayor's Court Docket, 1767–71, passim, City Archives, Philadelphia; *Colonial Records,* 9:699; Pennsylvania Commission Bk., A, 4:39–40, microfilm, HSP.

18. John Hughes to Benjamin Franklin, 8 September 1765, in Labaree, ed., *Franklin Papers,* 12:265–66; Samuel Purviance, Jr., to James Burd, 20 September 1765, in Thomas Balch, *Letters and Papers Relating Chiefly to the Provincial History of Pennsylvania* (Philadelphia, 1855), 208; *Votes and Proceedings of the House of the Representatives* (Philadelphia, 1775), 5:419–21. Theodore Thayer, *Pennsylvania Politics and the Growth of Democracy* (Harrisburg: Pennsylvania Historical and Museum Commission, 1964), 118–19, suggested that another Quaker motivation to send Bryan and Dickinson to New York was to get them out of town during the October elections.

19. Fox did not attend the congress. *Votes,* 5:437; Caesar Rodney to Thomas Rodney, 20 October 1765, in George H. Ryden, ed., *Letters to and from Caesar Rodney, 1756–1784* (Philadelphia: University of Pennsylvania Press, 1933), 25–26; Edmund S. Morgan and Helen M. Morgan, *The Stamp Act Crisis: Prologue to Revolution* (1953; reprint, New York: Macmillan, 1963), 138–54.

20. James Burd to Edmund Burd, 18 September 1765, Shippen Papers, 6:125, HSP; John Penn to Thomas Penn, c. November 1765, PPOC, 11:263, HSP; *Pennsylvania Journal,* 10 October, 19 and 28 December 1765. The London Coffee House was located on the corner of Front and Market streets and was a major meetinghouse for politicians, sea captains, merchants, and traders throughout the eighteenth century. It was owned by William Bradford, printer of the *Pennsylvania Journal.*

21. *Pennsylvania Journal,* 14 November 1765.

22. Ibid., 14 and 21 November 1765.

23. *Colonial Records,* 9:299–300, 309; Richard Penn to Thomas Penn, 15 December 1765, PPOC, 10:19, John Penn to Thomas Penn, 15 December 1765, PPOC, 10:23, HSP; *Pennsylvania Journal,* 2 January, 2 February 1766.

24. The seven who visited Hughes were William Bradford, Charles Thomson, James Tilghman (Secretary of the Land Office), John Cox, Jr., (a Presbyterian merchant), Archibald McCall, Robert Morris (both Anglican merchants), and William Richards (an Anglican druggist). The seven were accompanied by either John, James, or Andrew Allen, all sons of William Allen, the chief justice. Hutson, *Pennsylvania Politics,* 196; Richard Alan Ryerson, "Leadership in Crisis. The Radical Committees of Philadelphia and the Coming of the Revolution in Pennsylvania, 1765–1776: A Study in the Revolutionary Process" (Ph.D. dissertation, Johns Hopkins University, 1973), 659. The members of the merchants' committee were Thomas Willing, Samuel Mifflin, Thomas Montgomery, Samuel Howell, Samuel Wharton, John Rhea, William Fisher, Joshua Fisher, Peter Chevalier, Benjamin Fuller, and Abel James. *Pennsylvania Journal,* 14 November 1765. The Sons of Liberty were not very "numerous," because of the opposition of the "White Oaks" and the "Hearts of Oaks," ship carpenters and laborers who were loyal to Franklin and subsequently to Hughes and the Quaker party, and who were suspicious of their enemies. Hutson, *Pennsylvania Politics,* 198; also Morgan, *Stamp Act Crisis,* 259n.

25. Morgan, *Stamp Act Crisis,* 321.

26. William Franklin to Benjamin Franklin, 7 September 1765, and John Hughes to Benjamin Franklin, 8 September 1765, in Labaree, ed., *Franklin Papers,* 12:262, 264–65.

27. Hugh Roberts to Benjamin Franklin, 12 October 1765, in Labaree, ed., *Franklin Papers,* 12:313.

28. Elizabeth I. Nybakken, ed., *The Centinel Warnings of a Revolution* (Newark: University of Delaware Press, 1980), contains an excellent summary of the episcopacy crisis and Pennsylvania politics.

29. Thomas Bradbury Chandler, D.D., *An Appeal to the Public, in Behalf of the Church of England in America* (New York, 1767), 4, LCP. "Men may ridicule the Notion of *uninterrupted succession* as they please; but if the authority of the clergy is derived from Christ, (and if it is not, they are no ministers of Christ). . . . And if the succession be *once* broken, and the power of ordination *once* lost, not all the men on earth—not all the angels in Heaven, without an immediate commission from Christ, can restore it."

30. Ibid., 6–25, 34–35.

31. Ibid., 26–27, 33, 59, 79, 97, 105.

32. Nybakken, *Centinel,* 19–27.

33. Ibid., 10, 19. Nybakken also determined that other authors probably contributed to Centinel as well, especially numbers 20 and 21. Nonetheless, the three principal authors who assisted one another were Alison, Dickinson, and Bryan.

34. Ibid., 85, 88, 102, 107; Centinel no. 1, 24 March 1768; Centinel no. 3, 7 April 1768; and Centinel no. 4, 14 April 1768.

35. Nybakken, *Centinel,* 118, 126, 128; Centinel no. 6, 28 April 1768; and Centinel no. 8, 12 May 1768.

36. Nybakken, *Centinel,* 148–53; Centinel no. 12, 9 June 1768.

37. Nybakken, *Centinel,* 148–53.

38. Nybakken, *Centinel,* 142–47; Centinel no. 11, 2 June 1768.

39. Nybakken, *Centinel,* 142–47.

40. Ibid.

41. Ibid.

42. Ibid.

43. Philadelphia's role within the nonimportation movement between 1768 and 1770 is presented in Ryerson, "Leadership in Crisis," 93–110; Arthur M. Schlesinger, *The Colonial Merchants and the American Revolution* (1918; reprint, New York: Frederick Ungar, 1957), 116–20, 125–29; and Hutson, *Pennsylvania Politics*, 221–35.

44. *Pennsylvania Journal*, 4 August 1768, "An Address"; An Alphabetical List of Subscribers to the Non-Importation Agreement, 10 March 1769, in James and Henry Drinker Correspondence, Henry S. Drinker Papers, 1739–1779, HSP; Committee of Merchants of Boston to Committee of Merchants of Philadelphia, 11 August 1768, MSS. Relating to Non-Importation Resolutions, Philadelphia, 1765–1766, vol. 2, APS.

45. Ryerson, "Leadership in Crisis," 102–10; Doerflinger, *Vigorous Spirit*, 189–91; Samuel Coates to William Logan, 26 September 1770, Samuel Coates Letter Book, August 1763–December 1781, Coates-Reynell Collection, HSP.

46. Hutson emphasized the role of the Presbyterian party in the resistance movement of the early seventies, while Ryerson argued that a "patriot" party emerged from the Stamp Act protests, the nonimportation committees, and the tea embargo, and claimed partisans from a variety of ethnic, religious, and economic backgrounds. The Quakers, for example, were increasingly uncomfortable with the imperial crisis, argued Ryerson, while the Presbyterians were very comfortable with the conflict, but that did not mean that Presbyterians had their own wing within the resistance movement. Rather, the crisis cut across social lines and shaped new coalitions of interest groups that formed and reformed with each successive stage of the crisis. Hutson, *Pennsylvania Politics*, 236–38; Ryerson, "Leadership in Crisis," 109–10; and Ryerson, *Revolution Is Now Begun*, 73–75.

47. George Bryan to Rev. John Ewing, 8 July 1775, in *PMHB* 23 (1899): 405–6.

Chapter 5

1. Pennsylvania's revolutionary period is best described in Robert L. Brunhouse, *The Counter-Revolution in Pennsylvania, 1776–1790* (Harrisburg: Pennsylvania Historical Commission, 1942); Richard Ryerson, *The Revolution Is Now Begun: The Radical Committees of Philadelphia, 1765–1776* (Philadelphia: University of Pennsylvania Press, 1978); Owen Ireland, "The Ratification of the Federal Constitution in Pennsylvania" (Ph.D. dissertation, University of Pittsburgh, 1966); and Douglas McNeil Arnold, "Political Ideology and the Internal Revolution of Pennsylvania" (Ph.D. dissertation, Princeton University, 1976).

2. "Diary of James Allen, Esq., of Philadelphia," *PMHB* 9 (1885): 189.

3. Willi Paul Adams, *The First American Constitutions: Republican Ideology and the Making of the State Constitutions in the Revolutionary Era* (Chapel Hill: University of North Carolina Press, 1980), 148. Also, for Pennsylvania's ideological origins of the 1776 constitution, see Gordon S. Wood, *The Creation of the American Republic, 1776–1787* (1969; reprint, New York: W. W. Norton, 1972), 229, 248–49, 363–64, 450–51; Richard A. Ryerson, "Republic Theory and Partisan Reality in Revolutionary Pennsylvania. Toward a New View of the Constitutional Party," in Ronald Hoffman and Peter Albert, eds., *Sovereign States in an Age of Uncertainty* (Charlottesville: University Press of Virginia, 1981), 96–130.

4. For descriptions of the various delegates, see William H. Egle, "The Constitutional Convention of 1776: Biographical Sketches of Its Members," *PMHB* 3 (1879): 96–101, 194–205, 319–30, 438–46; Eric Foner, *Tom Paine and Revolutionary America* (New York: Oxford University Press, 1976), 109–32; Brooke Hindle, *David Rittenhouse* (Princeton: Princeton University Press, 1964); David Freeman Hawke, "Dr. Thomas Young—'Eternal Fisher in Troubled Waters': Notes for a Biography," *New York Historical Society Quarterly* 54 (1970): 7–29;

Pauline Maier, "Reason and Revolution: The Radicalism of Dr. Thomas Young," *American Quarterly* 28 (1976): 226–49; Lewis H. Meader, "The Council of Censors," *PMHB* 22 (1898): 265–300.

5. *Minutes of the Proceedings of the Convention of the State of Pennsylvania* (Philadelphia, 1776), 58–65.

6. John Adams to Benjamin Rush, 12 October 1776, in L. H. Butterfield, ed., *Letters of Benjamin Rush* (Princeton: Princeton University Press, 1951), 1:240; *Pennsylvania Packet*, 29 October 1776, "Christophilus Scotus," 8 October 1776, "Scipio."

7. *Pennsylvania Packet*, 24 September 1776, "K"; *Pennsylvania Journal*, 25 September 1776, "Demophilus," cited in John N. Sheaffer, "Public Consideration of the 1776 Constitution," *PMHB* 98 (1974): 432.

8. Benjamin Rush to Anthony Wayne, 24 September 1776, Wayne Papers, 1:101, HSP. Rush wrote that the state's unicameral constitution was "tho't by many people to be rather too much upon the democratical order, for liberty is as apt to degenerate into licentiousness, as power is to become arbitrary. Restraints therefore are as necessary in the former as the latter case."

9. Alexander Graydon, *Memoirs of His Time, with Reminiscences of the Men and Events of the Revolution* (Philadelphia, 1846), 286; Benjamin Rush to John Adams, 24 February 1790, in Butterfield, ed., *Letters of Benjamin Rush*, 1:532; David Hawke, *In the Midst of a Revolution* (Philadelphia: University of Pennsylvania Press, 1961), 186. Hawke believed that Robert Whitehill was an influential participant in the writing of the constitution.

10. Charles S. Hyneman and Donald S. Lutz, eds., *American Political Writing during the Founding Era, 1760–1805* (Indianapolis: Liberty Press, 1983), 1:340–67.

11. Although the evidence is not direct, the author has identified Bryan as "Whitlocke" because of the compelling similarity in Bryan's known works and the three "Whitlocke" articles that appeared between May and June 1777. John Whitlocke (1625–1709) was a Presbyterian minister during the Interregnum who frequently suffered for his dissenting faith after the Restoration. The referrence may also be to Bulstrode Whitelocke, a government official who served under Cromwell during the Interregnum. Edmund Ludwell (c. 1617–92), a republican who fought on the side of Cromwell and the army during the civil war, was one of the justices appointed to preside over the trial of Charles I and was a signer of the king's death warrant.

12. [Benjamin Rush], *Observations upon the present Government of Pennsylvania: In Four Letters to the People of Pennsylvania* (Philadelphia, 1777), LCP. The letters originally appeared in the *Pennsylvania Journal*, 21 and 28 May, 4 June 1777, under the pseudonym of "Ludlow."

13. *Pennsylvania Evening Post*, 24 May 1777, "Letter I. To Ludlow," by "Whitlocke."

14. Ibid.; *Pennsylvania Gazette*, 4 and 11 June 1777, "Letter II. To Ludlow," by "Whitlocke"; *Pennsylvania Packet*, 10 June 1777, "Letter III. To Ludlow," by "Whitlocke."

15. *Pennsylvania Evening Post*, 27 May 1777, "Letter I. To Ludlow," by "Whitlocke."

16. Ibid.; *Pennsylvania Gazette*, 4 and 11 June 1777, "Letter II. To Ludlow," by "Whitlocke."

17. *Pennsylvania Evening Post*, 27 May 1777, "Letter I. To Ludlow," by "Whitlocke"; *Pennsylvania Gazette*, 4 and 11 June 1777, "Letter II. To Ludlow," by "Whitlocke."

18. *Pennsylvania Evening Post*, 27 May 1777, "Letter I. To Ludlow," by "Whitlocke"; *Pennsylvania Gazette*, 4 and 11 June 1777, "Letter II. To Ludlow," by "Whitlocke."

19. *Votes and Proceedings of the House of the Representatives* (Philadelphia, 1776), 6:737.

20. *Minutes of the Proceedings*, 16, 37. Included among those who were appointed as Philadelphia justices were Benjamin Franklin, John Dickinson, Sharp Delaney, Christopher Marshall, Sr., Robert Knox, and James Young.

21. On the same day Bryan was elected as a councillor he was also elected as justice of the peace for the dock ward, Philadelphia City; *Minutes of the First General Assembly* (Philadelphia, 1777), 30. Also, an anticonstitutionalist argued that only seventy votes were cast in the election of Bryan (*Pennsylvania Journal*, 12 March 1777, "Phocion").

22. Bryan was not one of the defeated November candidates.

23. Brunhouse, *Counter-Revolution*, 20–22; Arnold, "Political Ideology," 70–75; *Minutes of the First General Assembly*, 32; *Pennsylvania Colonial Records* (Harrisburg, Pa., 1852), 11:174. For the mass meetings held in Philadelphia protesting the new constitution: *At a Meeting Held at the Philosophical Society Hall, on Tuesday evening, October 17, 1776* (Philadelphia, 1776); *At a Meeting of a Number of the Citizens of Philadelphia, at the Philosophical Society's Hall, November 2, 1776* (Philadelphia, 1776); and *At a Meeting of a Number of the Citizens of Philadelphia, at the Philosophical Hall* (Philadelphia, 1776), LCP. For a defense of the constitution and the convention: James Cannon, David Rittenhouse, and Timothy Matlack, "In Convention for the State of Pennsylvania, September 28, 1776," in *Pennsylvania Packet*, 15 October 1776.

24. Francis Alison to Robert Alison, 20 August 1776, in *PMHB* 28 (1904): 379.

25. *Minutes of the First General Assembly*, 13.

26. George W. Geib, "A History of Philadelphia, 1776–1789" (Ph.D. dissertation, University of Wisconsin, 1969), 56–59; Brunhouse, *Counter-Revolution*, 29–30; *Colonial Records*, 11:199–224 passim.

27. James Read to George Bryan, 30 July 1777, Archibald McClean to George Bryan, 13 August, 3 September, 18 October 1777, and William Lyon to George Bryan, 2 February 1778, in *Pennsylvania Archives* (Harrisburg, Pa., 1852), 1st ser., 5:463–64, 514–20, 575–77, 682, 6:228 (hereafter *Pa. Arch.*).

28. "Warrant for Arrest," George Bryan to Sheriff of Bedford County, 17 November 1777, *Pa. Arch.*, 1st ser., 6:12. Smith was not the only former official arrested for refusing to turn over the county papers to their successors. The council ordered, or threatened, the arrest of other recalcitrant officials in Lancaster, Chester, and York counties.

29. One anonymous contemporary summed up an impressive list of those who refused office or opposed the constitution: the majority of the state's Board of War, headed by Benjamin Richard Bache, the speaker of the assembly, John Bayard [who would change his position], and nine out of ten members of the state's Navy Board opposed the constitution, while two men refused the appointments of brigadier general of the state's militia [John Cadwalader, Samuel Meredith], two more refused prothonotary of Philadelphia, and numerous others refused the posts of lieutenants of the counties. *Pennsylvania Evening Post*, 27 May 1777.

30. Brunhouse, *Counter-Revolution*, 34–38; *Pa. Arch.*, 2d ser., 3:601; *Colonial Records*, 11:197, John Evans to George Bryan, 20 August 1777, Justices Associates Papers, HSP.

31. George Bryan to Nathan Sellers, 24 July 1777, in "Extracts from the Diary of Nathan Sellers, 1776–1778," *PMHB* 16 (1892): 192–93; George Bryan to Thomas Mifflin, 6 August 1777, John Evans to George Bryan, 16 August 1777, Jacob Morgan to George Bryan, 17 August 1777, George Bryan to B. Galbraith, 23 August 1777, Peter De Haven to George Bryan, 10 September 1777, *Pa. Arch.*, 1st ser., 5:490, 529, 530, 543, 607; *Colonial Records*, 11:242–93 passim. For a description of Howe's movements, see Christopher Ward, *The War of the Revolution* (New York: Macmillian, 1952), 1:334–71.

32. For a thorough description of the removal of the Quakers and disaffected persons to Virginia, and the role of the Congress and Pennsylvania government, see James D. Anderson, "Thomas Wharton, 1730/31–1784: Merchant in Philadelphia" (Ph.D. dissertation, University of Akron, 1977), 357–408; also Brunhouse, *Counter-Revolution*, 41–44. Penn and Chew were sent to New Jersey, while those Quakers who refused an oath provided specifically for this circumstance were sent to Winchester, Virginia.

33. Thomas McKean to John Adams, 19 September 1777, in Robert J. Taylor, ed., *Papers of John Adams* (Cambridge, Mass.: Belknap Press, 1983), 5:289. Referring to the arrest of the Quakers and proprietary officials, McKean observed that "the only authority for the confinement, that I saw, was the copy of a letter from the Vice-President [Bryan] to Colo: Lewis Nicola."

34. George Bryan, 8 August 1777, Gratz Collection, HSP.

35. George Bryan to President of Congress, 2 September 1777, in *Journals of the Continental Congress, 1777* (Washington, D.C.: Library of Congress, 1907), 7:707; *Colonial Records*, 11:286, 295–96; Thomas Gilpin, *Exiles in Virginia* (Philadelphia, 1848), 68–69, 91, 147, 149–50; *Minutes of the First General Assembly*, 89–90; James T. Mitchell and Henry Flanders, eds., *Statutes at large of Pennsylvania, 1682–1801* (Harrisburg, Pa.,1897), 9:139–40.

36. Anderson, "Thomas Wharton," 357–408. (Lovell quote 368); Gilpin, *Exiles*, 133–35; Anne M. Ousterhout, *A State Divided: Opposition in Pennsylvania to the American Revolution* (New York: Greenwood Press, 1987), 164–68.

37. "Excitement in Philadelphia on Hearing of the Defeat at Brandywine," *PMHB* 14 (1890): 64–67; *Diary of the Reverend James Sproat, DDS,* HSP; *Colonial Records,* 11:325.

38. Brunhouse, *Counter-Revolution,* 16; Arnold, "Political Ideology," 63; Roland M. Baumann, "The Democratic-Republicans of Philadelphia: The Origins, 1776–1797," (Ph.D. dissertation, Pennsylvania State University, 1970), 22; Ireland, "Ratification," 74.

39. See Ryerson, "Republic Theory," 99–130.

40. James M. Aldrich, "A Quantitative Reassessment of the Effects of Sectionalism in Pennsylvania during the War for Independence," *Pennsylvania History* 39 (1972): 334–61. Aldrich determined that the "radicals came almost equally from all sections" of the state, and that "conservatives" were fairly represented in the eastern and central counties with less support from the west. Aldrich concluded that an east-west factional interpretation of revolutionary Pennsylvania is unfounded. Useful for this study, however, are Aldrich's scalograms for 1776–79, which indicate an absence of a clearly definable Constitutionalist party.

41. *Minutes of the Proceedings,* 61.

42. *Pennsylvania Packet,* 15 October 1776, "Lucius," and 2 March 1779, "The Remonstrance"; *Pennsylvania Gazette,* 30 October 1776, "Consideration"; *Pennsylvania Evening Post,* 16 November 1776, "To the People."

43. *Pennsylvania Evening Post,* 20 May 1777, "An Additional Address presented to the House of assembly by the Whig Society." "It does not appear to us," concluded the Whig Society, "that the oath is to be considered as a necessary part of the Constitution, . . . and that the oath of abjuration, . . . to all intents and purposes," was "fully sufficient."

44. Ibid.; *Minutes of the Third General Assembly* (Philadelphia, 1779), 4–5.

45. *Statutes,* 9:110–12, 147–49, "An Act Obliging the Male White Inhabitants of this State to Give Assurances of Allegiance to the same . . . ," 13 June 1777, and "A Supplement to the Act, 'An Act Obliging the Male White Inhabitants . . . ,'" 12 October 1777.

46. *Statutes,* 9:238–45, 284–86, "An Act for the Further Security of the Government," 1 April 1778, and "A Supplement to the Act, Entitled, 'An Act for the Further Security . . . ,'" 10 September 1778.

47. *Statutes,* 9:303–8, "A Further Supplement to the Act Entitled, 'An Act for the Further Security . . . ,'" 5 December 1778; "Proclamation of Pardon to Prisoners under Test Laws, 1778," *Pa. Arch.,* 1st ser., 7:131–32.

48. *Statutes,* 9:404–7, "A Further Supplement to the Test Laws of this State," 1 October 1779. Also, *Statutes,* 9:346–84, "An Act for Repealing part of An Act, Entitled, 'A Further Supplement to the Act . . . ; and for Disarming Persons who shall not have given Attestations of Allegiance . . . ,'" 31 March 1779.

49. *Colonial Records*, 11:220; *Minutes of the First General Assembly*, 77–79, 90; *Pennsylvania Packet*, 20 March 1777, "At a Meeting of the Whig Society"; *Pennsylvania Evening Post*, 20 May 1777, "An Additional Address presented to the House of assembly by the Whig Society."

50. *Minutes of the Third General Assembly*, 66. The vote was forty-seven to seven.

51. George Bryan to John Weitzel, 22 May 1778, Alexander McDowel to George Bryan, 1 June 1778, *Pa. Arch.*, 1st ser., 6:541, 572; George Bryan to John Thorne, 25 May 1778, George Bryan to Joseph McIlvaine, 27 August 1778, George Bryan to Jacob Miller, 22 September 1778, *Pa. Arch.*, 2d ser., 3:169–70, 205, 210.

52. Ousterhout, *A State Divided*, 191–92.

53. George Bryan to Samuel Adams, 5 January 1780, Samuel Adams Papers, LC.

54. John Armstrong to George Bryan, 24 July 1778, *Pa. Arch.*, 1st ser., 6:663; *Colonial Records*, 11:564–66, 600–606, 611–12; Ousterhout, *A State Divided*, 187–88.

55. John Armstrong to George Bryan, 10 September 1778, *Pa. Arch.*, 1st ser., 6:744.

56. David Jackson to George Bryan, 13 July 1785, Bryan Papers, HSP.

57. Brunhouse, *Counter-Revolution*, 57, 247n.; *Colonial Records*, 11:632–33; *Minutes of the Third General Assembly*, 244; *Pennsylvania Journal*, 24 February, 3 March 1779, "A Republican." Brunhouse noted that there is no direct evidence for the compromise, but presented convincing circumstantial evidence for the supposition.

58. *Pa. Arch.*, 2d ser., 3:301–32; *Minutes of the Third General Assembly*, 65–66.

59. Andrew Boyd to James Young, 29 December 1779, *Pa. Arch.*, 2d ser., 3:298. Also, Robert Whitehill complained bitterly about the compromise, and believed that his county would collect a thousand signatures against it. William Duane, *Extracts from the Diary of Christopher Marshall* (Albany, N.Y., 1877), 210.

Chapter 6

1. Thomas Leiper to Hall and Sellers, 1784, Bryan Papers, HSP; L. H. Butterfield, ed., *Letters of Benjamin Rush* (Princeton: Princeton University Press, 1951), 2:1202, 1202n.; William Duane, *Extracts from the Diary of Christopher Marshall* (Albany, N.Y., 1877), 159.

2. George Bryan to John Weitzel, 22 May 1778, *Pa. Arch.*, 1st ser., 6:540–41; *Pennsylvania Colonial Records* (Harrisburg, Pa., 1852), 11:499; Thomas McKean to George Bryan, 27 May 1778, in Paul H. Smith, et al., eds., *Letters of Delegates to Congress, February 1–May 31, 1778* (Washington, D.C.: Library of Congress, 1982), 9:759–60.

3. *Colonial Records*, 11:506–30 passim.

4. Christopher Ward, *The War of the Revolution* (New York: Macmillan, 1952), 2:571–72; Henry Laurens to George Bryan, 10 June 1778, *Pa. Arch.*, 1st ser., 6:592–93.

5. George Bryan to John Carothers, 3 May 1778, *Pa. Arch.*, 1st ser., 6:467–68.

6. George Bryan to William Gibbon, 19 May 1778, to the Delegates of Congress, 20 May 1778, to Samuel Hunter, 21 May 1778, to the Board of War, 3 June and 20 June 1778, *Pa. Arch.*, 1st ser., 6:530, 535–36, 536–37, 576–77, 608–9.

7. Board of War to George Bryan, 20 May, 5 and 8 June, 20 July 1778, *Pa. Arch.*, 1st ser., 6:533, 581–82, 586–87, 655.

8. John Carothers to George Bryan, 28 June 1778, John Proctor to George Bryan, 27 August 1778, Robert Levers to George Bryan, 25 August 1778, John Armstrong to George Bryan, 24 July 1778, James Potter to George Bryan, 1 September 1778, *Pa. Arch.*, 1st ser., 6:620–22, 722, 719, 662–63, 729; John Armstrong to George Bryan, 25 August 1778, Reed Papers, NYHS.

9. Samuel Hunter to George Bryan, 1 June 1778, *Pa. Arch.*, 1st ser., 6:571.

10. George Bryan to Samuel Hunter, 29 May 1778, *Pa. Arch.*, 1st ser., 6:563–64.

11. Samuel Hunter to George Bryan, 14 June, 12 July 1778, George Armstrong to George Bryan, 23 June 1778, John Harris to George Bryan, 3 June 1778, Robert Levers to George Bryan, 6 July 1778, John Weitzel to George Bryan, 8 July 1778, Matthew Smith to George Bryan, 12 July 1778, Thomas Hartley to George Bryan, 1 August 1778, *Pa. Arch.*, 1st ser., 6:599, 637, 612–13, 574–75, 626–27, 629, 632–33, 674; Frederick A. Godcharles, *Pennsylvania: Political, Governmental, Military, and Civil* (New York: American Historical Society, 1933), 3:243–47.

12. Board of War to George Bryan, 27 May, 16 July 1778, John Armstrong to George Bryan, 6 August 1778, Samuel Hunter to George Bryan, 7 October 1778, *Pa. Arch.*, 1st ser., 6:556, 646, 680–81, 772–73; George Bryan to John Weitzel, 14 July 1778, Provincial Delegates, 4:13, HSP.

13. George Bryan to John Weitzel, 14 July 1778, Provincial Delegates, 4:13, HSP; Godcharles, *Pennsylvania*, 3:258–59; Division of Archives and History, *The Sullivan-Clinton Campaign in 1779* (Albany: University of the State of New York, 1929), HSP; Louise W. Murray, *Notes from Collections of Tioga Point Museum on the Sullivan Expedition of 1779* (Athens, Pa., 1929), HSP.

14. *Pa. Arch.*, 2d ser., 3:180. For his variety of functions on the council, see *Colonial Records*, 11:506–12:127 passim; *Pa. Arch.*, 1st ser., 6:525–7:745 passim.

15. [Bryan] Council to Assembly, 7 August, 9 November 1778, *Pa. Arch.*, 1st ser., 6:685–86, 7:77–81. Also, *Minutes of the Second General Assembly* (Philadelphia, 1778), 89; and *Minutes of the Third General Assembly* (Philadelphia, 1779), 10.

16. *Pa. Arch.*, 1st ser., 7:77–81.

17. Robert L. Brunhouse, *The Counter-Revolution in Pennsylvania, 1776–1790* (Harrisburg: Pennsylvania Historical Commission, 1942), 60–62; H. James Henderson, *Party Politics in the Continental Congress* (New York: McGraw Hill, 1974), chap. 8. See also H. James Henderson, "Constitutionalists and Republicans in the Continental Congress," *Pennsylvania History* 36 (1969): 119–44.

18. See the Matlack-Arnold correspondence for October 1778 in the Reed Papers, NYHS.

19. Willard M. Wallace, *Traitorous Hero: The Life and Fortunes of Benedict Arnold* (New York: Harper and Brothers, 1954), 180–92.

20. George Bryan to William Paca, 20 February, 5 March, and William Paca to George Bryan, 4 March 1779, Reed Papers, NYHS; George Bryan to William Paca, 25 February, George Bryan to John Jay, 4 March, John Jay to Joseph Reed, 5 March, and William Paca to George Bryan, 9 March 1779, microfilm M247, National Archives, Washington, D.C.

21. Charles Thomson to Joseph Reed, in Smith, *Delegates*, 12:219–21, 222n.; Daniel Roberdeau to George Bryan, 21 February 1779, *Pa. Arch.*, 1st ser., 7:198; Henry Laurens' Notes of Debate, 26 March 1779, in Smith, *Delegates*, 12:249–50, 250–53n.

22. Wallace, *Traitorous Hero*, 189–92.

23. Bryan also acted as a commissioner to Virginia from Pennsylvania to finally settle the boundary line between the two states. The state's delegates were the Presbyterians Bryan, the Rev. John Ewing, and David Rittenhouse. Bryan to Reed, 31 August 1779, Reed Papers, NYHS; *Pa. Arch.*, 1st ser., 8:352–53.

24. The three most important politicians in Pennsylvania were Reed, Bryan, and Matlack, as symbolized by their meeting with continental congressmen over the appearance of a suspected British agent John Temple in the city in December 1778. Smith, *Delegates*, 11:359.

25. Anne Bezanson, "Inflation and Controls, Pennsylvania, 1774–1779," *Journal of Economic History*, supplement 8 (1948): 1–20. Also, Anne Bezanson et al., *Prices and Inflation during*

the American Revolution: Pennsylvania, 1770–1790 (Philadelphia: University of Pennsylvania Press, 1951).

26. *Colonial Records,* 11:671.

27. *At a General Meeting of the Citizens of Philadelphia and Parts Adjacent, at the State House Yard in this city, on Tuesday 25 May 1779* (Philadelphia, 1779), LCP; *The Address of the Committee of the City and Liberties of Philadelphia, to their Fellow Citizens throughout the United States* (Philadelphia, 1779), LCP; Philadelphia Price Regulating Committee, *In Committee, July 14, 1779* (Philadelphia, 1779), LCP.

28. *Pennsylvania Packet,* 27 July ("Junius"), 5 August ("Robert Morris"), 12 August ("Blair McClenaghan"), 24 August ("John McLaughlin, Robert Hagan"), 28 August ("A Citizen"), and 11 September ("To the General Committee of the City and Liberties of Philadelphia" and "C. S.") 1779; *Pa. Arch.,* 1st ser., 7:621–22, 643.

29. *Colonial Records,* 11:545, 12:87.

30. George W. Geib, "A History of Philadelphia, 1776–1789" (Ph.D. dissertation, University of Wisconsin, 1969), 96–97.

31. Ibid., 123.

32. Steven Rosswurm, *Arms, Country, and Class: The Philadelphia Militia and the "Lower Sort" during the American Revolution, 1775–1783* (New Brunswick, N.J.: Rutgers University Press, 1987), 209–17; John K. Alexander, "The Fort Wilson Incident of 1779: A Case Study of the Revolutionary Crowd," *WMQ* 31 (1974): 589–612.

33. Rosswurm, *Arms, Country, and Class,* 217–27.

34. Brunhouse, *Counter-Revolution,* 75–76. Two months earlier, on 2 August, the Constitutionalists won a crushing victory over the Republicans for the 120 extralegal committee positions. *Pennsylvania Packet,* 5 August 1779.

35. Bryan was also elected to act as a commissioner of the Continental Congress's admiralty board by the Congress on 3 December 1779. Bryan, however, refused. Edward C. Bennet, ed., *Letters of Members of the Constitutional Congress* (Washington, D.C.: Library of Congress, 1928), 4:519n.

36. *Minutes of the Fourth General Assembly* (Philadelphia, 1780), 161, 165, 175, 182. The Act for Erecting an High Court of Errors and Appeals was passed 28 February 1780, while An Act for Regulating and Establishing Admiralty Jurisdiction was passed 8 March 1780; James T. Mitchell and Henry Flanders, *The Statutes at Large of Pennsylvania, 1682–1801* (Philadelphia, 1896), 10:52–58, 97–106. The 1779 assembly did not create a new loan office.

37. [Bryan] Council to Assembly, 7 August, 9 November 1778, *Pa. Arch.,* 1st ser., 6:685–86, 7:77–81.

38. Eric Foner, *Tom Paine and Revolutionary America* (New York: Oxford University Press, 1976), 133.

39. *Minutes of the Third General Assembly,* 121; *Colonial Records,* 11:722.

40. *Minutes of the Fourth General Assembly,* 169–70. The vote authorizing the arrears of purchase money originally owed to the proprietors and now to be paid to the state carried in the assembly, thirty-two in favor to fourteen opposed. Of those fourteen members, ten members, including Bryan, were from the city or county of Philadelphia and Bucks or Chester counties. The final vote on the entire bill carried with forty in favor to seven in opposition. Those seven opponents listed their dissent after the vote; the fourth item therein represents the original reasons for the opposition to the clause regarding the arrears owed to the proprietors.

41. *Minutes of the Fourth General Assembly,* 121, 143–46; *Colonial Records,* 12:58–59; *Pennsylvania Gazette,* 3, 17, and 31 March, 29 September 1779, "N. G."; *Pennsylvania Packet,* 25 November 1779, "A Universalist."

42. Edward Cheyney, *History of the University of Pennsylvania, 1740–1940* (Philadelphia: University of Pennsylvania Press, 1940), 107–8.

43. Bezanson, *Prices and Inflation,* 38–50.

44. *Minutes of the Fourth General Assembly,* 162, 167.

45. Benjamin Rush to James McHenry, 19 January 1780, in *PMHB* 29 (1905): 63–64.

46. George Bryan to Samuel Adams, 15 January 1780, Samuel Adams Papers, LC.

47. *Minutes of the Fourth General Assembly,* 182, 195–96.

48. Ibid., 229–30, 232, 246. Swing votes were those votes initially against the suspension, but changed to for the suspension. The geographic breakdown of delegates on the tender law votes:

	For suspension	Swing to suspension	Against suspension
(southeast):			
Phila. City	5	0	1
Phila. County	4	2	1
Chester	3	2	3
Bucks	2	3	0
(central):			
York	1	3	1
Lancaster	1	3	6
(north and west):			
Cumberland	4	2	0
Westmoreland	2	1	0
Northumberland	1	1	1
Northampton	1	0	2
Berks	0	2	2
Bedford	0	0	1
	24	19	18

49. Ibid., 205–17.

50. Foner, *Tom Paine,* 172–73.

51. Reed never believed price controls worked, but was unable to influence the party to his viewpoint. William Reed, ed., *Life and Correspondence of Joseph Reed* (Philadelphia, 1847), 4:139–40.

52. *Colonial Records,* 12:305.

53. George Bryan to Samuel Adams, 5 January 1780, Samuel Adams Papers, LC.

54. "An Act for the Gradual Abolition of Slavery," 1 March 1780, *Statutes,* 10:67–73.

55. *Pennsylvania Gazette,* 2 February 1791.

56. *Pa. Arch.,* 1st ser., 6:685–86.

57. Ibid., 7:79.

58. Ibid.

59. *Minutes of the Third General Assembly,* 302; *Pennsylvania Packet,* 4 March 1779.

60. *Pennsylvania Packet,* 4 March 1779. The authorship of this bill has been ascribed to various individuals, including Bryan. Others mentioned as possible authors are the lawyer and former Quaker William Lewis, and Anthony Benezett. Gary B. Nash and Jean R. Soderlund, *Freedom by Degrees: Emancipation in Pennsylvania and Its Aftermath* (New York: Oxford University Press, 1991), 101–2. The members of the committee that drafted the bill were George Clymer, an anticonstitutionalist Anglican from Philadelphia County; Robert Knox, a Presby-

terian from Philadelphia city; Joseph Gardner from Chester County; and Edward Biddle from Berks County.

61. *Minutes of the Fourth General Assembly,* 157, 158, 165.

62. Ibid., 165, 199, 212.

63. Ibid.

64. Nash and Soderlund, *Freedom by Degrees,* 106–8; Owen S. Ireland, "Germans Against Abolition: A Minority's View of Slavery in revolutionary Pennsylvania," *Journal of Interdisciplinary History* 3 (1973): 685–706. I am also grateful to Jean R. Soderlund for background data on the participating assemblymen.

65. *Statutes,* 10:67–73.

66. George Bryan to Samuel Adams, 5 January 1780, Samuel Adams Papers, LC.

67. Philip Marsteller to George Bryan, 13 March 1780, Bryan Papers, HSP.

68. Robert Smith to George Bryan, 6 May 1780, Bryan Papers, HSP.

69. Chester County Presbyterians presented the house with a petition opposing abolition (*Minutes of the Third General Assembly,* 365); the reasons for the dissent of the minority assemblymen over abolition are located in *Minutes of the Fourth General Assembly,* 212. Such prominent Presbyterian Constitutionalists as John Whitehill, Jonathan Hoge, and Christian Lower opposed emancipation.

70. *Pennsylvania Packet,* 25 December 1779, "A Letter to a Clergyman in the Country."

71. Ibid.

72. *Pennsylvania Packet,* 1 January 1780, "Another Letter to a Clergyman in the Country."

73. Ibid.

74. Ibid.

75. Ibid.

76. *Statutes,* 10:67–68.

Chapter 7

1. For example, John Thorne to John Bayard and George Bryan, 15 January 1780, Philip Marsteller to George Bryan, 13 March 1780, 23 March 1782, Robert Smith to George Bryan, 6 May 1780, John Hubley to George Bryan, [c. winter 1782], Henry Haller to George Bryan, 20 April 1782, Bryan Papers, HSP; George Bryan to Joseph Reed, 9 May 1780, Provincial delegates, Society Collection, HSP.

2. Joseph Gardner to George Bryan, 19 March 1785, Bryan Papers, HSP.

3. George Bryan to Joseph Reed, 9 May 1780, Society Collection, HSP; George Bryan to Joseph Reed, 13 May 1780, Stauffer Collection, Governors, 74, HSP; Joseph Reed to George Bryan, 11 and 18 May, 5 October, 4 November 1780, 23 May 1782, and George Bryan to Joseph Reed, 7 November 1780, Reed Papers, NYHS; Joseph Reed to George Bryan and Jonathan D. Sergeant, 5 September 1780, *Pa. Arch.,* 2d ser., 3:378; Joseph Reed to George Bryan, 11 May, 17, 23 and 26 July 1780, Bryan Papers, HSP.

4. Joseph Reed to George Bryan, 18 May 1780, Reed Papers, NYHS.

5. Joseph Reed to George Bryan, 11 May 1780, Reed Papers, NYHS.

6. Thomas McKean to Joseph Reed, 12 December 1780, two letters, and Joseph Reed to Thomas McKean, 13 and 15 December 1780, *Pa. Arch.,* 1st ser., 8:649–52, 645–55, 657–58; Joseph Reed to George Bryan, 4 November 1780, Reed Papers, NYHS.

7. G. S. Rowe, *Thomas McKean: The Shaping of an American Republicanism* (Boulder: Colorado Associated University Press, 1978), 265–66.

8. *Pennsylvania Packet,* 30 May 1780. Bryan resigned his Philadelphia assembly seat to become a Supreme Court justice.

9. Joseph Reed to George Bryan, 5 October 1780, Reed Papers, NYHS.

10. F. Johnston to [William Irvine], 16 October 1780, in *PMHB* 31 (1907): 249–50; Robert L. Brunhouse, *The Counter-Revolution in Pennsylvania, 1776–1790* (Harrisburg: Pennsylvania Historical Commission, 1942), 90.

11. William Harris to George Bryan, [c. winter] 1780, Bryan Papers, HSP.

12. See Owen S. Ireland, "Ratification of the Federal Constitution in Pennsylvania" (Ph.D. dissertation, University of Pittsburgh, 1966), 277, table 19, for Ireland's breakdown of the assembly's political composition.

13. *Minutes of the Fifth General Assembly* (Philadelphia, 1781), 3 November 1780, 527; Brunhouse, *Counter-Revolution,* 88.

14. Theodore G. Tappert and John W. Doberstein, *The Journals of Henry Melchior Muhlenberg* (Philadelphia, 1953), 625–26.

15. Owen S. Ireland, "The Ethnic-Religious Counter-Revolution in Pennsylvania, 1784–1786," paper presented before the Philadelphia Center for Early American Studies, 22 January 1988, 28–31.

16. Freeholder, *To the Inhabitants of Pennsylvania* (Philadelphia, 1782), LCP. Bryan's authorship of the pamphlet was suggested by an anti-Bryan article appearing on 8 October 1783 in the *Pennsylvania Gazette.* Contemporary speculations over authorship of anonymous articles were not necessarily accurate, but in this case, several of the discussions by Freeholder were similar to themes developed by Bryan in private correspondence prior to the pamphlet's publication. It seems, however, that Bryan had assistance, for the paragraph complimentary to him was probably inserted by friends.

17. Freeholder, *To the Inhabitants.*

18. Ibid.

19. Milton E. Flower, *John Dickinson, Conservative Revolutionary* (Charlottesville: University Press of Virginia, 1983), 165–88.

20. Freeholder, *To the Inhabitants.*

21. Ibid.

22. Ibid.

23. Ibid.

24. Brunhouse, *Counter-Revolution,* 123.

25. L. H. Butterfield, ed., *Letters of Benjamin Rush* (Princeton: Princeton University Press, 1951), 1:251.

26. *Pennsylvania Colonial Records* (Harrisburg, Pa., 1852), 13:413.

27. Thomas R. Meehan, "The Pennsylvania Supreme Court in the Law and Politics of the Commonwealth, 1776–1790" (Ph.D. dissertation, University of Wisconsin, 1960), 323; Benjamin Rush to John Montgomery, 15 October 1782, in Butterfield, ed., *Letters of Benjamin Rush,* 1:250; Joseph Reed to George Bryan, 25 December 1782, Reed Papers, NYHS. See also Rowe, *McKean,* 181–82.

28. *Minutes of the Proceedings of the Convention of the State of Pennsylvania* (Philadelphia, 1776), 65. For secondary sources on the Council of Censors, see Lewis H. Meader, "The Council of Censors," *PMHB* 22 (1898): 265–300; and John N. Sheaffer, "Public Consideration of the 1776 Pennsylvania Constitution," *PMHB* 98 (1974): 219–34.

29. Gordon S. Wood, *The Creation of the American Republic, 1776–1787* (1969; reprint, New York: W. W. Norton, 1972), 232, 335–439.

30. *Four Letters on Interesting Subjects* (Philadelphia, 1776), LCP.

31. *Pennsylvania Gazette,* 1 September 1784, "One of the Minority."

32. George Bryan, Unpublished Address to the Public, [n.d.], Bryan Papers, HSP.

33. Brunhouse, *Counter-Revolution*, 142–45, 278.

34. *Journal of the Council of Censors, First and Second Sessions, 1783–1784* (Philadelphia, 1784), 53–72.

35. Joseph Reed to Thomas Barclay, 20 April 1784, Society Collection, HSP.

36. James McLene to George Bryan, 10 February 1784, Bryan Papers, HSP.

37. *Council of Censors*, 174–75.

38. *Independent Gazetteer*, 26 June 1784; *Council of Censors*, 85; Brunhouse, *Counter-Revolution*, 161.

39. *Council of Censors*, 93, 111–79 passim.

40. Ibid., 82, 85.

41. Ibid., 177.

42. George Bryan, Unpublished Address to the Public, [n.d.], Bryan Papers, HSP.

43. *Council of Censors*, 177; Wood, *Creation*, 449–53; Robert F. Williams, "The Influences of Pennsylvania's 1776 Constitution on American Constitutionalism during the Founding Decade," *PMHB* 112 (1988): 46–48.

44. *Pennsylvania Gazette*, 1 September 1784, "One of the Minority."

45. *Council of Censors*, 177; George Bryan, Unpublished Address to the Public, [n.d.], Bryan Papers, HSP.

46. Brunhouse, *Counter-Revolution*, 100, 126–27; Joseph Reed to George Bryan, 3 December 1782, Reed Papers, NYHS.

47. Brunhouse, *Counter-Revolution*, 105–7; *Pennsylvania Journal*, 17 December 1781, "A Friend to Constitutional Government"; *Pennsylvania Packet*, 27 November 1781, "A Lover of Justice and Fair Enquiry"; *Freeman's Journal*, 2 January, "Censor," and 23 January 1782, "By a Constitutionalist."

48. George Bryan to William Atlee, 31 December 1781, Atlee Papers, Peter Force Papers, LC.

49. Brunhouse, *Counter-Revolution*, 105–7, 118–19; *Minutes of the Eighth General Assembly* (Philadelphia, 1784), 51, 90–94, 137, 145–46; Joseph Reed to William Bradford, 2 May 1784, in William Reed, ed., *Life and Correspondence of Joseph Reed* (Philadelphia, 1847), 2:414. Bayard was elected to the assembly of 1784 and was selected by the Constitutionalists as speaker. But his political comeback was short-lived, as he was defeated, like other city Constitutionalists, in the following year.

50. Rowe, *McKean*, 167; *Freeman's Journal*, 17 July, "Tenax," 25 July, "Legality," 1 August, "Philadelphia," 8 August, "Latimer," 15 August, "AntiQuibler," 22 August, 29 August, 12 September 1781.

51. John F. Roche, *Joseph Reed, a Moderate in the American Revolution* (New York: Columbia University Press, 1957), 213–19.

52. William Moore was another party leader who after the expiration of his term in 1782 would not be returned to state politics except for a year in the assembly in 1784. Also, Moore became associated with the interests of Robert Morris in the later half of the decade. James Potter was a well-known Constitutionalist but never achieved a position of leadership within the party as did Bryan and others.

53. *Minutes of the Sixth General Assembly* (Philadelphia, 1782), 511, 514–15, 543, 557–60.

54. James T. Mitchell and Henry R. Flanders, *The Statutes at Large of Pennsylvania, 1682–1801* (Harrisburg, Pa., 1896–1915), 10:376–78. The act was entitled An Act for the Support of Government, and the Administration of Justice.

55. William Moore to the Assembly, 12 April 1782, *Pa. Arch.*, 4th ser., 3:839–40. Also, John Hubley to George Bryan, [n.d., c. winter 1782], Bryan Papers, HSP.

56. George Bryan to William Atlee, 26 March 1781, Atlee Papers, Peter Force Papers, LC.

57. George Bryan to William Atlee, 31 December 1781, Atlee Papers, Peter Force Papers, LC.

58. *Minutes of the Seventh General Assembly* (Philadelphia, 1783), 954.

59. *Minutes of the Eighth General Assembly*, 202–3; *Colonial Records*, 14:43; Joseph Reed to William Bradford, 2 May 1784, in Reed, *Life of Joseph Reed*, 2:414.

60. *Pennsylvania Gazette*, 25 August 1784, "A Citizen of Pennsylvania."

61. Ibid., 8 October 1783, "Z."

62. Ibid., 25 February 1784, "Isaac Austin."

63. Ibid., 22 and 29 September 1784, "A Citizen of Pennsylvania." More so than other years, Bryan was targeted for additional abuse by his Republican counterparts during 1783 and 1784. The reasons are chiefly twofold: first, it was a time of heightened political passions as the Council of Censors met and deliberated; second, Bryan was not only a censor but the principal leader of the Constitutionalists, and his election occurred while he was serving as a supreme court justice. His opponents charged that a member of the judicial branch was prohibited by the constitution from serving on the censors—not to mention that technically Bryan was a resident of the Northern Liberties and not the city, for which he sat as a representative.

64. *Freeman's Journal*, 1 September 1784, "A Plebeian."

65. Ibid., 29 September 1784, "Bourbon." Also, 6 October 1784, "Bourbon."

66. Ibid., 10 March 1784, "Publius."

67. Ibid., 1 September 1784, "A Plebeian."

68. Ibid., 1 September 1784, "Junius."

69. Meehan, "The Pennsylvania Supreme Court," 305–9.

70. The following account is based on Meehan, "The Pennsylvania Supreme Court," 325–36.

71. Jacob Cox Parsons, ed., *Diary of Jacob Hiltzheimer of Philadelphia* (Philadelphia, 1893), 53–55.

72. *Freeman's Journal*, 15 January 1783, "Adrian."

73. Ibid., 29 January 1783, "Adrian."

74. *Pennsylvania Packet*, 25 January 1783, "One of the People." Also in Francis Hopkinson, *The Miscellaneous Essays and Occasional Writings of Francis Hopkinson* (Philadelphia, 1793), 194–218.

75. *Freeman's Journal*, 29 January 1783, "Adrian."

76. *Pennsylvania Packet*, 25 January 1783, "One of the People."

77. Hopkinson, "I've a Thought, What's It Like?" in *Miscellaneous Essays*, 228–38.

78. Ibid., 297–315.

79. Burton Alva Konkle, *George Bryan and the Constitution of Pennsylvania, 1731–1791* (Philadelphia: W. J. Campbell, 1922), 269–70; *Pennsylvania Gazette*, 24 November 1784, "Projector"; Hopkinson, *Miscellaneous Essays*, p. opposite 296.

80. Alexander J. Dallas, *Reports of Cases Ruled and Adjudged in the Courts of Pennsylvania Before and Since the Revolution* (Philadelphia, 1830), 1:330.

81. Brunhouse, *Counter-Revolution*, 88; Douglas McNeil Arnold, "Political Ideology and the Internal Revolution in Pennsylvania, 1776–1790" (Ph.D. dissertation, Princeton University, 1976), 149, 193.

82. Ireland, "Ethnic-Religious Counter-Revolution." Also, Owen S. Ireland, "The Ethnic-Religious Dimensions of Pennsylvania Politics, 1778–1779," *WMQ* 30 (1973): 423–48; Wayne L. Bockleman and Owen S. Ireland, "The Internal Revolution in Pennsylvania: An Ethnic-Religious Interpretation," *Pennsylvania History* 41 (1974): 125–59; Owen S.

Ireland, "The Crux of Politics: Religion and Party in Pennsylvania, 1778–1789," *WMQ* 42 (1985): 453–75.

83. Eric Foner, *Thomas Paine and Revolutionary America* (Oxford: Oxford University Press, 1976); Charles S. Olton, *Artisans for Independence: Philadelphia Mechanics and the American Revolution* (Syracuse, N.Y.: Syracuse University Press, 1975); and Steven Rosswurm, *Arms, Country, and Class: The Philadelphia Militia and the "Lower Sort" during the American Revolution, 1775–1783* (New Brunswick, N.J.: Rutgers University Press, 1987).

84. Brunhouse, *Counter-Revolution*, 338; Ireland, "Ratification," table 19; and Owen S. Ireland, "The People's Triumph: The Federalist Majority in Pennsylvania, 1787–1788," *Pennsylvania History* 56 (1989): 93–109; *Council of Censors*, 26.

85. Samuel Bryan to George Bryan, [n.d., c. winter, 1785] and 3 November 1785; Arthur Bryan to George Bryan, 3 November 1785, Bryan Papers, HSP.

Chapter 8

1. Samuel Bryan to George Bryan, May 1785, Bryan Papers, HSP.

2. Douglas McNeil Arnold, "Political Ideology and the Internal Revolution in Pennsylvania, 1776–1790" (Ph.D. dissertation, Princeton University, 1976), 241–43; Owen S. Ireland, "The Ratification of the Federal Constitution in Pennsylvania" (Ph.D. dissertation, University of Pittsburgh, 1966), 11–65.

3. Robert L. Brunhouse, *The Counter-Revolution in Pennsylvania, 1776–1790* (Harrisburg: Pennsylvania Historical Commission, 1942), 338.

4. Ireland, "Ratification," 207–19.

5. Positions on the proposed constitution broke along party lines in Pennsylvania: the Republicans were primarily Federalists and the Constitutionalists were generally Antifederalists. See Ireland, "Ratification"; also, Robert A. Rutland, *The Ordeal of the Constitution: The Antifederalists and the Ratification Struggle of 1787–1788* (Norman: University of Oklahoma Press, 1966); Steven R. Boyd, *The Politics of Opposition: Antifederalists and the Acceptance of the Constitution* (Milwood, New York: Krauss International, 1979); and Gordon S. Wood, *The Creation of the American Republic, 1776–1787* (New York: W. W. Norton, 1969).

6. *An Address to the Subscribers: Members of the late House of Representatives to their Constituents* (Philadelphia, 1787), in John B. McMaster and Frederick D. Stone, *Pennsylvania and the Federal Constitution, 1787–1788* (Philadelphia, 1888), 73–79; *Independent Gazetteer,* 10 October 1787, "The Couching Needle"; *Freeman's Journal,* 17 October 1787, "From the Chronicles of Early Times," and 31 October 1787, "An Old Whig."

7. *Independent Gazetteer,* 13 October 1787, "A Gaul." The other men the author listed were Dr. James Ewing, Charles Pettit, Jonathan B. Smith, and John Smilie.

8. George Bryan to John Ralston, 7 March and 13 March 1788, printed in the *Pennsylvania Gazette,* 26 March 1788.

9. Ibid.

10. Bryan was referring to a mob of pro-Federalist rioters in the city. Gathering outside the home where seven Constitutionalists were staying during the ratifying convention, the rioters threw stones at the windows, shouted epithets, and threatened the Constitutionalists with death. None of the rioters were caught, nor was there a serious attempt made to catch them. *Debates of the Convention of the State of Pennsylvania on the Constitution* (Philadelphia, 1787). For the Carlisle riots, see Brunhouse, *Counter-Revolution,* 210–11; and Saul Cornell, "William Petrikin and the Carlisle Riot: Popular Opposition to the U.S. Constitution in the

Pennsylvania Backcountry," paper presented to the Philadelphia Center for Early American Studies, 26 September 1986.

11. George Bryan to John Ralston, 7 March and 13 March 1788, printed in the *Pennsylvania Gazette*, 26 March 1788.

12. *Pennsylvania Gazette*, 2 April 1788, "A Pennsylvanian" and "Sidney."

13. Benjamin Rush to John Montgomery, 9 April 1788, in L. H. Butterfield,ed., *Letters of Benjamin Rush* (Princeton: Princeton University Press, 1951), 456.

14. Samuel Bryan (1759–1821).

15. Centinel No. 1, in McMaster and Stone, *Pennsylvania*, 567, 569.

16. Centinel No. 4, ibid., 603–4.

17. Centinel Nos. 1 and 2, ibid., 565–91.

18. Centinel No. 5, ibid., 610–12.

19. Arnold, "Political Ideology," 261–62. Also, Bernard Bailyn, *Ideological Origins of the American Revolution* (1967; reprint, Cambridge: Belknap Press of Harvard University Press, 1982), chap. 4.

20. Centinel Nos. 1–3, 10–15, 17–18, 20–22, in McMaster and Stone, *Pennsylvania*. Quotations from Centinel Nos. 2 and 3, 591, 594.

21. The following account of the Oswald case is taken from Thomas P. Meehan, "The Pennsylvania Supreme Court in the Law and Politics of the Commonwealth, 1776–1790" (Ph.D. dissertation, University of Wisconsin, 1960), 490–508.

22. Cited in Meehan, "Pennsylvania Supreme Court," 498. Also in Alexander J. Dallas, *Reports of Cases Ruled and Adjudged in the Courts of Pennsylvania Before and Since the Revolution* (Philadelphia, 1830), 1:329–30.

23. Paul Leicester Ford, *The Origin, Purpose and Result of the Harrisburg Convention* (Brooklyn, N.Y., 1890), 6–7.

24. George Bryan to George Clinton, 9 February 1788, quoted in Ford, *Harrisburg Convention*, 13.

25. Circular Letter of East Pennsborough, Cumberland County, 3 July 1788, in Ford, *Harrisburg Convention*, 15–19.

26. Brunhouse, *Counter-Revolution*, 213–14; Arthur Bryan to George Bryan, 9 April 1788, and Samuel Smith to George Bryan, 26 April 1788, Bryan Papers, HSP.

27. Ford, *Harrisburg Convention*, 30–32.

28. Ibid., 35–39.

29. See Owen S. Ireland, "The People's Triumph: The Federalist Majority in Pennsylvania, 1787–1788," *Pennsylvania History* 56 (1989): 93–113.

30. Wood, *Creation*, 467. Wood noted that the "move for a stronger government thus became something more than a response to the obvious weakness of the Articles of Confederation. It became as well an answer to the problems of the state governments."

31. Centinel No. 9, in McMaster and Stone, *Pennsylvania*, 626–30.

32. Benjamin Rush to Timothy Pickering, 30 August 1787, in Max Farrand, ed., *The Records of the Federal Convention of 1787* (New Haven: Yale University Press, 1966), 4:75.

33. Benjamin Rush to John Montgomery, 27 March 1789, in Butterfield, ed., *Letters of Benjamin Rush*, 1:569

34. Merrill Jensen, *The New Nation: A History of the United States during the Confederation, 1781–1789* (1950; reprint, New York: Vintage Books, n.d.), 60–63, 227–31; Thomas M. Doerflinger, *A Vigorous Spirit of Enterprise: Merchants and Economic Development in Revolutionary Philadelphia* (Chapel Hill: University of North Carolina Press, 1986), 296–310; E. James Ferguson, *The Power of the Purse: A History of American Public Finance, 1776–1790* (Chapel Hill: University of North Carolina Press, 1961), 121–24.

35. For the discussion of the bank and Pennsylvania politics, see Bray Hammond, *Banks and Politics in America from the Revolution to the Civil War* (Princeton: Princeton University Press, 1957), chap. 4; George David Rappaport, "The Sources and Early Development of the Hostility to Banks in Early American Thought" (Ph.D. dissertation, New York University, 1970); George David Rappaport, "The First Description of the Bank of North America," *WMQ* 33 (1976): 661–67; Lawrence Lewis, Jr., *A History of the Bank of North America: The First Bank Chartered in the United States* (Philadelphia, 1882); Arnold, "Political Ideology," 216–24; Janet Wilson, "The Bank of North America and Pennsylvania Politics: 1781–1787," *PMHB* 66 (1942): 3–28.

36. Located in the Bryan Papers is a floor speech written and delivered by William Findley. The speech was presented before the House in 1786 and represents an excellent statement of the Constitutionalist position toward the bank and its charter.

37. Bryan was referring to the creation of a rival bank in 1784 and the BNA's opposition to it. The BNA chose to buy out the new bank. The assembly in 1785 responded to the depression among farmers by creating a loan office backed by £50,000 of paper money, as well as issuing £100,000 in paper money to discharge state debts. To the horror of the Republicans and bank directors, the issues were legal tender, threatening the specie deposits within the bank. Brunhouse, *Counter-Revolution,* 150–51, 171.

38. Joseph Gardner to George Bryan, 19 March 1785, Bryan Papers, HSP; George Bryan to William Atlee, 29 March and 23 June, 1785, Atlee Papers, Peter Force Papers, LC.

39. Joseph Hart to George Bryan, 2 January 1787, Bryan Papers, HSP. Hart was upset with Bryan for not responding quickly by the creation and circulation of petitions against the bank. "Yours of February 13 came to hand in a few days, but to my surprise found no instructions respecting a remonstrance at the bank." Bryan did not alter his opposition toward the bank charter, and he may have forwarded the expected news by a later date. But Bryan must have been aware that the cause was lost, and he might have simply resigned himself to the inevitable. Joseph Hart to George Bryan, 7 March 1787, ibid.

40. *Minutes of the Thirteenth General Assembly* (Philadelphia, 1789), 160–62. On 24 March the assembly authorized by a vote of forty-one to seventeen the calling of a convention. The Constitutionalist dissent is registered on 203–5.

41. Robert Whitehill to George Bryan, 3 August 1789, William Findley to George Bryan, 3 August 1789, Francis Bryan to George Bryan, 24 October 1789, Bryan Papers, HSP; George Bryan to Albert Gallatin, 29 August 1789, Reed Papers, NYHS.

42. *Independent Gazetteer,* Centinel No. 25, 27 August, Centinel No. 26, 29 August, Centinel No. 27, 4 September, Centinel No. 28, 8 September, Centinel No. 29, 9 September, Centinel No. 30, 10 September, Centinel No. 31, 12 September, Centinel No. 32, 15 September, Centinel No. 33, 28 September, and Centinel No. 34, 28 October 1789.

43. William Findley to George Bryan, 3 August 1789, Bryan Papers, HSP.

44. William Brooke Rawle, "The Last Assembly under the Pennsylvania Constitution of 1776: Extract from the Diary of William Rawle, Esq.," *PMHB* 25 (1901): 223.

Conclusion

1. For a discussion of James Wilson, see C. Page Smith, *James Wilson* (Chapel Hill: University of North Carolina Press, 1956); for a discussion of Wilson's political philosophy, two sources are Cecelia Kenyon, "Men of Little Faith: Anti-Federalists on the Nature of Representative Government," *WMQ* 12 (1955): 3–43; and Daniel J. McCarthy, "James Wilson and the American Republicanism" (Ph.D. dissertation, University of Notre Dame, 1981).

2. *Pennsylvania Colonial Records* (Harrisburg, Pa., 1852), 11:599–614 passim; *Pa. Arch.,* 1st ser., 7:21–58.

3. *Independent Gazetteer,* 4 September 1784, "A Friend to Mercy" and an unsigned article.

4. *Colonial Records,* 11:564–65.

5. George Bryan to Joseph Reed, 7 November 1780, and Joseph Reed to George Bryan, 4 November 1780, Reed Papers, NYHS.

6. George Bryan, in summation of *Commonwealth v. Well, etc.,* to the jury, 13 November 1788, Washington County, Bryan Papers, HSP.

7. Ibid. See also verdict by George Bryan in oyer and terminer at Newtown, Bucks County, 25 May 1787, in *Commonwealth v. Dyer,* Bryan Papers, HSP.

8. The following is based on George Bryan to Mr. Claypoole, [n.d.], Bryan Papers, HSP.

9. Ibid.; David Jackson to George Bryan, 22 June 1785, Bryan Papers, HSP. Also, for reference to penal reform, see Michael Meranze, "The Penitential Ideal in Late Eighteenth-Century Philadelphia," *PMHB* 108 (1984): 419–50.

10. Answer to the request of the assembly concerning the granting of patents, by George Bryan, 23 March 1789, Bryan Papers, HSP.

11. Burton Alva Konkle, *George Bryan and the Constitution of Pennsylvania, 1731–1791* (Philadelphia: W. J. Campbell, 1922), 350n.

12. Samuel Bryan to Albert Gallatin, 13 May 1790, Reed Papers, NYHS.

13. *Pennsylvania Gazette,* 20 October 1790. Also, J. R. Pole, "Election Statistics of Pennsylvania, 1790–1840," *PMHB* 82 (1958): 219.

14. Konkle, *George Bryan,* 354–55.

15. Ibid., 357n., 358n.

Index

Brown, William, 130
Brunhouse, Robert L., 137
Brunswick, N.J., 5
Bryan, Anne, 2, 161–62 n. 1
Bryan, Arthur, 2, 161–62 n. 1
Bryan, Eliza, 2, 161–62 n. 1
Bryan, Elizabeth, 10, 159–60, 163 n. 38
Bryan, Francis, 163 n. 38
Bryan, George, xiii–xiv, 1, 2, 3, 5, 10, 41,
  98, 105, 107, 131, 160, 180 n. 24, 181
  n. 35
  and Admiralty law in America, 71–72
  as "Adrian," 134–35
  attacks on, 132–34, 186 n. 63
  and Bank of North America, 149–50
  bankruptcy of, 11–12, 74, 164 n. 42
  and "Centinel," 69–71, 144
  on church governing committees, 17, 29,
  31
  as commissioner to Virginia, 180 n. 23
  and Council of Censors, 125–26, 140
  and election of 1764, 50–52
  and election of 1765, 55, 173 n. 18
  and election of 1766, 55, 173 n. 18
  and election of 1776, 177 n. 22
  and election of 1779, 104–5
  and election of 1782, 123
  on Franklin's appointment, 171 n. 68
  as "Freeholder," 119, 184 n. 16
  and French and Indian War, 6–7, 169 n.
  36
  and Great Awakening, 16
  Harrisburg Convention presiding officer,
  148
  and illegal trade, 8
  and Indians, 44–45
  as a jurist, 12
  justice of the peace for dock ward, 177 n.
  21
  on law and social order, 153–58
  and loyalty oaths, 90–92
  and militia laws, 107–8
  ministers relief fund trustee, 26
  and nonimportation agreement, 73
  overseeing river construction, 11
  and Parliament, 75
  and Pennsylvania Constitution of 1776,
  80–85
  Pennsylvania Supreme Court justice, 108
  Philadelphia County justice, 57, 61, 85

  and Philadelphia ratifying convention,
  142–43
  port officer of Delaware River, 85
  and Presbyterian politics, 56, 57, 75
  Princeton trustee, 23
  and Quaker party, 44
  and second Constitutional Convention,
  90, 92–93
  1764 Assembly member, 53–54
  and slavery, 109–14
  and Stamp Act, 55, 64–66
  on Supreme Executive Council, 86, 87
  and "tender" laws, 107
  and test acts, 94–95
  University of Pennsylvania treasurer, 106
  as "Whitlocke," 80–85
Bryan, George, Jr., 159, 163 n. 38
Bryan, Jonathan, 163 n. 38
Bryan, Mary, 163 n. 38
Bryan, Nancy, 2, 161–62 n. 1
Bryan, Samuel (brother of George), 2, 161–
  62 n. 1
Bryan, Samuel (father of George), 2–4, 9
Bryan, Samuel (son of George), 140–41,
  144–45, 148–49, 159–60, 163 n. 38
Bryan, Sarah, 163 n. 38
Bryan, Sarah Dennis, 2, 9
Bryan, Thomas, 163 n. 38
Bryan, William, 2
Bryan, William (son of George), 163 n. 38
Bryan, William (brother of George), 161–62
  n. 1
Bucks County, Pa., 36, 50, 52, 110, 137,
  140, 143, 167 n. 4, 181 n. 40, 182 n.
  48
Bull, John, 64
Bunker Hill, Battle of, 76
Burr, Aaron, 21

Cadwalader, John, 177 n. 29
Canada, 7
Cannon, James, 79–80, 105, 177 n. 23
Carlisle, Pa., 5, 86, 143
Carlisle, Abraham, 154, 157–58
"Centinel," 69–73, 144
Chandler, Dr. Thomas Bradbury, 68–70, 174
  n. 29
Charles I (king of England), 176 n. 11
Charming Sally, the, 6
Chesapeake Bay, 88, 101